Helion & Company Limited
Unit 8 Amherst Business Centre
Budbrooke Road
Warwick
CV34 5WE
England
Tel. 01926 499 619
Email: info@helion.co.uk
Website: www.helion.co.uk
Twitter: @helionbooks
Visit our blog http://blog.helion.co.uk/

Text © Bojan Dimitrijević 2021
Photographs © as individually credited
Colour profiles © Tom Cooper 2021
Maps © Tom Cooper 2021

Designed & typeset by Farr out Publications,
    Wokingham, Berkshire
Cover design Paul Hewitt, Battlefield Design
    (www.battlefield-design.co.uk)

ISBN 978-1-913336-30-1

British Library Cataloguing-in-Publication
    Data
A catalogue record for this book is available
    from the British Library

We always welcome receiving book
proposals from prospective authors.

CONTENTS

Acknowledgements		2
Abbreviations		2
Introduction		3
1	The Serb Air Force dominates Bosnian skies, 1992	4
2	NATO establish control, 1993-1994	15
3	Parallel Air Wars 1995	37
4	Operation Deliberate Force	46
5	The Aftermath of the NATO Air Campaign	69
Conclusion		80
Bibliography		81
Notes		83
About the Author		88

Note: In order to simplify the use of this book, all names, locations and geographic
designations are as provided in *The Times World Atlas*, or other traditionally accepted major
sources of reference, as of the time of described events.

ACKNOWLEDGEMENTS

The author wishes to thank: Generals Božo Novak, Milan Torbica, Jovica Draganić and Dušan Kukobat, and Colonels Rajica Bosković and Gostimir Popović, who helped the author by providing access to their own materials and documentation. Very special thanks to Dr Nikica Barić (Croatian History Institute) who provided the author with his research on the Srpska Vojska Krajine air force. Thanks also extend to Bojan Ristić, Zvonimir Despot, Dr Milan Gulić and Danko Borojević for providing various items of literature. The author wishes to thank all of his oral sources who provided valuable insight into the Bosnian air war (see bibliography for details).

For photo materials, the author wishes to thank Milan Micevski and Milorad D. Ristić (Belgrade, Serbia), Drago Vejnović and Ranko Ćuković (Banja Luka, Republika Srpska) and Vinko Šebrek (Brežice, Slovenia) who took the photos during the war in 1992-1995. To Mario Raguž (Dubrovnik, Croatia), Dean Čanić and Zoran Delibašić (Zagreb, Croatia) who provided their photo materials. Also, to Rebeccah A. Woodrow, TSgt, Public Affairs, 31st Fighter Wing, USAF who provided the author with guidance on USAF photo material. Finally, special thanks to editor Tom Cooper, who initiated and helped finalise this project and supported the author's efforts to fulfil the high expectations of Helion's readers.

ABBREVIATIONS

AA	anti-aircraft (artillery)
AAC	Army Air Corps (British)
ABCCC	Airborne Battlefield Command and Control Centre
ABG	Air Base Group
AdA	Armée de l'Air (French Air Force)
AGM	Air-to-Ground Missile
AEW	Airborne Early Warning
A-FAC	Airborne Forward Air Controller
AFRES	Air Force Reserve
AFSOUTH	Allied Forces Southern Europe
AIRSOUTH	Allied Air Force Commander in South Europe
ALAT	Aviation légère de l'armée de Terre (French Army light Aviation)
AM	Aeronautica Militare (Italian Air Force)
ANG	Air National Guard
AS	Airlift Squadron
ATAF	Allied Tactical Air Force
ATGM	Anti-Tank Guided Missile
ARBiH	Armija Bosne i Herccgovine (Army of Bosnia and Herzegovina)
ARS	Air Refuelling Squadron
ARW	Air Refuelling Wing
AW	Airlift Wing
AWACS	Airborne Warning and Control System
BAI	Battlefield Air Interdiction
BiH	Bosna i Hercegovina (Bosnia and Herzegovina)
BS	Bomber Squadron
BW	Bomber Wing
C-ALCM	Conventional Air Launched Cruise Missile
CAG	Carrier Air Group or Commander Air Group
CAOC	Combined Air Operations Centre
CAW	Carrier Air Wing
CAP	Combat Air Patrol
CAS	Close Air Support
CINCSOUTH	Commander-in-Chief, Allied Forces Southern Europe
COMAIRSOUTH	Commander Allied Air Forces Southern Europe
CONUS	Continental United States
CSAR	Combat Search and Rescue
DF	Deliberate Force
DoD	Department of Defense (US)
ECR	Electronic Combat and Reconnaissance
ECM	Electronic Countermeasures
ELINT	electronic intelligence
FAC	Forward Air Controller
FRY	Federal Republic of Yugoslavia
FS	Fighter Squadron
FW	Fighter Wing
HARM	High Speed Anti-Radiation Missile
HAS	Hardened Aircraft Shelter
HTS	HARM Targeting System
HRZ	Hrvatsko Ratno Zrakoplovstvo (Croatian Air Force)
HV	Hrvatska Vojska (Croatian Army)
HVO	Hrvatsko Vijeće Odbrane (Croatian Defence Council, in Bosnia and Herzegovina)
ICTY	International Criminal Tribunal for the Former Yugoslavia
IFOR	Implementation Force
JNA	Jugoslovenska Narodna Armija (Yugoslav People's Army)
J-STARS	Joint Surveillance Target Attack Radar System
LANTIRN	Low Altitude Navigation and Targeting Infrared for Night
MANPADS	Man-portable air defence system/s
MEDEVAC	Medical Evacuation
NAC	North Atlantic Council
NAC/DoD	National Archives Catalogue/US Department of Defense
NATO	North Atlantic Treaty Organisation
NAEWF	NATO Airborne Early Warning Force
NFZ	No-Fly Zone
Object	A facility, base, installation or item of infrastructure
PGM	Precision-Guided Missiles
PVO	protivvazdušna odbrana (air defence)
RAF	Royal Air Force
RED HORSE	Rapid Engineer Deployable Heavy Operational Repair Squadron Engineer

ROE	Rules of Engagement
RNLAF	The Royal Netherlands Air Force
RRF	Rapid Reaction Force
R-StON	radarska stanica za osmatranje i navođenje (early warning and fire-control station)
RS	Reconnaissance squadron
RV i PVO	Ratno Vazduhoplovstvo i Protivvazdušna Odbrana (Air Force and Air Defence of the SFRJ)
RW	Reconnaissance Wing
SACEUR	Supreme Allied Commander Europe
SEAD	Suppression of Enemy Air Defence
SFRJ	Socijalistička Federativna Republika Jugoslavia (Socialist Federal Republic of Yugoslavia)
SHAPE	Supreme Headquarters Allied Powers Europe
SIGINT	Signals Intelligence
SLAM	Stand-Off Land Attack Missile
SVK	Srpska Vojska Krajine (Serbian Army of Krajina)
TACP	Tactical Air Control Party
TLAM	Tomahawk Land Attack Missile
TO	Teritorijalna odbrana (Territorial Defence)
UNSC	United Nations Security Council
V i PVO	Vazduhoplovstvo i protivvazdušna odbrana (Air Force and Air Defence)
VJ	Vojska Jugoslavije (Yugoslav Army)
VRS	Vojska Republike Srpske (Army of Republika Srpska)
UAV	Unmanned Aerial Vehicle
UN	United Nations
UNPA	United Nations Protected Areas
UNPROFOR	United Nations Protection Force
UNHCR	United Nations High Commissar for Refugees
USAF	United States Air Force
USAFE	United States Air Force in Europe
USMC	United States Marine Corps
USN	United States Navy

INTRODUCTION

The inter-ethnic war – or 'civil war' – that occurred in the former Socialist Federal Republic of Yugoslavia (*Socijalistička Federativna Republika Jugoslavia*, SFRJ) from 1991 until 1995, attracted much media coverage, both while ongoing and ever since. The long list of publications, monographs, analyses, and other kind of titles almost overwhelms the international scene and ranges from the most serious and important works, to trivial and propaganda titles. The involvement of the International Criminal Tribunal for the former Yugoslavia (ICTY) expanded the coverage through the emergence of numerous original documents nowadays available on the ICTY's website. Ironically, while most of the foreign participants proclaimed the outcome of the war – concluded through the General Framework Agreement for Peace in Bosnia and Herzegovina, also known as the Dayton Agreement or the Dayton Accords – as a 'success', the local participants regard it until this very day as a 'defeat', although all such conclusions are both an oversimplification and an indication of a shift in perception of the backgrounds, the context, and the reason for the beginning and the end of the war in Bosnia and Herzegovina (BiH), and in the former Yugoslavia.

Although an element of the same conflict, the air war, air campaigns, and aerial operations run within the scope of the war in Bosnia and Herzegovina in particular, are actually not directly comparable to the ground operations – which ranged from large-scale conventional battles to ugly campaigns of ethnic cleansing and war crimes on a scale not seen in Europe since 1945. Nevertheless, their influence was highly important and, ultimately, decisive for bringing that war to its end. Unsurprisingly, this aspect of the war in BiH has attracted much attention: numerous authors have researched the deployment of airpower by the North Atlantic Treaty Organisation (NATO) and have analysed and described it in great detail. Because all of the usual analysis is based on NATO-related sources, the result was one-sided: the local participants have largely escaped attention, and their involvement was reduced to three roles: that of the Bosnian Muslims as the 'victims', the Serbs (whether from Bosnia and Herzegovina, Croatia, or Serbia) as 'aggressors', and Croats (regardless if from Croatia or BiH) as 'turncoats', switching positions as they found opportune. Another factor that is frequently superimposed – and not

only by foreigners such as nationals of the NATO member states, but by the Bosnian Muslims (colloquially known as 'Bosniaks'), Croats and Serbs alike – is that regardless of established borders, the war in BiH was usually seen as the same theatre of operations as the war in the Serbian-controlled parts of Croatia.

From the author's standpoint, this is not only an oversimplification, but also a misinterpretation: after all, the Bosnian War – and so also its aerial component – involved more than just the three well-known belligerents, and lasted five years, while the NATO aerial campaign, Operation Deliberate Force, was merely its culmination. This study is thus not only an attempt to sort out the complexity of the Bosnian War, but also an effort to reconstruct a largely unknown story of the air war raging between the Bosnian Muslims and their allies, Croats and their allies, and Serbs in BiH.

In the course of preparing this project, the author made extensive use of domestic and foreign documentation and literature. Foremost amongst foreign sources were two classic works of the British journalist Tim Ripley, one of which was titled almost identically to this volume, but also a range of studies published by the historians of the Historical Branch of the United States Air Force (USAF), at Maxwell Air Force Base (AFB). The final report on the *Balkans Air Campaign Study* edited by Robert Owen and his separate works, and those by Mark Bucknam and a few other authors have provided further, in depth analyses of the deployment of NATO – and US – airpower, including all of its constraints and benefits. Various monographs by Dutch and German authors have contributed to the description of these air forces. Finally, the Central Intelligence Agency (CIA) study *Balkan Battlegrounds* proved an essential source of information in providing an overview of the US – and NATO – involvement.

That said, the centrepiece of this project is the extensive use of documentation about local air forces, and a series of interviews with local participants and eyewitnesses. The documentation used was drawn from the Croatian State Archives, the ICTY online materials, the (partial) archive of the Army of the Republic Srpska (*Vojska Republike Srpske*, VRS), and from numerous private collections. Additional information was obtained from monographs published in the Croatian and Serbian languages. Particular attention was also paid to the involvement of the local air forces – and this is likely to become the most significant contribution of this volume: the provision of entirely new insights into an extremely complex air war fought over Bosnia and Herzegovina – and the Serb-controlled parts of Croatia – in the period of 1992-1995.

Much of the documentation obtained from various Serbian sources is still considered 'classified'. Access to this provided much exclusive information, never previously published, and an entirely new interpretation of many crucial events: indeed, this enabled a complete reconstruction of the widely unknown aspects of the air war over Bosnia.

My hope is that readers might find these explanations satisfactory and retain their full confidence in the narrative that follows.

1

THE SERB AIR FORCE DOMINATES BOSNIAN SKIES, 1992

The civil war that exploded in 1991 in the former SFRJ, marked the end of this state after 73 years of existence. It began when the two westernmost administrative units of the country – the Socialist Republics of Slovenia and Croatia, respectively – decided to abandon the Federation in 1991. They were followed by the easternmost Socialist Republic of Macedonia, which declared itself independent in September of the same year.

While the Federal government in Belgrade might have let Slovenia go, the separation of Croatia – where a large portion of the population consisted of Serbs – made an armed conflict inevitable. The war in Slovenia was sharp and short, lasting from 27 June to 2 July 1991. However, in late August and early September 1991, the conflict in Croatia escalated into full-scale hostilities, with months-long battles and massive casualties. Under diplomatic pressure of the European Community (EC), a ceasefire came into effect on 3 January 1992: by this time, up to one third of Croatia – mainly the territories along the border with the Socialist Republic of Bosnia and Herzegovina (colloquially 'BiH') – came under the control of the Serbs, who self-proclaimed an independent Republic Serbian Krajina (*Republika Srpska Krajina*, RSK). Having already evacuated its garrisons in Slovenia, in July and August 1991, and most of those in Croatia during the rest of that year, the Yugoslav National Army (*Jugoslovenska Narodna Armija*, JNA) was then ordered to withdraw from the RSK too: in February 1992, a peacekeeping force of the United Nations (UN) – the United Nations Protection Force (UNPROFOR) – began deploying with the aim of separating the belligerents in Bosnia and Herzegovina.

Initially at least, the Socialist Republic of Bosnia and Herzegovina had managed to keep itself out of the war, but tensions between its three principal ethnic and religious groups – Bosniaks, Croats, and Serbs – soared: each began establishing its own paramilitary forces, always with the official explanation of intending to safeguard its own territory within the Republic. Moreover, many of the units of the Yugoslav National Army from BiH became engaged in the war in Croatia: indeed, a few of the JNA's units predominantly staffed by local Serbs were then 'left behind' in the Republic. The longer the conflict went on, the more members of the various ethnic and religious minorities defected, in turn making the JNA's units more and more Serbian-dominated. With the leaders of all the differing parties pursing their own interests, an armed confrontation became inevitable and indeed: the first clashes between the Bosniaks, Serbs, and Croats took place in the spring of 1992.

At this point in time, the international community – foremost the EC and the UN – reached the decision that Bosnia and Herzegovina should become an independent state. This premature arbitration only served the purpose of fuelling the conflict: the Serbs and the Croats of Bosnia and Herzegovina quickly proclaimed their own states, which had aims that were entirely different from those of the government in Sarajevo. Indeed, their aims were at odds with the intentions of the international community: absurdly, while the international community had not only tolerated but even supported the collapse of the *multinational* SFRJ, it proved unwilling to tolerate the collapse of the *multinational* Bosnia and Herzegovina.

Withdrawal of the JNA

Until 1992, the Air Force and Air Defence Force of the SFRJ (*Ratno Vazduhoplovstvo i Protivvazdušna Odbrana*, RV i PVO) had numerous air bases and other facilities in BiH. The most important of which was the one in Bihać – which included a huge underground complex, and the forward operations base in Udbina (which since 1991 had been within the RSK) – followed by Mostar (home of the Air Force Academy units), Rajlovac (Technical School of the RV i PVO outside

A line-up of Galeb G-4s of the 249th Fighter Bomber Squadron at Udbina Air Base. The Federal forces abandoned this air base during April 1992. (Milorad D. Ristić)

Sarajevo), and Tuzla.[1]

As the clashes from late March continued during April 1992, the RV i PVO took part in combat operations, mainly through supporting the JNA (and later Serb) units on multiple frontlines: in Posavina (the area along the Save River, in northern Bosnia), in the Kupres area (southern Central Bosnia and western Herzegovina), and all over Herzegovina. Notably, most of the time the RV i PVO flew ground-strikes against units of the – now 'regular' – Croatian Army (*Hrvatska Vojska*, HV), deployed on the territory of BiH since late March 1992. However, as BiH became an independent state, in May 1992 the rump Federal Yugoslav government in Belgrade decided that the RV i PVO, as part of the Federal forces, would abandon BiH and withdraw to the 'shortened' Federal Republic of Yugoslavia (consisting of Serbia and Montenegro). The evacuation of RV i PVO garrisons started in the second half of April and continued during the early days of May.

The three MiG-21 squadrons, a light AA air defence regiment and parts of the air base from Bihać moved to Ponikve, a non-operational air base in Serbia, between 22 April and 16 May 1992. The runways and almost iconic underground *object* were destroyed on 16 May. The empty air base, being in the administrative sense between Croatia and BiH, remained partly controlled by the Serb forces from Krajina and BiH and under the constant threat of Muslim territorial forces from their neighbouring villages.[2]

At Mostar, two helicopter squadrons moved to Podgorica Air Base in Montenegro, while two aviation squadrons and an air defence missile regiment moved to Serbia, by 13 May 1992. The runway and vital objects were demolished by 19 May. The air base remained under the control of local Serb forces, until the Croat offensive initiated on 11 June 1992.[3]

In Tuzla, the MiG-21 squadron that had arrived earlier from Pula in Croatia along with a light air defence regiment and the remaining personnel of the air base withdrew to Pristina Air Base, in Serbia, between 12 and 18 May 1992, and the runway was demolished.[4] A few days later, Muslim Territorial Defence forces entered the ruined facility.

At Rajlovac, south-west from Sarajevo, most of the training and logistic facilities were evacuated, and the emptied air base remained under Serb control until the end of the war. Air defence and communications assets at Mount Jahorina remained functional and under Serb control.

Most of the RV i PVO units stationed in Banja Luka remained. Although many of the active personnel arriving from BiH decided to abandon their units and go to Serbia, enough officers and other ranks remained to establish the core of a nascent Serbian military flying branch in the republic.[5] The last of the 'Federal' RV i PVO personnel left BiH on 19 May 1992: even then, this force continued flying sporadic air support and transport operations until 31 May 1992.[6]

V i PVO

A full understanding the air war over Bosnia and Herzegovina, and over the Serbian-controlled parts of Croatia requires an analysis of the local participants: after all, it was the deployment of local air forces that provoked an intervention by the international community and led to the involvement of NATO from 1993, thus opening the way for Operation Deliberate Force in late summer 1995.

The war was already rampaging over most of BiH when the government of what was officially re-named as the Federal Republic of Yugoslavia (FRY, essentially: Serbia and Montenegro), in Belgrade, announced that the remaining units of the JNA would leave the nascent nation, effective from 19 May 1992. Correspondingly, the Bosnian Serbs decided to create their own army, using assets handed

to them by the JNA when it withdrew from Bosnia and Herzegovina. Following a decision of the Parliament of the Republic Srpska, on 12 May 1992 the Army of the Republic Srpska (*Vojska Republike Srpske*, VRS) was established with Lieutenant-General Ratko Mladić as its first commander.[7] The flying branch of the VRS became the Air Force and Air Defence Force (*Vazduhoplovstvo i Protivvazdušna Odbrana*, V i PVO). The majority of the personnel of both the VRS and the V i PVO were Serbs born in BiH.

The first commander of this force was the newly promoted General Živomir Ninković, a former Commanding Officer (CO) of the Mostar-based 97th Aviation Brigade. He arrived in Banja Luka on 19 May 1992, and immediately assumed his duties.[8] Although Mladić demanded that Ninković establish the HQ closer to his own HQ in Han Pijesak (the wartime HQ of the Yugoslav RV i PVO was originally planned to be positioned on Mount Jahorina, close to Sarajevo), the latter kept his headquarters in the north: the reason was that most of his units were either at the nearby Mahovljani AB, or inside Banja Luka. Instead, he took care to establish an Air Force Department within Mladić's HQ, to coordinate the cooperation between the VRS and the V i PVO.[9]

The other former RV i PVO bases (Tuzla, Mostar and Bihać) were seized in May-June by Muslim or Croat forces. The air base at Banja Luka had been constructed before the war started in 1991 but was not in regular use: located north of the town, near the village of Mahovljani, it was a reserve air base with all the facilities but without active units. In August 1991, the 474th Air Base and 82nd Aviation Brigade were redeployed there from Cerklje AB in Slovenia. Because of the lack of personnel, the 82nd Brigade was disbanded and its assets reorganised as No. 238 Fighter-Bomber Squadron of the 117th Aviation Brigade with HQ at Bihać Air Base (AB). The squadron was equipped with Soko J-22 Orao and Soko J-21 Jastreb strike aircraft.[10]

In mid-October 1991, another unit arrived at Banja Luka. It was the 111th Aviation Brigade, withdrawn from air bases of Pleso and Lučko near Zagreb. On 20 October 1991, this was reorganised as the 111th Helicopter Regiment, including the 711th Anti-Tank Helicopter Squadron (Aerospatiale SA-341/342 Gazelles in their locally-manufactured armed Gama variant), and the 780th Transport Helicopter Squadron (Mil Mi-8, ASCC/NATO-codename Hip). They were based at Zalužani barracks, north from Banja Luka.[11]

Later, in December 1991, additional units of the RV i PVO were deployed in and around Banja Luka. These were the 149th Self-Propelled Missile Air Defence Regiment (from Pleso), the 155th Missile Air Defence Regiment (formerly responsible for protection of Zagreb), elements of the former 151st Air Base in Pleso, 258th Air Base at Pula and the 289th Communications Battalion from Zagreb.[12] Finally, the HQ of the 51st Air Surveillance Battalion was evacuated from Bihać to Banja Luka on 11 May 1992. Other major elements of the RV i PVO still present in BiH included air surveillance units at Mount Kozara (a company of the 51st Battalion), Mount Jahorina and Nevesinje (companies of 20th Battalion, which had its HQ in Serbia), and the remnants of the 321st Communications Battalion at Mount Jahorina.[13] While remaining under the control of the Yugoslav Air Force, they closely cooperated with the V i PVO. Nevertheless, the build-up of the latter proved a difficult task, foremost because – regardless of where born – the mass of the flying- and ground-personnel preferred to withdraw to the FRY (and Serbia in particular). The result was that numerous units literally collapsed: their equipment was left in place, but fewer than half of the original personnel of flying units, and fewer than one third of the personnel of air defence units were still around. Pilots were especially a problem: for example, there were only a handful of fliers trained to fly Oraos at Banja Luka.

Table 1: V i PVO, 1993-1995[16]		
Unit	Base	Equipment & Notes
HQ V i PVO, Banja Luka		
ELINT Platoon	Banja Luka	
Aviation Depot Kosmos	Banja Luka	Maintenance and overhaul of radars and air defence equipment
Aviation Depot Orao	Rajlovac	Maintenance and overhaul of aircraft engines
474th Air Base	Mahovljani, Zalužani	Includes 474th Light Air Defence Regiment (Bofors L-70; M-55; 9K32M Strela-2M/SA-7 'Grail'; 9K38 Igla/SA-18 'Grouse'; Strela-1M/SA-9 'Gaskin'; Strela-10M/SA-13 'Gopher')
92nd Mixed Aviation Brigade	Mahovljani	
27th Fighter-Bomber Aviation Squadron	Mahovljani	J-22 Orao
28th Fighter-Bomber Aviation Squadron	Mahovljani	J-21/IJ-21 Jastreb
89th Mixed Helicopter Squadron	Zalužani	SA.341H Gazele/Gama, Mi-8
92nd Light Multi-Purpose Aviation Squadron	Banja Luka, Prijedor	Utva-66, Utva-75, Piper, Cessna, Zlin, Vilga
76th Air Base	Bratunac	The chain of command unclear; mostly controlled by the Serbian State Security – including the 76th Air Base
76th Light Combat Aviation Squadron	Bratunac	J-20 Kraguj, An-2
155th Air Defence Missile Regiment	Banja Luka	
1st Battalion	Čelinac	S-75M Volkhov/SA-2 'Guideline'
4th Battalion	Novakovići	S-75M Volkhov/SA-2 'Guideline'
Technical Battalion	Čelinac, Novakovići	Unit incomplete
51st Aerial Surveillance Battalion	Banja Luka	
Communications Company	Mount Jahorina	
Radar Company	Mount Plješevica	Marconi S-600 radar
Radar Company	Mount Kozara	Marconi S-600 radar
Radar Company	Mount Jahorina	Marconi S-600 radar
Radar Company	Nevesinje	Marconi S-600 radar
Air Assault Company		Disbanded in 1993

Similarly, the 155th Regiment was only capable of staffing one of its battalions in an operational condition. Although the VRS authorities repeatedly requested help from Belgrade, demanding that officers and other ranks born in BiH be sent back, the authorities of the FRY only reluctantly rotated some of their personnel to the V i PVO, and thus the force never had more than 60% of the necessary staff.[14]

Eventually, 27 Gazelle and Gama helicopters, 14 Mi-8s, 13 Oraos, and nine Jastrebs were left at Banja Luka. By the end of May 1992, these had all received new markings, which distinguished them from the aircraft and helicopters operated by what was now the air force of the FRY. Ninković and his staff then went a step further and reorganised all the units as listed in Table 1: this structure would remain almost unchanged throughout the whole duration of the war. The only major change occurred in 1993-1994, when air defences were expanded through the re-deployment of a number of units equipped with 2K12 Kub (ASCC/NATO-codename SA-6 'Gainful') from the FRY.[15]

Air Force of the Armija BiH

In June 1992, the government in Sarajevo established a predominantly Muslim force, the Army of BiH (*Armija BiH*) using paramilitary groups – such as the 'Patriotic League' or 'Green Berets' – and whatever elements of the former

New Serbian V i PVO markings were introduced in late May 1992, to distinguish the Serb combat aircraft from those of the FRY air force. (Milan Micevski)

Jastrebs over Bosnia

While the V i PVO operated a small number of faster and more powerful Soko J-22 Oraos, its backbone was the older, slower and less capable Soko J-21 Jastrebs. Developed in the late 1950s by the Aeronautical Technical Institute at Zarkovo, and in production by the Soko aircraft factory in Mostar from 1965 until 1977 the Soko G-2 Galebs and J-21 Jastrebs shared the same design, which emphasised the simplicity of maintenance and operation. The G-2 Galeb was a two-seat jet trainer armed with two 12.7mm Browning AN/M3 machine guns and four underwing hardpoints with a capacity of 300kg (661lbs) in total. The J-21 Jastreb was a single-seat light attack aircraft with strengthened structure and a more powerful variant of the Rolls-Royce Viper engine, armed with three 12.7mm machine guns and eight hardpoints: inboard hardpoints could carry bombs of up to 250kg (550lbs), while six outboard pylons were usually used for 127mm (5in) VRZ-157 unguided rockets. A total of 248 G-2s and 224 J-21s, reconnaissance IJ-21s, and NJ-21 two-seat conversion trainers were manufactured, a large number of which were exported to Libya and Zambia. During the 1980s, the JRV i PVO began replacing them with more advanced Soko Galeb-4: this process was never completed due to the outbreak of the war in Yugoslavia. As a consequence, both types were still available in significant numbers and this is why a number of J-21s (though no G-2s) served with the 28th Fighter-Bomber Aviation Squadron of the V i PVO at the Mahovljani AB.

Serb Jastrebs were extensively used during the strike missions in 1992. To allow better performance they did not used tip-tanks, as with this NJ-21 serialed 23518. (D Vejnović)

Territorial Defence it could scratch together. Although poorly trained and armed, the Armija BiH established itself in control over several sport airfields and the former RV i PVO Tuzla AB. While having no aircraft or helicopters early on, the Armija BiH did manage to obtain several Mi-8s by 1995, and to slowly build-up an operational structure.

As such, it was never able to compare with other local players, except in regards of the courage of its staff.

The JNA abandoned Tuzla AB on 22 May 1992. Three days later a group of Bosniak airmen entered the air base and officially established Air Group Tuzla: this unit had no flying equipment and was mainly responsible for keeping the facility safe from looting, repairing the sabotaged runway and organising regular military life. In June 1992, the Air Group requisitioned nine light aircraft – including three Utva-75, two Vilgas, two Pipers, one Utva-66, and one Zlin – from the local aero-club, while runway repairs were completed by August. The unit started flying during about the same time (and, indeed, suffered its first loss when the sole Utva-66, serial number 51112, was shot down by Serb groundfire while on a mission of medical evacuation to Zagreb

Mi-8 transport helicopters of the V i PVO seen at Zalužani airfield, Banja Luka. (Drago Vejnović)

A pilot poses near one of the 89th Mixed Helicopter Squadron's SA-341 Gazelles. (M. Micevski)

evacuating 52 troops of the Armija BiH to Croatia.[20] Indeed, by the autumn of 1992 the air bridge was in full swing, An-2s undertaking 12 missions in November, and 63 in December, primarily to Ćoralići. In turn, the Armija BiH sent parts for 203mm artillery ammunition and a stock of British-made Hunting BL.755 cluster bomb units to Croatia. All operations were undertaken by night – which was a precaution to avoid not only groundfire, but also the long-range artillery of the VRS. Only early training flights were undertaken by day. The air bridge came to a sudden end on 30 December 1992, when UN observers arrived and imposed the no-fly policy.[21]

on 18 July 1992), but never attempted to equip any of its aircraft with weaponry. Moreover, once the UN imposed a no-fly zone (NFZ) over BiH in October 1992, its operations were severely curtailed.[17]

Cazinska Krajina: the Bihać Pocket

The other area where the Bosnian Muslims established a flying unit was the so-called Cazinska Krajina: a pocket in western BiH, an area predominantly populated by the Bosniaks, that found itself cut off and besieged by Serb forces. The former underground air base south of the town was sabotaged upon the withdrawal of the RV i PVO: subsequently, its – extensive – overground facilities were partially controlled by the Serbs, and partially by Bosniak forces, or considered 'no-man's land'.[18] However, the staff of the former RV i PVO included many Muslims, most of whom joined the local Territorial Defence (*Teritorijalna Odbrana*, TO) of BiH, and the latter requisitioned an Utva-75, a Piper 18, and three gliders from the local aero-club. These aircraft flew their first 'combat' sorties between Dolovo and Ceravci-Bihać on 18 May 1992. A month later, a Bosnian pilot flew the first mission with the Utva-75 from 'Begova Kafana', near Cazin, to Lučko airport outside Zagreb, with the aim of establishing contact with the nascent Croat Air Force (*Hrvatsko Ratno Zrakoplovstvo*, HRZ). As a result, starting from the night of 21 to 22 June 1992, an air bridge was established connecting Lučko with Ćoralići airfield near Cazin, which subsequently came under the control of the unit designated 'Airport Hub Bihać', which controlled all three flying installations in this part of Muslim-controlled Bosnia. On 4 August 1992, the 'Hub' was reorganised as the 1st Air Squadron, and later expanded into the Air Group Bihać.[19]

In June 1992, a group of Armija BiH airmen had been sent to Zagreb to undergo conversion training on Antonov An-2 biplane transports and – later on – on Spanish-made CASA C.212CD light transports. A second group followed in November 1992. Their training was completed during early 1993, by when a few new pilots had also been trained to fly the Utva-75 and Piper 18 at Ćoralići airfield. In August 1992, a Bosnian businessman obtained a single CASA C.212CD Aviocar and donated it for the air bridge. Flown and maintained by the HRZ, by December 1992 the aircraft had flown 79 sorties delivering 90 tonnes of cargo and 330 passengers to Cazinska Krajina, while

Hips to the Rescue

Meanwhile, the government of BiH was searching for ways to reinforce its fledgling flying branch through new acquisitions abroad. This resulted in the purchase of two Mi-8T helicopters (ASCC/NATO-codename Hip) on the market in the former Union of Soviet Socialist Republics (USSR or Soviet Union). Delivered and assembled in Croatia, they were flown to Visoko in BiH on 17 February 1993, before, two days later, being ferried to Tuzla. Two additional Mi-8s arrived between 10 and 14 March and, ultimately, the fleet was increased to 12. Like all the Mi-8s acquired by Croatia around the same time, all had belonged to former Soviet civil operators such as Aeroflot, Mi-Inter and others. Due to the great hurry with which they were pressed into service, most retained their civilian livery: examples acquired by the Armija BiH received local registrations pre-fixed by T9, followed by three-letter codes between HAA and HAL. All Armija BiH-operated Mi-8s were assigned to the Air Group Tuzla that, in 1995, was reorganised as the 1st Air Brigade RV i PVO, Armija BiH.[22]

With no sources of fuel or spares of their own, the Bosniak Mi-8s were subjected to the direct control of the Supreme Command of the Armija BiH and used only for 'special' purposes. The first two were almost immediately pressed into service for supplying two Muslim enclaves besieged in eastern Bosnia: Srebrenica and Žepa. Between 27 February and 30 March 1993, they transported 20 tonnes of ammunition and 5,000kg of other equipment, and evacuated wounded in a total of 17 sorties. Attrition was heavy: one Mi-8 crashed at Mount Konjuh, on 10 March 1993, injuring the crew and passengers, while another was damaged by groundfire and its pilot wounded while overflying VRS positions on 24 March 1993, but managed to continue the mission.[23]

Operations inside the territories controlled by the Armija BiH were frequently important but remained rather sparing – to no small degree because of the subsequent confrontation with forces of the Croatian Defence Council (*Hrvatsko Vijece Odbrane*, HVO), which erupted in Herzegovina in the late summer of 1993. There, one Bosniak Mi-8 was captured on the ground, together with its crew, and subsequently deployed by the HVO.

Utva 75 belonging to the Armija BiH Bihać Air Group at Ćoralići airfield. (Felić Bejdo)

The backbone of the air bridge between Croatia and the Bihać Pocket in later 1992 was this CASA 212 (JetsPhotos. Net, Roberto Benetti)

HRZ: Croatian Air Force

Unlike the VRS and the Armija of BiH, the HVO did not poses its own air arm: instead, it was supported by the regular Croatian Air Force (*Hrvatsko Ratno Zrakoplovstvo*, HRZ) throughout the entire war in Bosnia and Herzegovina, from 1992 until 1995. The HRZ was established during the war in Croatia, in 1991: initially, it was a branch of the Croatian Army (*Hrvatska Vojska*, HV) and operated several light aircraft drawn from civilian aero-clubs. Its first fighter squadron was officially established on 17 January 1992 and included only pilots, but no aircraft.[24] This was soon to change: the first MiG-21bis of the RV i PVO was flown to Croatia by a defecting pilot on 4 February, followed by two more on 15 May 1992. Although the squadron lost one of its aircraft in clashes with the VRS forces in the Posavina area on 24 June 1992, the unit then moved to Pula AB, and commenced training of its pilots and ground crews.[25]

For the time being, the Croatian-operated transport and light aircraft were thus to play a much more important role in the fighting. As part of the assistance to the official government of BiH in Sarajevo, starting from 22 June 1992, the HRZ took part in establishing an air bridge between Croatia and improvised airfields in Cazinska Krajina. In the beginning, Antonov An-2s and Air Tractor AT-400s were used in these flights, mostly carried out by former RV i PVO pilots, veterans from war in 1991. The RS Krajina was entered by UN peacekeeping forces and during this period there was no threat from the ground: this would emerge only later in 1993, when the Serbs began reactivating

their forces. Nevertheless, even then the transportation missions were carried out from Lučko and Pula during the night, always at different times.[26]

In late autumn of 1992, the HRZ obtained several second-hand Mil Mi-8 (ASCC/NATO-codename 'Hip') transport helicopters, mostly from the Russian Aeroflot, or civil companies such as Jakutaiva, OLVI or Slovakian Slov-Air, or in Poland. The helicopters would enter the inventory of the mixed squadrons in Pleso-Zagreb and Split. Two of them would be used by the Police/Ministry of Interior.[27]

In the same period a number of light aircraft and helicopters were obtained on the civil market for the Special Unit of the HV Main Staff. Those included MD-500 Helicopters, Cessna 201Ns, Schweizer 269C light helicopters and Aviasud Albatros ultralight aircraft. This unit had been regularly supported by a detachment of Mi-8s since April 1993 and flew observation and reconnaissance missions against the RS Krajina.

Between June 1993 and spring 1994 HRZ obtained a total of 15 Mil Mi-24D/V attack helicopters (ASCC/NATO-codename 'Hind') in Ukraine. They were shipped to Krk Island and then brought to Pleso for assembly at the nearby Air Technical Centre in Velika Gorica. Ten of them entered service with the 29th Combat Helicopter Squadron, HRZ. In the same period, Croatia obtained 23 MiG-21bis and four MiG-21UMs from the same source. Once again, all were delivered by ship to Krk and from there to the Air Technical Centre in Velika Gorica (which, while still called the Zmaj, had overhauled all of the MiG-21s for the former Yugoslav Air Force before 1991). The curious UN observers were told that the MiGs were left by the Yugoslav Air Force in 1991, and that the Mi-24s were to be used for MEDEVAC purpose. The armament pylons were removed and provisional red crosses were painted on the fuselage: it was in this condition that they were shown in the public for the first time in late 1994.[28]These purchases enabled the expansion of the HRZ into seven squadrons (Nos 20-22, 26-29), among them two equipped with MiG-21bis fighters (Nos 21 and 22).

As a retaliation for the Croatian attack on RS Krajina in Medački Džep in mid-September 1993, the SVK launched missile attacks on several cities in Croatian territory. In an attempt to hit back by destroying one of the Serb ammunition depots outside Vrgin Most, on 14 September that year two HRZ MiGs took off from Pleso, each armed with four 250kg FAB-250M-54 bombs. The first pilot managed to drop his bombs, but the second reported that he was hit and lost communication: his aircraft – HRZ serial number 103 (former 17167

Antonov An-2 No 014, of the Croatian Air Force (HRZ), seen in mid-1993. (Author's collection)

The HRZ MiG-21bis No 103 was claimed by Serbian air defences on 14 September 1993. (via Dean Čanić)

during 1993 in operations against the SVK and in support of the HVO in autumn 1993 deep in Central Bosnia. One of them was damaged by the Armija BiH on 2 September 1993 during a medical evacuation of injured troops in the Busovača area. Later on, starting in November 1994, HRZ Mi-8s were also involved in the renewed air bridge to Cazinska Krajina.

Outside the HRZ there was a Special Unit of the HV Main Staff which operated light aviation and helicopters. They were used in special missions against Krajina and in BiH, supporting the local Croat HVO forces and elements of the regular HV forces that operated there. In September 1993, two Mi-8 MTV-1s (Nos H-252 and 253) were passed to the HVO, while they managed to capture another one from the ARBiH (T9-HAA) in November 1993 in Herzegovina.[30]

One peculiarity of Croatian aviation in the war of 1992-1995 was the usage of numerous indigenous drones/UAVs constructed by air enthusiasts and in March 1993, at Slavonski Brod, the 280th Platoon HV was formed to operate drones/UAVs. The usage of these aerial vehicles

of the RV i PVO) – was most likely hit by a Serb-operated SA-6 surface-to-air missile (SAM), deployed near Trepča, and crashed near Stipan, killing its pilot.[29]

Besides the obvious improvement of the HRZ's combat capabilities, the Mi-8 helicopters improved their air mobility. They were used

was intensive in 1995 during preparations for the operations against the RS Krajina and in the final phases of the war in Bosnia against the VRS forces. VRS military intelligence assessed in 1995 that the HRZ, 'grew up to the level in which we should respect their capabilities'.[31]

Two unmarked MiG-21bis seen during take-off from Pleso-Zagreb, in autumn 1993, after being assembled in the Air Technical Centre in nearby Velika Gorica. (Vinko Šebrek via Z. Despot)

A few Mi-8MOUNTV helicopters were provided to the Croatian police and were used in support of their special purpose units, as here at Mount Velebit in 1993. (Stjepan Milković, *Alfe žive vječno*, p.271)

RV i PVO of the Federal Republic of Yugoslavia

Proclaimed on 27 April 1992, the Federal Republic of Yugoslavia included the remaining two former republics of the SFRJ: Montenegro and Serbia. The army of the new state was named correspondingly; the Army of Yugoslavia (*Vojska Jugoslavije*, VJ), effective from 19 May 1992. Essentially, the VJ consisted of all the assets and equipment that remained in the territory of the two republics and parts of the units that were earlier transferred from other former Yugoslav republics. The Yugoslav Air Force, or RV i PVO, consisted of units already stationed in Serbia and Montenegro and of those withdrawn from the republics that abandoned the SFRJ in 1991-1992.

By late May 1992, the FRY was subjected to an arms embargo imposed by the UN. Based on accusations that it was maintaining a military presence – and exercising influence – inside BiH, this embargo included the deployment of observers from the EC and the UN at all of the RV i PVO's bases: they continued to control all the activities of the air force well into late 1995. Moreover, in July 1992, NATO warships deployed in the Adriatic Sea began exercising control of the shipping from, and bound for, the ports of Montenegro within the framework of Operation Sharp Guard. They were supported by maritime patrol- and reconnaissance aircraft – including Lockheed P-3C Orions of the US Navy (USN), P-3s of the Dutch, Portuguese and Spanish Air Forces, Lockheed CP-140 Auroras of the Royal Canadian Air Force, Breguet 1150 Atlantics of the French and German naval aviation, and British Aerospace (BAE) Nimrods of the Royal Air Force (RAF) – deployed at the US-controlled Naval Air Station (NAS) Sigonella, on Sicily, and at Cagliari AB in Italy.[32]

The RV i PVO did not take part in the Bosnian War after 31 May 1992. However, it did indeed – and very much – support the two newly-established Serbian air forces: V i PVO in BiH, and the one of the RSK in Croatia, through provision of (mostly obsolete) equipment, and through rotating its personnel (mostly officers born in BiH or Croatia). Moreover, the aerial surveillance of the RV i PVO retained links to radar stations on Bosnian territory for the entire duration of the war.

Operation Corridor 92

The first serious challenge to the young Republika Srpska, its army, and air force, was Operation Corridor. As the JNA withdrew, Muslim forces and Croat forces from the country, reinforced by units of the regular HV, established themselves in control of the Posavina area, cutting off the west of the RS from the east, and thus its vital link to Serbia. The V i PVO went into action against targets in this area on the morning of 27 May 1992, when a pair of Oraos attacked the Bosniak forces at Pudin Han, outside Ključ.[33] By the end of that day, Serb pilots had flown a total of 16 attack sorties – which is why henceforth 27 May is celebrated as Air Force Day. Additional sorties against Muslim and Croat forces followed, resulting in the loss of an armed Gama helicopter on 9 June, and a two-seat NJ-21 Jastreb on 11 June 1992, with both crews.[34]

Following extensive preparations, on 24 June 1992 the VRS launched Operation Corridor, with the intention of establishing a land connection between the western and eastern parts of the Republika Srpska. This was a massive operation, including not only all the major units of the VRS, but also units of the Krajina Militia (*Milicija Krajine*) from Serb-controlled parts of Croatia – and the HRZ: on the first day of the Serb operation, the VRS claimed the Croatian MiG-21bis serial 101 (ex 17133 of the RV i PVO), flown by Colonel Radoš. The jet was flying an airstrike on the Serb positions outside Plehan and crashed about 10 kilometres from Derventa.[35] Subsequently, the HRZ withdrew from action and is not known to have flown any further combat sorties. Nevertheless, on 28 June, Croat forces claimed the downing of a single Orao (serial 25105) near Odžak. Its pilot, Captain Lukić, was killed – apparently – after ejecting safely and landing under his parachute.[36]

After five days of bitter fighting, the Serbs punched through and re-established their link to western Bosnia, and thus to Serbia.[37] The V i PVO engaged the complete available fleet, including the attached Krajina Militia 56th Helicopter Squadron. The list of strikes from July to early October 1992 is long. There were CAS missions to support the advancing VRS troops, and missions against important targets in the enemy territory (including a refinery in Brod, a ferry on the River Sava, concentrations of Croatian forces on both sides of this river) until the Serb forces captured the city of Bosanski Brod on 6 October. The final missions were conducted on 10 October 1992.

The V i PVO was heavily involved in supporting Operation Corridor and logged following numbers of sorties by type:

- J-22 Oraos: 528 sorties (316.20hrs)
- Jastrebs: 490 sorties (375.02hrs; not including reconnaissance operations)
- Gama: 72 sorties (242.42hrs) – during which they used 154 9M14 Malyutka (ASCC/NATO-codename AT-3 Sagger) anti-tank guided missiles.

Part of the tail of Croatian MiG-21bis No 101 that was claimed on 24 June 1992 in Posavina, now displayed in Banja Luka VRS Museum. (Bojan Dimitrijević)

Amongst the ordnance deployed by fighter-bombers were 492 Munja 128mm unguided rockets and 303 BL.755 cluster bomb units (CBUs), as well as four US-made Hughes AGM-65 Maverick guided missiles. The Mi-8s and Gazelles were engaged in MEDEVAC and supply missions and flew a total of 2,909 sorties (5622.09hrs), ferrying 1,070 passengers, transporting 215 tonnes of cargo, and evacuating 1,894 wounded.[38]

From 12 June 1992, the V i PVO was reinforced through the addition of the 56th Helicopter Squadron with five Gazelles and two Mi-8s of the Ministry of Interior RS Krajina, from Serb-controlled parts of Croatia. With all of its helicopters painted in blue and white, and based at the football stadium of Prnjavor, the helicopters were used along with those from Banja Luka, without any difference in tasks and treatment. However, they suffered heavily: two Mi-8s were shot down and nine crewmembers killed. The first was lost on 17 July near Gradačac, with a crew of three; the second on 18 August near Doboj, with its crew of three, and a replacement crew it carried. Most Krajina helicopters remained in Prnjavor until 1 August 1992: then nearly all were withdrawn, bar a few left behind at the request of General Talić, commander of the 1 Krajiški Corps VRS: they were to continue serving in Bosnia until the end of the war. One of the latter, a Gazelle, crashed on 17 November 1992 while underway from Udbina to Knin, killing the commander of the unit and three technicians. Thus, within only a few months, the *Milicija* (Police) of the Krajina lost three helicopters and 13 pilots and ground personnel, and even its commander. Nevertheless, it remained operational and continued deploying its Gazelles, foremost for liaison.[39]

One of two Mi-8 helicopters of the 56th Helicopter Squadron of the RS Krajina Ministry of Interior, used during Operation Corridor from Prnjavor football stadium, summer 1992 (D. Vejnović)

Once the land communications with the FRY were not only secured but also re-opened, on 1 July 1992, helicopters of both the V i PVO, and from the Krajina Militia, flew to Belgrade to pick up urgently needed medical supplies for the hospital in Banja Luka. One of them was hit from the ground causing many dead and wounded among the crew, but it managed to land safely. In the narrowest part of the corridor, in the later period they had to fly at extremely low altitudes of 25 metres, to avoid Armija BiH groundfire.

Other Targets

Beside the operations in support of Operation Corridor, the V i PVO carried out numerous strikes against targets and close air support for VRS units all over the BiH frontlines until the late autumn 1992. In certain cases, the strikes were pivotal in enabling the local Serb forces to hold the lines against the quantitatively superior Muslim Armija BiH forces, especially in Eastern Bosnia – around Goražde and at the Smoluća (Serb) enclave, west of Tuzla.

Other targets were the factories of the former Yugoslavia defence industry which continued to produce ammunition or other equipment for Croat or Muslim forces. These were "Bratstvo" at Novi Travnik (26 August, including usage of two AGM-65s) and later, the factory

The characteristic "half-roundel" of the RS Krajina Militia adopted in spring 1992 on its Gazelle and Mi-8 helicopters. (M. Micevski)

One of the J-20 Kragujes that were used by the Light Strike Squadron in the Bratunac area in 1992-1993. It carries a Cyrillic inscription 'Militia', and personal name "Milić". (M.D. Ristić)

The other J-20 Kraguj used from Bratunac was 03, named "Vulić". Here, seen prior to take-off for a mission. (M.D. Ristić)

Four J-20 Kragujes that were used for ground crew training in Rajlovac Air Technical Academy were taken to the Bratunac area, but were used for spare parts. (M.D.Ristić)

at Vitez, "Slavko Rodić" in Bugojno, the iron works in Zenica which were attacked between 26 September and 3 October. In the separate Cazinska Krajina, soon to be known as the Bihać Pocket, the V Corps of the Armija BiH developed local production of ammunition and equipment in several factories or small enterprises. They were targeted between 25 August and 14 September in successful attacks which downsized the production for some time and included the usage of AGM-65 Mavericks, such as during the attack on the Krajina Metal factory in Bihać. The Serb air force also carried out strikes against the improvised airfield at Ćoralići near Cazin, during September and October to prevent the established air bridge between Croatia and the Bihać pocket. Durandal runway-penetration bombs were not effective since the Muslim forces repaired the airfield through the night, and instead BL-755 cluster bombs were the standard ordnance against this target.[40]

Overall, between 27 May and 5 December 1992, fighter-bombers of the V i PVO flew 1,205 combat sorties, delivering 612.5 tons of ordnance. On average each pilot flew 83 combat sorties that lasted a total of 40 hours and delivered 40 tons of ordnance. Both Jastrebs and Oraos were used with the same tempo, but Oraos were usually deployed against better-defended targets. Contrary to peace-time practice, now it became normal for pilots to carry out three or four mission in one day; some of the more experienced fliers managed even six or seven, while the absolute record was eight missions by one pilot in one day.[41] Pilots on many occasions remained in the cockpit, waiting for the ground crew to fix a new set of armaments and continued to another sortie. Although most of the missions were flown against targets about 150-200 kilometres away from Mahovljani, and thus were rather short in duration, pilots had to regularly overfly areas controlled by the Muslims and Croats. The longest sortie ever recorded lasted for 1.45hrs. Thus, instead of fuel, the biggest problem

experienced by pilots was the lack of accurate intelligence on enemy positions and post-strike damage assessment.[42]

Conflicts over the V i PVO

Autumn of 1992 brought an increase in pressure from the international community against the Serbian side in the Bosnian War and demands for the V i PVO to be grounded. The extensive use of airpower in Operation Corridor from June to the beginning of October, as well as against targets in other parts of the Bosnia and Herzegovina theatre, influenced the representatives of the international community to raise the question of banning Serb airpower entirely. Gauging by General Mladić's notebook (available via the ICTY), pressure was exercised

An RAF AWACS AEW 1 Sentry of No 23 Squadron RAF. (British MoD)

Mi-8 Helicopters of the 89th Squadron VRS parked at Zalužani airfield, winter 1993. (D. Vejnović)

Ninković for a further meeting with Owen but, regardless how much pressure was exercised upon him, the Serbian officer resisted. Eventually, Karadžić issued a written order for the removal of all combat aircraft to the FRY, but Ninković still refused: on the contrary, he issued an order for all the pilots and ground personnel to remain at Banja Luka regardless of who said what. Furious, Karadžić attempted to remove the commander of the V i PVO. However, the Supreme Command of his own air force not only refused to carry out the related order, but – with backing from Mladić and the Supreme Command of the VRS – even threatened to bomb Pale, the 'capitol' of the RS. Eventually, on 28 October 1992, a decision was taken for combat aircraft to remain at Banja Luka, but to be monitored by the UN representatives there. This was a kind of 'pyrrhic victory' for the Serb Air Force in Bosnia, which was to have far-reaching consequences in the long term: indeed, it was to lead directly to Operation Deliberate Force.[45]

Meanwhile, irrespective of all the domestic and international pressure, the V i PVO not only retained its two squadrons of strike aircraft, but also continued carrying out combat sorties. In autumn 1992, it was primarily active in the Gradačac area, but also flew reconnaissance around Mostar, and helicopter operations in all directions. Its last recorded combat sorties by Oraos, Jastrebs, and even a Super Galeb during this period took place on 3 December 1992. However, it is more likely that operations went on for two days longer, and that the last one was flown by a G-4 only on 5 December.[46] Indeed, the Light Combat Squadron from Bratunac continued flying for weeks longer, regardless of immense political pressure.[47] General Satish Nambiar – commander of UNPROFOR and the UN monitors – received a report that all the combat aircraft were, finally, parked inside hardened aircraft shelters at Banja Luka AB and operations stopped. Of course, they continued to be maintained by ground crews that, from time to time, also powered up their engines, in order to keep them in airworthy condition. Moreover, Mladić obtained permission from General Nambiar for undisturbed use of helicopters for MEDEVAC and other emergency operations.[48]

Operation Sky Monitor: the first No-Fly Zone

In place of the combat aircraft of the V i PVO, UNSC Resolution 781 brought new aircraft into the skies over Bosnia and Herzegovina. Henceforth, contingents from different air forces – mainly those of NATO – became involved in Operation Sky Monitor, the task of which was to make sure that no combat sorties would be flown unobserved. The first related flight was undertaken on 16 October 1992, by a Boeing E-3A Sentry Airborne Early Warning and Control (AWACS) aircraft of the NATO Airborne Early Warning Force (NAEWF) forward deployed in Italy. Starting from 31 October 1992, Operation

as early as of May 1992, first upon the president of the RS, Karadžić. However, Mladić did not care all that much and thus the V i PVO flew as intensively as described above.[43]

Finally, on 9 October 1992, the UN Security Council issued Resolution 781, banning all military flights over Bosnia and Herzegovina – except those by the UNPROFOR contingents and other operations by the United Nations.[44] Since the other two sides did not possess any kind of serious airpower, this effectively meant a ban on Serb military operations and, indeed, the V i PVO ceased flying strikes on 10 October 1992, just days after the final phase of Operation Corridor. However, the UN was still not satisfied and insisted on the V i PVO removing all of its combat aircraft from Banja Luka AB. Correspondingly, on 13 October 1992, Lord David Owen, special EC emissary, and president of the RS, Karadžić, agreed for all the aircraft to be flown out to the FRY and to remain there under the inspection of the UN monitors. At this point in time, it was the generals of the VRS who refused to obey the related orders: Karadžić thus sent General

Sky Monitor included an AWACS orbiting over southern Hungary: later on, in addition to E-3s of the NAEWF, Sentries from the US Air Force (USAF), RAF of the United Kingdom, and the Armée de l'Air (AdA, French Air Force) also became involved. Of course, the Serbs did their best to monitor such operations with whatever suitable equipment was on hand. Operation Sky Monitor lasted until 12 April 1993, when it was replaced by the much more intensive Operation Deny Flight, that included armed fighter-bombers from NATO.49

2
NATO ESTABLISH CONTROL, 1993-1994

The international airport in Sarajevo became the hub of international humanitarian and other transport flights from mid-1992. In the initial period of clashes, the Federal JNA and later Serb side controlled the airport, but Lockheed C-130 Hercules and C-141 StarLifter transports of the USAF – followed by C-130s of the AdA – were granted permission to deliver humanitarian aid. As pressure from the international community continued to rise, the Serbs were forced to abandon the airport on 29 June 1992, and it was secured by UNPROFOR. Within hours, C-130Hs of the AdA, followed by Transall C.160s, began landing there to deliver additional cargoes of humanitarian aid.[1]

Operation Provide Promise
During the following days, transport aircraft from numerous other air forces joined the effort of delivering relief aid to Sarajevo: thus, starting from 3 July 1992, an air bridge came into being – run within the framework of Operation Provide Promise, controlled by the headquarters of the UN Refugee Agency (UNHCR) in Zagreb, and the NATO-controlled Joint Air Operations Centre in Ancona, in Italy. After some 1,000 flights throughout the summer of 1992, one event changed the situation. On 3 September 1992, an Aeritalia G.222 transport from the 46 Aerobrigata of the Italian Air Force (*Aeronautica Militare*, AM) was shot down by a man-portable air defence system (MANPADS), some 25 kilometres from Sarajevo, over the territories that were controlled by the HVO and the Armija BiH forces. The four-man crew was killed. Moreover, Croat forces opened fire upon the US rescue party that consisted of two Sikorsky CH-53 Sea Stallions and two Bell AH-1W Super Cobras.[2] The consequence of this tragedy was that Sarajevo airport was closed for a month, and the air bridge re-launched only months later. Although eventually becoming 'routine', it was never such for the involved crews due to the threat of ground fire from one of the hills surrounding the airport. Indeed, at least 270 'minor incidents' were recorded by January 1996, by when 12,951 flights had landed in Sarajevo. Only one aircraft was lost, however: an Ilyushin Il-76 (ASCC/NATO-codename 'Candid') crashed on 1 January 1995, but its crew was rescued.[3]

The next step in humanitarian flights and the presence of the wider NATO air forces over BiH airspace was Operation Provide Promise. It could be regarded as being a unilateral US

operation, which later expanded with certain NATO assets. The cargo missions were organised to deliver food to the Muslim population in surrounded enclaves in north-eastern Bosnia and the first missions were carried out on 28 February 1993 by USAF C-130E transports of the 37th Airlift Squadron of the 435th Airlift Wing, taking off from Rhein-Main near Frankfurt. On the previous night, clouds of leaflets were dropped to warn the inhabitants. The missions were carried out at night, as a precaution against Serb air defences. Soon, another squadron, the 38th (Provisional) Airlift Squadron – also known as 'Delta Squadron' – was formed at Rhein-Main from the other Hercules that were deployed there on temporary duty (TDY). At first the Provide Promise missions were carried out in the three- and then in six-ship formations, as the missions became more routine. Once the 38th Squadron became operational the missions were expanded into nine-ships for Provide Promise over Eastern Bosnia and four-ships to Sarajevo. The supplies were loaded at Taszar AB in Hungary or Falconara AB in Italy. From mid-March 1993, the German Luftwaffe and French *Armee de l'Air* joined the operation with its Transall C.160 transport, and the RAF followed with its fleet of Hercules transports of the Lyneham Wing fleet in Operation Cheshire.[4]

From the first mission carried out on the night of 27-28 February 1993, the Serbian V i PVO carefully monitored the operations with help of radar sites at Plješevica, Kozara and Jahorina. They identified the procedures, paths of the sorties, drop zones and activities of other aviation which supported the missions (AWACS, or Carrier Air Wings aboard US aircraft carriers in Adriatic). The drop zones in Eastern Bosnia were primarily aiming to deliver to the wider area of Tuzla, and the two besieged Muslim enclaves in Srebrenica and Goražde. The packages were dropped from altitudes between 3,500 and 4,000 metres. The Serb V i PVO estimated that the humanitarian

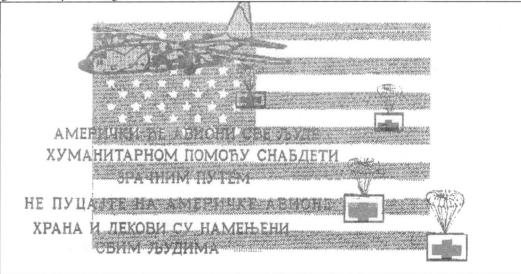

One of the leaflets that were dropped during Operation Provide Promise to warn the locals not to open fire on aircraft carrying humanitarian aid. (Author's collection)

nature of these flights could soon change into deliveries of ammunition and military equipment, or preparation to carry out airstrikes.[5]

Operation Provide Promise continued until 19 August 1994, by when it was expanded to the Bihać Pocket. The final airdrop mission was flown by the 37th AS, alongside Luftwaffe C.160Ds over this area, before further missions were put 'on hold' because of the heavy Serb anti-aircraft fire. Overall, a total of 2,828 missions were carried out by the USAF, Luftwaffe and Armée de l'Air: Germany was the largest donator of the supplies that were parachuted to the Muslim enclaves.[6]

UNPROFOR Fliers

From November 1992, the RAF and French Army aviation (ALAT) deployed their helicopter detachments to support the UNPROFOR units on the ground. They initially operated from Divulje helicopter base near Split in Croatia, but later they were seen almost everywhere in BiH where the UN forces were deployed.[7]

To follow the development of the events, the first US reconnaissance platforms appeared in the theatre: on 4 July, US Navy EP-3 Aires SIGINT platforms flew their first missions from Souda Bay in Crete. A week later, USAF SIGINT RC-135 Rivet Joints were deployed to the region and on 10 July 1992, they carried out their first mission. Later they became part of Operation Provide Promise, logging over 600 missions monitoring Serb communications and activities. In addition, U-2Rs taking off from Istres or Aviano supported the mission.[8]

Hercules of the 37th AS were the backbone of the USAFE in Operation Provide Promise. They flew constantly from February 1993 to January 1996. Here, a C-130 lands at Sarajevo on 8 May. (NAC/DoD)

Groundcrew at Split Airport use a farm tractor to pull a Ground Power Unit to a C-130 Hercules aircraft from the 118th Airlift Squadron, Tennessee Air National Guard, 5 December 1993. (NAC/DoD)

The RAF participated in humanitarian aid deliveries to Sarajevo, and Bosnia in general, from mid-1992. Here one of the C-130s takes off from Split Airport and heads to Sarajevo in 1993. (NAC/DoD)

Illegal Flights

As the Serbs expected, numerous illegal overflights by transport aircraft were registered, starting in early 1995. The most obvious of the aircraft involved – also noticed by UN and EC observers – were those by unidentified C-130s, apparently from the Royal Saudi Air Force, which landed up to a dozen times at Tuzla AB and in the Bihać Pocket. Of course, NATO quickly denied any responsibility for these flights,

which – quite certainly – delivered cargoes that consisted of anything but humanitarian aid. However, NATO interceptors are not known to have undertaken any action to curb such operations.[9]

Operation Deny Flight

As the local actors of the Bosnian War continued to use mostly helicopters, they repeatedly violated the NFZ. Eventually the number of violations of UNSC Resolution 781 passed over 500, prompting

The 53rd FS of the Bitburg-based 36th FW was the first USAFE fighter unit deployed to Aviano Air Base to carry out CAP missions in Operation Deny Flight. (NAC/DoD)

The RNLAF was first non-US NATO member to contribute to Operation Deny Flight. Here, F-16A (J-510) taxis out at Villafranca AB for a mission in support of Operation Deny Flight on 9 April 1993. (NAC/DoD, Photo by Sgt Chris Putman)

the Security Council to issue Resolution 816. This prohibited all flights inside the airspace of Bosnia and Herzegovina except those expressly authorised by the UN Flight Coordination Centre in Zagreb. Adding much weight to this decision was the fact that Resolution 816 authorised all UN member states to 'take all necessary measures… to ensure compliance' with the NFZ.[10] This decision resulted in NATO launching Operation Deny Flight: this time, it not only monitored activities in the airspace over Bosnia and Herzegovina, but also exercised active control by deploying combat aircraft – mostly interceptors, but also including fighter-bombers – to fly combat air patrols (CAPs), and if necessary these could be authorised to open fire. Operation Deny Flight began at noon on 12 April 1993 and was initially carried out by McDonnell Douglas (later Boeing) F-15C-MSIP-II Eagle interceptors of the 36th Fighter Wing, USAF, forward deployed at Aviano AB, in Italy.[11]

The first missions raised the question of how to use the NATO fighters against the violators of the No Fly Zone. The decision was taken that the execution of the missions should be controlled by the Combined Air Operations Centre (CAOC) at the HQ of the 5th Allied Tactical Air Force (ATAF) HQ, at Vicenza in Italy. The Rules of Engagement for the aircrews involved were extremely tight: any use of force during the interception should be approved by a three or four-star general who would be present in CAOC. The Supreme Allied Commander of NATO in Europe turned over the responsibility to Commander-in-Chief of the Allied Forces in South Europe (AFSOUTH) and, in turn, he then turned over responsibility to the Allied Air Force Commander in South Europe (AIRSOUTH), both with their HQ in Naples, Italy.

The operation was run on a day-to-day basis by CAOC 5th ATAF NATO and nearly all of the generals in this chain of command were American. In 1995, the CO of 5th ATAF was an Italian general, while all others from SHAPE to CAOC were Americans. Coordination with the UNPROFOR HQs in Zagreb and Sarajevo was conducted through the 5th ATAF liaison officers. Up until 1995, all of the UNPROFOR

The AN/TSC-94A tactical satellite communications terminal of the 603rd Air Control Squadron that was deployed in Aviano and remained to support the CAOC 5th ATAF in Vicenza and later resident 31st FW. (B. Dimitrijević)

many questions about relocating it to Naples or Ramstein into the US facilities, where better conditions were present, but the operation had to be a NATO effort, and it remained in Vicenza. The number of personnel would quickly rise from 73 in April 1993, to 364 at the end of 1993, and to 531 by mid-1995.[13] The USAF 603rd Air Control Squadron was deployed to Aviano to enable communications and command between the different "players" in the air over the theatre.

The Serb side monitored the appearance of the NATO fighters over the BiH airspace sceptically. In the late evening broadcast on Serb TV, General Mladić and his aides became acquainted the uneasy notion of the presence of NATO over the 'Republika Srpska'. General Ninković, the CO of the V i PVO explained that Operation 'Provide Promise'

commanders were European ground forces generals and most of them were not in favour of the usage of wider airpower against the Serbs. Their familiarity with airpower was limited – mainly – to the understanding of the application of close air support. Such a situation would produce much frustration among the American generals responsible for Deny Flight.[12]

In this period, the CAOC and the AFSOUTH HQs were still small Cold War-style HQs without the personnel and equipment necessary to command and control Operation Deny Flight. It raised

was a prelude to Deny Flight', while Mladić stated that the VRS would remain 'maximally restrained and shall perform nothing to provoke any incident in the Republika Srpska airspace'.[14]

However, when the NATO fighters began conducting low-altitude overflights, and then even made sonic booms over Banja Luka, the Serbs became anxious: they considered this a power demonstration, and not the control of airspace. Thus, on 20 April 1993, General Mladić protested to General Wahlgreen of UNPROFOR – to no avail: the low-altitude and supersonic overflights continued until 12 June 1993, when, during a meeting in Belgrade, Wahlgreen promised to stop them, and that henceforth NATO fighters would remain above an altitude of 3,000 metres. Of course, the aerial surveillance units of the V i PVO remained alert and continued monitoring the activities of Deny Flight, eventually realising that the NATO aircraft had not only continued operating at often much lower altitudes than agreed, but had also flown several simulated attacks on their positions. [15] Despite protests from the Serbs, Operation Deny Flight was not only expanded, but also intensified through the addition of fighter-bombers equipped with precision-guided munitions (PGMs). Moreover, on 2 August 1993, the NATO Council expanded the initial responsibilities of Operation

From late July 1993, the fighters on CAP missions started to carry strike ordnance. Here, an RNLAF F-16 is armed with a Mk-82 bomb under its wing. (Author's collection)

Deployed NATO Air Contingents

Operation Deny Flight brought contingents from multiple NATO air forces into the skies over Bosnia and Herzegovina. As well as the Americans, British and the French, the Dutch and Turkish air forces were also involved right from the start, as were E-3s of the NAEWF. Later on, in 1994, elements of the Spanish Air Force were to join the scene, followed by the German Luftwaffe. The mass of aircraft involved, and their crews, were based in Italy, the most important base of which became Aviano. Originally constructed during the Cold War as a temporary duty (TDY) facility only, in 1993

Deny Flight through adding the possibility of authorising airstrikes. Mostly advocated by US officials, this was a significant change, which NATO explained as a requirement to react should the UNPROFOR forces come under attack.

Before long, fighter-bombers from multiple NATO air forces began arriving at Italian air bases, while tactical air control parties (TACPs) were deployed with most of UNPROFOR's contingents. The latter were small teams tasked to act as forward air controllers should the need arise. To improve communication between the HQ 5th ATAF, TACPs and UNPROFOR contingents on the ground, and all the involved aircraft, NATO began deploying EC-130H Airborne Battlefield Command and Control Centre (ABCCC) aircraft over Bosnia.[16] To control any possible airstrikes, NATO and the UN established a 'dual key' control, under which an approval had to be granted by both the UN Secretary-General (or his representative), and the commander of UNPROFOR. While this was a well-thought-out solution, by 1994 the situation frequently called for a much quicker process of approvals.

this installation was reactivated to receive F-15Cs of the 36th FW, then home-based at Bitburg AB in Germany. For a while during the summer of 1993, aircraft of the US Navy's Carrier Air Wing 8 (CVW-8) – including Grumman F-14A Tomcats (from fighter squadron VF-84) and McDonnell Douglas (later Boeing) F/A-18C Hornets – embarked aboard the aircraft carrier USS *Theodore Roosevelt* (CVN-71) flew CAPs over Bosnia. Meanwhile, on 2 July 1993, F-15Cs were replaced by General Dynamics F-16C Fighting Falcons of the 23rd FS/52nd FW, home-based at Spangdahlem AB, which in turn were reinforced by Fairchild A-10A Thunderbolt IIs of the 81st FS, from the same wing. Following other units, in February 1994, Aviano became a temporary duty base for McDonnell Douglas F-15E Strike Eagle fighter-bombers of the 492nd FS/48th FW, home-based at Lakenheath AB in the UK: this was to become one of the most important USAF assets in subsequent operations against VRS forces.

Meanwhile, by early 1994, Aviano AB was expanded to a degree where the USAF decided to make it the home base of one of its fighter-

Men of a Special Purpose Marine Air Ground Task Force participate in physical training on the flight deck of the nuclear-powered aircraft carrier USS *Theodore Roosevelt*, spring 1993. A-6s, and an EA-6B, armed with AGM-88 HARMs can be seen in the background. (NAC/DoD)

An F-14 Tomcat belonging to VF-84 takes off from USS *Theodore Roosevelt* for a CAP mission over Bosnia and Herzegovina, 1 April 1993. (NAC/DoD)

Following soon after the F-15C and F-16C fighters, the USAFE deployed its strike A-10As from the 81st Fighter Squadron at Spangdahlem. In December 1994, the 110th Fighter Group ANG was deployed to Aviano to relieve the 81st FS in time for the Christmas holidays. (NAC/DoD)

An A-6 Intruder of VA-85 stands-by on the flight deck of the aircraft carrier USS *America*, Adriatic Sea, 26 October 1993. (NAC/DoD)

role in all USAF operations over the Balkans in 1994-1999.

Later in 1994, additional USAF assets were deployed within range of the Balkans, including Boeing KC-135 Stratotankers at Naval Air Station Sigonella on Sicily, Milano-Malpensa and Pisa; ABCCCs from the 7th and then the 42nd Airborne Command and Control Squadrons; Sikorsky HH-53 combat search and rescue (CSAR) helicopters and Lockheed HC-130 CSAR aircraft, and Lockheed AC-130H Spectre gunships, forward deployed at Brindisi. Moreover, the 31st Tactical Fighter Wing was reinforced through regular deployments of General Dynamics/Grumman EF-111A and Grumman EA-6B Prowler electronic warfare aircraft and, from time to time, relieved by aircraft carriers of the US Navy.

Among the European NATO allies, the first to deploy to Italy was the Netherlands. Its Royal Air Force (Koninklijke Luchtmacht, KLu) had deployed a combined detachment of 18 F-16As from its Nos. 306 and 315 Squadrons at Villafranca AB starting in late 1992: indeed, the Dutch pilots were the first to fly a nocturnal CAP over Bosnia, on 25 April 1993. Since 25 August 1993, six of their F-16s were devoted to CAS and strike missions with personnel on rotation. On 14 February 1994, four reconnaissance RF-16As replaced four regular F-16s. Despite being just 18-strong, the RNLAF contingent eventually took part in fighter, strike and reconnaissance missions, logging 10,000 hours in Operation Deny Flight by 20 May 1994, and 20,000 by 18 September 1995.[18]

The Royal Air Force of the United Kingdom deployed its first contingent for Operation Deny Flight from 19 April 1993, when No. 11 (Composite) Squadron – including personnel from Nos. 11, 23 and 25 Squadrons – equipped with Panavia Tornado F.Mk 3 interceptors arrived at Gioia del Colle AB. Between 26 June and 16 July 1993, a strike component was added in the form of 12 SEPECAT Jaguar GR.Mk 1s from the Coltishall Wing, the units of which – Nos. 6, 41 and 45 Squadrons – maintained TDY-shifts of two months each. Later on, No. 6 Squadron, RAF, became responsible for running all Jaguar-

bomber wings. Correspondingly, the base received 48 F-16C/Ds drawn from the 512th and 526th FS/86th FW formerly based at Ramstein AB, in Germany, and from the 301st FW of the Air Force Reserve (formerly based in the USA), and the HQ of the 401st FW from Torrejon AB in Spain. Through a merger and re-organisation of these assets, a new unit came into being in form of the 31st Fighter Wing, including the 510th FS, activated in September 1994, and the 555th FS, activated in May 1994.[17] Aircraft from the 31st FW not only flew 1,644 sorties under Operation Deny Flight but were to play a pivotal operations over the Balkans, and these were supported by Vickers VC.10 tankers of No. 101 Squadron, to be replaced by Lockheed TriStars from No. 216 Squadron in June 1993. Moreover, two Hawker-Siddeley (later British Aerospace, BAE) Nimrod MR.Mk 2Ps were regularly forward deployed at NAS Sigonella – initially within the framework of Operation Sharp Guard – while Royal Navy aircraft carriers made frequent cruises in the Adriatic Sea, from where their Hawker-Siddeley (later BAE) Sea Harrier FRS.Mk 2s flew CAPs over Bosnia and Herzegovina.[19]

The Armée de l'Air referred to its deployment as Operation Crecerelle. On 12 April 1993, a batch of Mirage 2000Cs from EC.5 landed in Cervia and five reconnaissance Mirage F-1CRs belonging to ER.33 landed in Istrana. For support, a Boeing C-135FR from 1.93 at Istres was dedicated to the operation, alongside a single Boeing E-3F AWACS which operated from Avord in France or Trapani in Italy. The French contingent was subject to poor publicity when on the first day of Deny Flight a Mirage 2000C (No 75, marked 5-NI, from EC 1/5 Vendee) crashed into the sea, though the pilot was rescued. As was the case with the RAF contingent, the French contingent was strengthened with eight SEPECAT Jaguar strike aircraft in July 1993 from EC.11, which landed at Rivolto Air Base. Three more Lockheed C-130s and/or C-160 Transalls and hundreds of surplus ground crew personnel were devoted to operation. For ELINT/SIGINT missions, the French sent C-160G Gabriels (EET 11.54) and Douglas DC-8 Sarigues (EE.51) to Italian air bases.

The French Navy deployed their aircraft carries *Foch* and *Clemenceau* to the Adriatic where they operated in shifts from 1993-1995 in Operation Balbuzard. The escadrilles

The Armée de l'Air sent its Mirage 2000C fighters to Cervia to take part in Deny Flight from its initial missions. (NAC/DoD)

Another Armée de l'Air component was the reconnaissance detachment from 33 Escadre. (Author's collection)

The RAF deployed its TriStar tankers of No 216 Squadron to Ancona. (British MoD)

A Turkish F-16C seen at the refuelling station over the Adriatic. The Turkish contingent arrived on 20 April 1993 at Gioia del Colle where it remained throughout the whole duration of Operation Deny Flight. (NAC/DoD)

A Volhov (SA-2 'Guideline') missile of the 155th Air Defence Missile Brigade in a firing position around Banja Luka, 1994. (D. Vejnović)

aboard the carriers operated Dassault Breguet Super Étendard, Étendard IVP and Breguet 1050 Alizee combat aircraft and a mix of Aerospatiale SA-360 Dauphin, SA-321 Super Frelon and SA-330 Puma helicopters.[20]

The RAF and Armée de l'Air had already engaged their air assets in the humanitarian air bridge to Sarajevo in operations Sharp Guard and Provide Promise, and British, French and Dutch helicopters were engaged in support of UNPROFOR. All three armies dispatched their Special Forces personnel to act as UNPROFOR TACP/FAC teams. Finally, the Turkish Air Force deployed its No 142 Filo with F-16Cs to Gioia del Colle on 20 April 1993. They were late in joining the operation as the Greek government would not approve Turkish fighters to overfly its airspace.[21]

Improvement of the Serbian Air Defences

UNSC Resolution 781 and the establishment of the NATO presence in BiH airspace were sufficient to prohibit operations by strike aircraft by the V i PVO in support of VRS ground forces. For this reason, it can be said that – even if indirectly – the NATO presence helped suppress further Serbian advances on the ground. Nevertheless, the NFZ was frequently violated by helicopters of all three of the involved parties. These were a unique challenge for the AWACS or radar crews who monitored BiH airspace, as contacts would appear on the radar screens and soon after disappear as the Bosnian hills and mountains provided cover that radars found difficult to monitor. The UN representatives, who monitored the activities from the ground, complained that the Muslims and Croats used helicopters in civilian colours, usually blue and white, while the Serbs sported large red crosses on their helicopters, no matter the mission or passengers that they were carrying. Fast NATO fighters were almost helpless and did not intercept any of the violating helicopters.

Much more danger would come from the ground forces of the warring parties. In one liaison flight on 2 August 1993, a Serb Mi-8 helicopter was shot down along the Posavina corridor, near Brčko, by the 107th Brigade of the Armija BiH. It was a heavy loss for the V i PVO, killing six fliers and three passengers – including the commanders of the 92nd Aviation Brigade and the 28th

Royal Navy crew aboard HMS *Invincible* preparing a Sea Harrier for a CAP mission over Bosnia. (British MoD)

Fighter-Bomber Squadron, and the deputy commander of the 89th Helicopter Squadron.[22]

However, as the Serb fixed wing aviation was grounded and increasing numbers of NATO combat aircraft became present in BiH airspace, the Serb air defence became an ever more important asset. Indeed, the everyday presence of NATO aviation prompted the Serbs into consolidating their SA-2 units of the 155th Missile Regiment.[23]

First Kubs

Back in December 1991, the 149th Air Defence Missile Regiment was withdrawn from Croatia to Banja Luka and disbanded. While most of its personnel were then redeployed to Novi Sad, in Serbia, some of its equipment was left behind and stored inside the Air Depot Kosmos. In spring 1993, the V i PVO decided to overhaul it and return it to service because the SA-6 SAM-system was, potentially, the most advanced of its kind in BiH. While inspecting the stored equipment, the Serbs found two SURN fire-control radars (ASCC/NATO-codename 'Straight Flush') (mounted on GM 578 tracked chassis), one such system was the centrepiece of every SA-6 SAM battery which usually also included four transporter-erector-launchers (TELs) each with three launch rails for the 599kg continuous-wave/semi-active radar homing 3M9M Kub missiles. Lacking enough TELs, the V i PVO used the two SURNs (locally designated R-StON) and six TELs to establish two sites. Later on, a third half-sized SAM battery was established with the help of a SURN provided by the FRY. These three units were operated with personnel drawn from the 155th Regiment and additional officers rotated from the FRY. All entered service with the 155th Missile Brigade, which thus became – for Serb circumstances – a unique asset: one operating two different SAM systems, including the fixed-position SA-2 and the mobile SA-6. Before long, all three SA-6 batteries found themselves in action: as well as being deployed in the Banja Luka area, they were frequently forward-deployed near the Tuzla area, where they attempted to set up ambushes for helicopters and – later on – transports bringing in supplies for the local Muslim garrison.[24]

Meanwhile, the Air Depot Kosmos – which used to overhaul all radars in service with the former RV i PVO – also constructed some six 'angle reflectors': essentially decoys emitting signals similar to those of the SURN fire-control radar with the aim of mimicking operational SAM batteries and decoying anti-radar missiles.[25] Finally, around the same time the 474th Light Air Defence Regiment was split from the 474th Air Base and reorganised as an independent unit. Henceforth, it was not only responsible for air defence of Banja Luka AB, but also the entire area between that town and the Sava River, which marked the border with Croatia.

172nd Self-Propelled Air Defence Missile Regiment

While all the heavy SAM systems of the V i PVO were concentrated in the west of the Republika Srpska, the eastern part was protected only by numerous MANPADS teams dispersed among the VRS. In February 1994, the Supreme Command VRS requested that its colleagues in Belgrade provide additional Kub-M systems and thus 'close the gap' in air defence over the eastern BiH. On 17 February 1994, the air force of the FRY decided to react positively and thus a new unit came into being: the 172nd Self-propelled Air Defence Missile Regiment. Home-based in Sokolac, north-east of Sarajevo, this unit had its command post deployed in Čavarine, and consisted of three fully deployed SAM batteries based in Sokolac, Han Pijesak, and on Mount Romanija. However, due to an intervention by president of the FRY, Slobodan Milošević, the 172nd Regiment never received its full complement: instead, it had to use half-batteries of the 155th Brigade

The Kub-M (SA-6 'Gainful') missile system was reactivated in 1993 and three independent batteries were formed. Seen here is "Self-propelled Launching Vehicle" No 22217 with its crew. (M. Micevski)

The heart and eyes of each Kub-M battery was its 1S91 radar, known in the former Yugoslavia as R-StON, or the NATO name 'Straight Flush'. This example is seen at a position near Banja Luka. (D. Vejnović)

on a rotational basis. It was only much later, after August 1995, that it received three complete SA-6 SAM batteries.[26]

Change of Strategy

It is important to note that due to Operation Deny Flight, through 1993 and 1994 the leadership of the V i PVO changed its threat assessments. From that time onwards, it ceased regarding the Croats and Bosniaks as its prospective enemies, and fully concentrated on confronting NATO. Upon the initiative of its Chief-of-Staff, Colonel (later Major-General) Novak, the force switched its strategy from that of 'territorial air defence' to 'air defence attack', the essence of which was to inflict as many losses to NATO as possible, instead of confronting it frontally, and attempting to defend specific areas or objects. The emphasis in this strategy was constant manoeuvre – re-deployment of SAM batteries at least every night – short operations of all radars, construction of many reserve firing positions (especially at unexpected, or even 'inaccessible' locations), and construction of at least as many dummy firing positions.[27]

Correspondingly, by 1993 the V i PVO also reorganised the four early warning radar stations under its control. Henceforth, all four radar companies – the 1st at Mount Plješevica, the 2nd at Mount Kozara, the 3rd at Mount Jahorina (which operated 24/7) and the 4th at Mount Nevesinje (which worked only 12 hours a day) – were linked to the Operations Centre of the 51st Aerial Surveillance Battalion in Banja Luka, the HQ of which also served as the Operations Centre of the entire V i PVO.[28] Moreover, using three old, Soviet-made P-12 Yenisey (ASSC/NATO-codename 'Spoon Rest A') and four P-15 (ASCC/NATO-codename 'Flat Face A') surveillance radars of the 155th Missile Brigade, it created a reserve radar network, while keeping several older US and Soviet-made systems (including AN/TPS-63s and AN/TPS-70s, and a few P-12s and PRV-11s) in reserve.[29]

In May 1994, the fifth radar station was added in the form of an independent unit equipped with an old Marconi S-605 radar and was established and deployed at Mount Ozren to monitor 'NATO transports operating in support of the

Armija BiH'.[30] Finally, around the same time the V i PVO established a platoon for electronic intelligence (ELINT). Based in Banja Luka, this started to monitor the activities of NATO's air forces during Operation Deny Flight. By 1995, it was one of the most important assets of the Serb air defences in BiH, capable of providing real-time information crucial for the survival of numerous units.[31]

A Krajina Militia Gazelle at the alert, Udbina Air Base, 1993. (M.D. Ristić)

The first Krajina RV i PVO combat aircraft was this G-2 Galeb, former gate-guardian at Zadar Zemunik Air Base. It was named "Krajišnik" at Udbina in 1993. (M.D Ristić)

A light liaison Utva 66 at Udbina Air Base. It was impossible to differentiate SVK from VRS aircraft according to the markings. (M.D. Ristić)

A former *Pan Adria* Piper Pawnee was also on the inventory of the Krajina Serb air force. (M.D Ristić)

Meanwhile, in September of 1993 the question of training for pilots of the V i PVO was resolved. They were dispatched to Udbina AB in the 'Republic of Serbian Krajina' in Croatia: because Operation Deny Flight applied only to the airspace of BiH, it proved possible for the Serbs to re-activate the small local air force (officially designated the RV i PVO; see below for details), equipped with a couple of G-2 Galebs and Gazelles. In early 1994, the V i PVO then clandestinely redeployed some of its Oraos, G-4s, and helicopters to the same base: eventually, these were not only to be used in the continuation of training of existing pilots and the advanced training of new pilots, but also to fly airstrikes against the Croat forces inside Croatia.[32]

Serb RV i PVO in 'Republic of Serb Krajina'
Once the JNA completed its withdrawal from Croatia, in April and May 1992, former air bases of the RV i PVO at Zemunik (Zadar) and Udbina came under the control of the RSK Milicija. Using the available helicopters, the latter established the 56th Mixed Helicopter Squadron, subordinated to the Special Purpose Milicija Unit (a sort of SWAT asset) that had taken part in Operation Corridor in June-July 1992. By the beginning of December 1992, the former Serb Krajina TO was reorganised into the Serbian Army of Krajina (*Srpska Vojska Krajine*, SVK), which took-over the control of the sole flying unit of the force. Reinforced by a few armed Gama helicopters, the 56th Squadron then took part in attempting to repel the Croatian Army offensive in late January 1993. However, and although – as recalled by the deputy squadron commander, Major Kecman – 'performing well' against Croat armour, it failed to prevent the fall of Zemunik AB to the Croat forces.[33]

On 11 April 1993, the RV i PVO established the 105th Air Brigade at Udbina AB, with the aim of centralising command over all the elements of this facility: the support battalion, a light air defence battalion, an infantry company, a platoon of military police, and others. Initially, the only flying unit assigned was the 728th Mixed Helicopter Squadron, which operated a handful of Gazelle and Gama helicopters – all 'donated' by the Milicija Squadron. However, the Brigade's HQ received a few different aircraft from official and non-official sources, including a G-2 Galeb that had been a gate-guard at Zemunik AB, an Utva-66 from Prijedor aero-club, an abandoned former Pan Adria Piper Pawnee, and another G-2 drawn from the Aeronautical Museum of Belgrade. Finally, in autumn 1993, the FRY donated a batch of J-21 Jastreb light strikers (these were transported by road all the way from Serbia, and then assembled at Udbina AB),

followed by a few Gazelles and a single Mi-8. Thus came into being the 249th Fighter-Bomber Aviation Squadron of the 105th Brigade.[34]

The cooperation between the V i PVO and the RV i PVO was continued, and thus one of the latter's Galebs saw action during the Croat Army offensive against the Medak Pocket, from 9 until 15 September 1993. Having been informed about an air-traffic corridor used by NATO aircraft to enter the airspace over BiH, the Serb pilot flew along it to carry out three airstrikes on HV positions between Medak and Gospić. The same trick was then also used by Gama crews.[35] Eventually, and with some help from the Canadian and French contingents of UNPROFOR, the Croat offensive was stopped by international pressure short of its target, and the HV forced to withdraw. Moreover, during the subsequent exchange of artillery and rocket-fire, a MiG-21 of the HRZ was shot down and its pilot killed by one of the Bosnian Serb SA-6s outside Gvozd. Nevertheless, the – initially successful – short Croat intrusion left a deep impression upon the Supreme Command of the SVK, prompting it to seek for ways to further reinforce its air force. Following negotiations with Belgrade, a batch of nine J-21 Jastrebs (later reinforced to 14) was passed to Udbina AB during the following weeks.[36]

Further Reinforcements
On 27 October 1993, the creation of the 44th Air Defence Missile Brigade in Knin started. By the beginning of 1994, a single missile battalion was passed from VJ equipped with the Dvina (ASCC/NATO-codename SA-2 'Guideline') system, which had officially been taken out of the VJ service as obsolete. One of four disbanded battalions and part of the missile-technical battalion were sent to Krajina and deployed in the Kordun area. In 1994 it was moved to the Banija area and to Mount Petrova Gora.[37]

In the same period two batteries of the Kub-M system were also delivered to Krajina from FR Yugoslavia (the third one would be delivered in 1995). The initial deployment was at Padjene, and later when the batteries were consolidated they would change their firing positions, maintaining one at Udbina Air Base for its protection, while the other one was tasked to prevent the mostly nocturnal supply flights to Armija BiH in the Bihać Pocket from the Croatian side, and operated from the wider area of Slunj. On 2 August 1994, one of the Kub-M batteries claimed an Armija BiH-leased Antonov AN-26 (ASCC/NATO-codename 'Curl') transport aircraft. After unloading supplies to V Corps Armija BiH at Cazin airfield, it took off for the Croatian side. At 01:26 and an altitude of 4,000 metres the AN-26 was hit and fell into the almost inaccessible zone of the Plitvice Lakes. The ferry flights to Bihać pocket were halted for some time.[38]

By March of 1994 the RV i PVO was completed with the creation of the 45th Air Surveillance Battalion. It was equipped with outdated Soviet surveillance radars; one P-12, two P-15s, and a PRV-11 altitude radar; and used radar positions at Petrova Gora (near the Dvina battalion), Kninska Plješevica and a few temporary positions around Knin and Benkovac.[39]

That all said, the build-up of the Krajina RV i PVO was anything but easy. The local authorities were chronically short on funding, and there was a widespread lack of the necessary personnel and equipment. Under immense pressure from abroad, Belgrade was only able to pass over outdated and obsolete equipment, and obviously unwilling to provide enough pilots and ground personnel. With there being very few pilots born within the 'Krajina', the RV i PVO found itself with only nine aviation pilots and five helicopter pilots available most of the time. This produced a situation where the force had only 20% of the fliers it wanted and was never able to simultaneously deploy more than a third of its theoretic firepower. The requests of the SVK that the VJ should deliver potent aircraft from its inventory – such as Galeb G-4s, Oraos, or the MiG-21PFMs – were never fulfilled. On the other side, the representatives of the VRS repeatedly attempted to convince the SVK authorities that the best solution would be to concentrate all the assets under the control of Banja Luka: this design was never fulfilled though due to the personal preferences of different politicians. Still, despite their formal separation, the two Serbian air forces in Croatia and BiH maintained as close a cooperation as possible.[40]

A new Plot

The training of VRS pilots at Udbina continued during early 1994. Since Krajina (Croatia) was not included in the NFZ, they were able to regularly maintain their flying proficiency. Indeed, to bolster related activities, two Oraos and single G-4 were redeployed from Banja Luka to Udbina, on 31 January 1994.[41]

However, February 1994 was the time of several changes in the overall military situation in Bosnia and Herzegovina. The Armija BiH and the HVO were meanwhile involved in brutal mutual clashes which ended only due to a major intervention of the administration of the US president William J Clinton. Related negotiations were concluded with the Washington Agreement, on 18 March 1994, which resulted in a ceasefire and the creation of a loose Federation of BiH, with the intention of redirecting their future efforts entirely against the VRS. In the light of these developments, the Supreme Command of the VRS developed the idea of reigniting the Croat-Muslim conflict through the deployment of strike aircraft from Udbina AB. The plot was for these to attack Armija BiH facilities approaching 'from the Croat side', and thus renew the Croat-Muslim dispute. With hindsight, it is clear that this was a very naïve point of view: worst of all, it resulted in the most serious loss that the V i PVO would ever suffer.

Airstrikes on Travnik and Bugojno

On the morning of Sunday, 27 February 1994, six pilots drawn from both squadrons of the 92nd Brigade – including its commander, Lieutenant-Colonel Perić, and his Chief-of-Staff – were ferried from Banja Luka to Udbina AB. Once there, they were briefed on the mission by the staff of the 92nd Brigade VRS and the 105th Brigade SVK. The briefing caused quite some debate amongst the pilots, but they were told that NATO would not open fire if their aircraft were not intercepted deep over BiH – and certainly not before warning them to leave the airspace over Bosnia and Herzegovina. Eventually, two Serb Krajina RV i PVO pilots joined the group, and a decision was made to launch the mission.[42]

Early on 28 February 1994, six Jastrebs and two Oraos were prepared at Udbina, and Perić was advised that the Operations Centre in Banja Luka would radio the code-word 'Sunshine' if the the airspace over BiH was free, or 'Cloud' if there were any NATO aircraft airborne. With the Operations Centre doing nothing, Perić decided to take the initiative and make a telephone call to Banja Luka: all of these remained unanswered, simply because it proved impossible to reach any of the officers acquainted with the secret mission. Eventually, Perić ordered the mission to start, despite uncertainty. The six Jastrebs and a pair of Oraos rolled for take-off at 06.00hrs, and then turned north-east, flying low between the hills until reaching the area between Jajce and Ključ.

At that moment, at 06:21, they were spotted by the AWACS that orbited in Hungarian airspace. The visibility was excellent. The leader of the Orao pair soon realised that NATO fighters were approaching, but the leader of the Jastrebs replied, 'I see. We are continuing!' Immediately after, six Jastrebs dived and attacked the Bratstvo armament factory in Travnik, while the Oraos proceed to attack the Slavko Rodić armament factory in Bugojno. The pair of Oraos conducted the attack at Bugojno while two F-16s passed nearby entirely oblivious of them. The two Serb jets continued south and then to the north-west and soon landed separately at Udbina: at that point in time, the mission appeared to be a success. However, before long everybody realised that there was no sign of the Jastrebs. The tension rose when only one of them appeared over Udbina and immediately landed since it was badly damaged and with its engine shut down. The pilot reported that all of the others had been shot down over the Travnik area by NATO fighters.[43]

Five Jastrebs Down

What happened over Travnik? For the NATO pilots underway over BiH the first sign of trouble occurred at 06.35hrs, was the AWACS alerted a pair of F-16Cs from the 526th FS/86th FW USAF (from Ramstein AB but redeployed to Aviano since 5 February 1994). They abandoned their CAP zone over Mostar and headed north-west to intercept the intruders. The patrol, callsigns Black 03 and 04 included Captains Bob Wilbur Wright and Scott O'Grady. By then, the AWACS should have radioed two warnings for the Serb pilots to land or to abandon the NFZ: reportedly, both were ignored, though actually, the Jastreb pilots could not hear them because their radios could not receive the frequency used. Due to the complex chain of command, the two US pilots had to wait for the Jastrebs to finish their multi-prong attack before they were granted permission to open fire. Thus, they caught the low-flying light strikers as they were heading back to Udbina at an altitude of 1,500m (~5,000ft). At 06.42hrs, Wright locked on one of the Jastrebs and fired a single AIM-120 Slammer active-homing air-to-air missile. The weapon hit the rearmost Serbian jet, causing it to crash outside the village of Bratsko. Five minutes later, Wright approached to within the range of his AIM-9M Sidewinders and fired one of these: the missile hit another Jastreb, which crashed near the village of Crkveno (15 kilometres outside Ključ). By now, the surviving Jastrebs had scattered, attempting to avoid the assailants by flying low between the hills. Nevertheless, Wright then caught one of the Serbs and, at 06.48hrs, fired his second Sidewinder, which scored a direct hit, disintegrating the target. Meanwhile, O'Grady acquired another Jastreb and fired a single AIM-9M, but the missile missed its hard-turning target. Meanwhile, the AWACS directed another pair of Fighting Falcons – radio callsigns Knight 25 and 26, led by Captain Stephen Allen – to intercept the remaining Serb jets. At 06.50hrs, Allen acquired two of the Jastrebs and claimed both as shot down,

A two-seat NJ-22 Orao of the V i PVO seen on finals, above the start of the runway of Udbina AB. Since early 1994, the V i PVO maintained a detachment of its combat aircraft in the Serb-controlled part of Croatia. (M. D. Ristić)

A group of V i PVO Jastrebs in flight. Other than the lack of ordnance and clouds, the mission on 28 February 1994 would have looked very like this scene. (D. Vejnović)

Captain Bob Wright's F-16C, serialed 89-137, in which he claimed three Serb Jastrebs, seen here in September 1995 during Operation Deliberate Force. (NAC/DoD)

but the pilot retained control and made an emergency landing in Udbina. Indeed, one of the F-16s approached it to take a closer look, before – realising he was about to exit Bosnian airspace – making a gesture with his hand and then peeling away. Short of approaching Udbina AB, the engine stopped and the Jastreb glided to its landing with the engine shut down.[45]

After the incident became public, the Supreme Command VRS and the General Staff of VJ denied their involvement. Although promptly reporting the take-off of four Jastrebs from Udbina AB, UNPROFOR was unable to determine the identity of the aircraft. Moreover, NATO was not certain from which air base the Jastrebs took off because of their low-level flight and late discovery by the AWACS. Certainly enough, the surviving three Serb pilots gathered in Banja Luka and the VRS set up a special commission to investigate what had happened, concentrating foremost on tactical mistakes. In the SVK, the 105th Air Brigade CO was grounded because his command ordered a combat deployment of six precious Jastrebs without a prior approval from higher commanders. However, three months later, all the involved pilots were decorated.[46]

On the other side, NATO and the USAF could be satisfied. After 11 months of patrolling and chasing incidental intruders consisting of helicopters and light aviation, now they had shot down five intruders: though the official claim remains at four. For the F-16 pilots involved, the mission was the fulfilment of a most-unlikely dream, and for NATO, it was the first combat operation in almost 50 years of that alliance. Unsurprisingly, this success strongly bolstered not only NATO, but also the top brass of the US military to plan further, similar operations.

NATO Airstrikes around Goražde and the loss of a Sea Harrier

After the five Serbian combat aircraft were shot down on 28 February 1994, this unusual air war continued and NATO took another step

even if officially being credited with only one 'kill'. The last J-21 was meanwhile inside Croat airspace, and thus left to escape.[44]

With their aircraft lacking radar warning receivers, the first indication that they were under attack for the Serb pilots was when they would hear a dull thump, and then lose control over their jets: none of them ever saw the F-16s. Three of them were killed: Ranko Vukmirović, Goran Zarić, and Zvezdan Pešić, while two others managed to bail out safely. The sixth Jastreb was damaged by a proximity-fusing missile, in the involvement in the Bosnian War. Earlier, in January 1994, the Secretary-General of the UN introduced the differences between the Close Air Support (CAS) in defence of UNPROFOR, and "airstrikes" to be used in punishment. But in the communication with NATO, the Secretary-General stressed that he could not ask for the usage of such airstrikes, until the NAC approved that NATO forces could be deployed in such missions. It was concluded that Resolution No 836 enabled NATO to conduct such missions, but still needed NAC approval.[47]

A Sea Harrier aboard a Royal Navy aircraft carrier, prior to taking off on a mission. (Brit MoD)

The first test of the threat of airstrikes against the Serbs came in mid-February, when the Serbs were issued an ultimatum after the alleged mortar shelling of Markale market in Sarajevo on 5 February, with 68 killed and up to 200 wounded civilians, to withdraw their artillery and armour from an exclusion zone of 20 kilometres around Sarajevo. It was the first real threat of using airstrikes against the VRS.[48]

The usage of airstrikes/CAS came two months later. During the VRS counteroffensive in April 1994 against the East-Bosnian city of Goražde, NATO carried out the first airstrikes in its history. The airstrikes were considered as necessary to protect UNPROFOR under UNSC Resolutions 836 and 844.

Sea Harrier XZ498 which was lost over Goražde. (Peter Nicholson, Airport-Data.com)

The Serbian counteroffensive against Goražde was a huge VRS effort to finally reduce the threat from the Armija BiH forces which made occasional offensives out of the city which had been regarded as a UN Safe Zone since 1993. After wide international public and media pressure, and alleged attacks upon the UNPROFOR forces in the enclave, its commander, General Rose, decided to react.

On 10 April Rose asked for close air support from NATO upon the signal 'Blue Sword'. The military-political procedure was complicated and the approval had to be granted by the UN Secretary-General. Finally, at 16:55 the approval to attack VRS positions reached the UNPROFOR HQ in Sarajevo. As Rose described, NATO for the first time headed into bombing. He warned General Mladić to withdraw his forces from the city, threatening airstrikes under Resolution 836. The Serbs continued with their attacks.[49]

Despite an SAS FAC TACP (Forward Air Control/Tactical Air Control Party) being in the city, the presence of numerous AA artillery pieces, heavy weather and terrain made this debut difficult. At 17:00 a pair of USAF A-10s were unable to locate their targets, following AA fire from the ground. Since they were directed to refuel, two F-16Cs

of 555th FS joined the action. General Rose insisted that no moving targets should be attacked, but only the VRS command posts. Soon after, at 18:26 two aircraft targeted one such "command post" killing some nine VRS officers and medical staff. It was the first NATO strike mission in 50 years of the organisation's history, as Rose describes. General Mladić was furious, threatening that no UN soldier would come out of Bosnia alive.[50]

The airstrikes continued on the following day, 11 April, since the Serb forces did not halt their offensive. French Mirages, which appeared first, did not come out below the clouds. Then, US Marine F/A-18s belonging to VMFA-251 from Aviano, arrived on the scene and carried out bombing against VRS positions. They left the scene at 14:45. More attacks and sonic booms were conducted over the VRS positions around the city. Despite the casualties and a few destroyed combat vehicles on the Serb side, the attacks were not carried out with accuracy or without technical problems. Some of the ordnance did not explode and one bomb remained beneath the wing of an F/A-18. Mladić and Rose exchanged harsh words but the air attacks ceased.[51]

Lt. Nick Richardson, pilot of the downed Sea Harrier. (Nick Richardson, *No Escape Zone*)

The VRS attacks continued on 15 April and two UNPROFOR troops were killed. A VRS report describes that two pairs of F-16s appeared over the city at 08:35 and 09:40 but without conducting strikes. At 11:35 another group of NATO aircraft appeared at low-level, climbed to 3,000 metres and attacked VRS artillery positions. The Serbs fired two Strela 2Ms MANPADS and hit one of the attackers in the tail section. Later, at 14:35, a pair of NATO combat aircraft attacked VRS artillery positions and were fired upon with six Strela 2M MANPADS from different positions.[52] After the pressure from Yasushi Akashi, the Personal Representative of the UN Secretary-General, upon President Karadžić, the VRS attacks stopped and enabled two Puma helicopters to evacuate wounded UN personnel from Goražde.

The damaged NATO aircraft was a French Aéronavale Étendard IVP (serialed No 115) belonging to 16 Escadrille aboard the aircraft carrier *Clemenceau*. Pilot Captain de Corvette Pierre Clary managed to exit the area with his wingman and continued with the damaged aircraft at an altitude of 4,000 metres to the carrier. Despite the serious damage to its tail section, Clary managed to land safely.[53]

The deployment of several Serb MANPADS was not taken seriously, most likely due to these being the initial combat operations. On the following day, airstrikes were continued upon the request of the General Rose. During the afternoon a pair of OA-10As tried to attack VRS targets around Goražde, but due to the weather conditions and lack of fuel they aborted the attack after 15:30. Soon after, Royal Navy Sea Harriers appeared. Flying very low below the clouds to find their targets, they made four overflights, guided by an FAC that was in contact with General Rose and the UNPROFOR HQ in Sarajevo. Finally, both Sea Harriers released their bombs but then, at 16.45hrs, one of them was hit by ground fire.[54]

The pilot of the damaged aircraft, serial XZ498, was Lieutenant Nick Richardson from NAS 801 embarked aboard the aircraft carrier HMS *Ark Royal*.[55] Much to the dismay of the Armija BiH troops who cheered the attacks, his aircraft caught fire, prompting Richardson to eject. The parachute opened and pilot landed safely among the Muslim troops at the hamlet of Oštro.[56] General Rose later described that his staff, who listened the FAC's radio communication, were speechless from the sudden shock. Nobody could believe that relatively modest VRS air defences could claim a NATO combat aircraft. Admiral Leighton Smith, Commander-in-Chief Allied Forces Southern Europe (CINCSOUTH) – NATO's 'Southern Flank' – was on the telephone ordering that the airstrikes should stop until the downed pilot could be found, and General Rose reported that he had landed at a friendly site. Richardson was evacuated on the following night – together with members of the SAS FAC team (TACP).[57]

Political intervention eventually resulted in the Goražde crisis calming down: the VRS forces withdrew their heavy weaponry, while UNPROFOR was granted permission to deploy inside the enclave. Following the incident with its Étandard, France decided to reinforce its assets in Italy through the addition of seven Mirage 2000D-NK2s from EC 2/12, EC 2/3 and EC1/3 and five Mirage F.1CTs.[58]

According to General Rose's memoirs, Admiral Leighton Smith was furious at this loss and would not allow more CAS missions at the tactical level, though he would approve targets of higher strategic value, such as command posts, communications and logistic units and ammunition stores in particular. Rose intervened, insisting on the need for CAS sorties, but they agreed that the area of Goražde should be avoided. In a later meeting between the UN Secretary-General and two UNPROFOR commanders, Rose and De La Presle, it was concluded that shooting down of NATO aircraft would no doubt change the military and political situation in Bosnia. The UN forces would be under pressure, while more airstrikes would enlarge the danger and threats. But Goražde was the turning point: NATO started to use it airpower against the Serb forces.[59]

An A-10 on the ramp at Aviano. During this period, a few CONUS-based ANG A-10 units were deployed on TDY to the base and took part in operations over Bosnia. This A-10 of the 104th FW Massachusetts ANG took part in air attack against VRS forces on 5 August 1994. (USAF)

More NATO Airstrikes against the VRS forces

In later summer of 1994, NATO carried out two more airstrikes on VRS units in the wider area of Sarajevo: one on 5 August and another on 22 September. The first case was at Ilidža, in the south-western suburbs of Sarajevo, where the VRS decided to take control of a number vehicles previously controlled by UNPROFOR. As Rose recalled, it was the first time that the Serbs violated the agreement on the Exclusion Zone: nevertheless, he and De La Presle decided to retaliate with the use of force. The British general was much in favour of the gradual usage of airstrikes against individual targets, rather than a massive air action as demanded by Admiral Smith, who pressed the UNPROFOR commanders to demand a wider air operation, including attacks on VRS communication and storage facilities.[60]

Eventually, because of his opposition, Rose was excluded from the chain of approval in this attack. The strike package was in the air orbiting and awaiting the approval of UN HQ in Zagreb. This was a serious NATO strike force comprised of four OA-10As, four French Jaguars and four Mirage F-1s, six Dutch F-16s (including two equipped for reconnaissance), a single EA-6B, two AWACS, one ABCCC, and several tankers. Due to the bad weather, the aircraft remained airborne for hours, their pilots waiting for the order to attack, which was finally issued at 18.40hrs, and the pilots went in. First a pair of A-10s from the 131st FS/104th Fighter Group (Massachusetts Air National Guard) targeted a single M18 self-propelled gun of the 2nd Light Infantry Brigade, VRS, at Ovčarevac. By then, the daylight had passed and thus the rest of the strike package withdrew.

Five days later, on 10 August a single Armija BiH tank was moving out of its position at the entry to the tunnel connected to besieged Sarajevo in order to shell Serb positions. General Rose immediately requested an AC-130 gunship to cruise over the city and attack the Muslim tank. However, the USAF replied that no such mission was possible. Moreover, US Chairman of the Joint Chiefs of Staff, General Shalikashvilli, accused the Serbs of violating the truce, and informed General Rose that the heavy weaponry would be targeted only by the USAF aircraft. Rose concluded that this explanation just confirmed the widespread belief that the Serbs were the only ones to be attacked since the violations of the ceasefire.[61]

Meanwhile, the airstrike of 5 August provoked a dispute between Lieutenant-General Michael Rose, who insisted on limited action, and Admiral Leighton Smith. The latter felt 'frustrated' by the approach of the Briton, explaining: 'I tried my damnest to get him to understand that you've got to do more than to go after some derelict tank in the middle of a field!'[62]

The second attack, which occurred on 22 September, came after the clash between the VRS and French contingent of UNPROFOR, in which one French vehicle was knocked out by Serb tanks. Permission for a strike was granted by General de La Presle because Rose was in Britain at the time. Two Mirages of the AdA could not find any targets and withdrew, but then a pair each of USAF A-10s and Jaguars of No. 41 Squadron RAF, deployed 500kg bombs. The Jaguars missed due to the low sun, while the results of the attacks by the Thunderbolts remain unclear. Later on, Rose commented negatively on the abilities of NATO pilots, while Mladić accused General de La Presle of conducting an unauthorised attack and decided to prohibit the use of Sarajevo airport for all UN transports. As a consequence, the air bridge to the capital of BiH was interrupted until 7 October 1994.[63]

Serb V i PVO supports the Jutro Counteroffensive

During the autumn of 1994, the V i PVO continued improving its air defences by training and deploying its three SA-6 half-batteries all over the territory of the RS. Meanwhile, it began deploying its SA-2 missiles against ground targets. The missile could be guided in 'empty' mode, then commanded 'down' and, at about 20-50 metres (65-164ft) above the ground activated and exploded, producing a kind of cluster bomb effect on targets. After two first unsuccessful firings from area at the Armija BiH positions in the Brčko area, starting from 2 October and all through November other rounds were deployed against targets in the Cazin, Bužim and the wider area of the Bihać Pocket, primarily from a position outside Bušević, near the town of Otok.[64]

The situation in the Bihać area became particularly complex once the V Corps Armija BiH launched its Offensive Grmeč 94 on 24 October 1994. By then, the Bihać Pocket was declared a 'Safe Zone' by UNPROFOR, which was supposed to mean that no such operations were to be undertaken. The Muslims thus took the VRS by surprise and advanced in two directions: along the Una river in the north, and towards the town of Petrovac in the south-east. The thinly-deployed Serbian siege positions were overrun, causing a mass-panic and an exodus of civilians leaving nearby: the VRS only managed to recover some of its positions after bringing in reinforcements and launching a counteroffensive codenamed Jutro (Morning).[65] Despite the NFZ, Jutro received extensive aerial support from V i PVO fighter-bombers deployed at Udbina AB. The range was short, and the terrain rugged, enabling them to undertake numerous low-altitude 'hit-and-run' strikes. From 8 and 9 November, Oraos and Jastrebs of the V i PVO – reinforced by RV i PVO Jastrebs and Galebs – hit several armament factories in and around Bihać, and also used J-22s deploying a number of AGM-65 Mavericks in the process. The SA-2 SAM site at Bušević joined the fray a few days later, firing pairs or trios of SA-2s, and at least four Gama attack helicopters were widely used. One of the latter was claimed by the ground fire of the Armija BiH, on 16 November 1994, when the VRS carried out a heliborne assault on enemy positions at

The sole G-4 Galeb of the V i PVO Galeb was this example, photographed at Udbina AB while still wearing the serial number 23725. In addition to training, it was used for combat and on 2 June 1992 it was deployed for a liaison mission to Belgrade: underway at a critically low altitude, it hit the powerlines, forcing the pilot to make an emergency landing at Banja Luka. The jet was repaired using the tailfin from G-4 serial 23685 and remained in service with the V i PVO for years longer. (M. D. Ristić)

Kamenak and Bugar, both of which were secured and thus for the first time under Serbian control since 1992.[66]

Airstrikes conducted by VRS Oraos from Udbina continued on 18 and 19 November. On the 18th, in a short sortie at around 11:00 they targeted the Armija BiH barracks and HQ of the V Corps in the city of Bihać with BL.755 CBUs and PLAB-250 incendiary bombs: this strike was not particularly successful though and most of the ordnance failed to detonate. However, while the V Corps reported no casualties, the Prime Minister of BiH, Haris Silajdžić accused the Serbs of massacring 15 civilians. Unsurprisingly, NATO aircraft appeared overhead soon after: too late to catch the Oraos, but still in time to prevent further Serb airstrikes – at least on that day.[67] Indeed, the Serbs continued violating the NFZ the next day: at 15.47hrs, two Oraos were scrambled from Udbina to bomb two ammunition factories in the town of Cazin. Their mission was supported by two Gazelle helicopters that flew visual reconnaissance of the target zone and, if necessary, to provide search and rescue (SAR). Armed with US-made Mk.82 bombs, the first Orao hit its target, but the second – piloted by Captain Nović – went in too low: it clipped the chimney of the Incel Works, and crashed nearby, killing the pilot. While the lead jet was back to Udbina AB by 15.58hrs, the UN observers quickly converged on the site of this strike, only to conclude that the killed Serbian pilot was born in Serbia proper and was flying a jet of the V i PVO, but from an air base of the 'Republika Srpska Krajina' – in Croatia.[68]

Serb anti-tank Gamas were extensively used against the Armija BiH forces in the clashes around Bihać in October and November 1994. (Radivoje Pavičić)

An Orao takes off from Udbina Air Base. The average duration of strike sorties against targets in the Bihać Pocket was about 12 minutes. (M. D. Ristić)

NATO Strike at Udbina AB

Had the mission by two Oraos on 14 November 1994 ended without such an obvious accident, the involvement of the V i PVO in Operation Jutro might have gone 'under the radar'. However, with evidence of the Serbs using their strike aviation once again being obvious, the situation for the international community was clear: the UN Security Council thus quickly passed Resolution 958, authorising NATO to operate against targets in Croatia.[69] Acting under this authorisation, on 21 November 1994, NATO decided to strike Udbina AB.

The General Secretary of the UN, Boutros Boutros Gali, was in favour of a limited operation. However, two of the loudest promoters of the air campaign – Admiral Leighton Smith and General Michael Ryan (Commander Allied Air Forces in Smith's area of responsibility, i.e. COMAIRSOUTH) – demanded permission not only to hit the Serb aircraft on the ground, but also to destroy Udbina AB, and hit the local air defence positions, too. Indeed, Smith later stressed, 'I wanted to make a parking lot out of that place!' Similarly, General de La Presle

insisted on attacks on the Serb air defence system inside BiH. Amid such pressure, Rose's recommendation to attack only the aircraft parked at Udbina AB was declined, even if the higher authorities – including the NATO Council and the Security Council of the UN – granted permission for Smith and Ryan to act against the Serb air base in Croatia only.[70]

With all the necessary aircraft and planning in position, the operation was launched almost immediately. The strike package was launched late on the morning of 20 November, and refuelled in the air from tankers above the Adriatic Sea but was then forced to abort due to bad weather: 12 of the involved aircraft passed high above Udbina AB at 12.50hrs. This, as well as the fact that all the UN observers had abandoned the facility warned the Serbs that 'something was going on'. At 11.00hrs the next day, the UN observers were alerted again, and one of their parties then blocked the road to the air base, explaining to the local civilians that they were prohibited from entering a 'danger zone'. For the Serbs, this was a clear sign that an attack was imminent. A few minutes later, the commander of the 105th Air Brigade ordered his ground crews to set fire to a number of old car tyres, positioned around the aircraft parked on the tarmac of Udbina AB, while the sole G-4 was re-positioned inside a hardened aircraft shelter, and other jets dispersed all over the site. The commander then took care to evacuate most of his personnel.[71]

By then, the strike package – consisting of 39 different US, British, French, and Dutch combat aircraft – was airborne. Supported by Boeing KC-135 Stratotankers of the 100th and the 319th ARW, French KC-135FRs, and British TriStars of No. 216 Squadron, it included two

Television report footage shows how one of two J-22 Oraos involved in airstrikes on 19 November 1994 hit a chimney in Cazin, and its wreckage. The jet wore the serial number 25201, and former markings of the Yugoslav RV i PVO were still visible on its wings. (Author's collection)

The mobile air control tower in the rugged conditions of the air base at Udbina, known as "Canadian Girl". (M.D Ristić)

AdA and four RAF Jaguars, two Mirage 2000N-K2s, four F-16As of the Dutch No. 315 squadron, six F/A-18Ds of VMFA-332 of the US Marines, six F-15Es of the 492nd FS, ten F-16Cs of the 555th FS, and one EF-111A of the 429th Electronic Combat Squadron (ECS). These were guided by one EC-130E of the 42nd ACC Squadron, and NATO and RAF E-3s. Combat search and rescue was provided by A-10As of the 81st FS, MH-53Js and HC-130s of the USAF, and Pumas of the French air force. While the Turkish contingent was prevented from taking off due to the fog over its base in Ghedi, the pilots of the strike aircraft found their target in clear weather and good visibility.[72]

The next sign of trouble for the Serbs was the deployment of massive volumes of electronic countermeasures against their radars and radio communications – primarily from an EF-111A, which approached at an altitude of 7,000m (~23,000ft): while radars of the SVK had already been switched off, the radars of the VRS continued emitting, and the personnel of the 1st Radar Company at Mount

 Plješevica managed to detect and monitor the approach of the first attacking formation. However, fearing his site might be a target, the local commander then ordered his crew to turn off the S-600 radar. From that moment onwards, it was up to the crew of the 2nd Radar Company at Mount Kozara to follow subsequent developments. Between 12.50 and 13.15hrs, both the S-600 system of that site, and that of the 3rd Radar Company were jammed by strong broad-band noise interference. Simultaneously, radio contact between Plješevica and Udbina AB was paralysed by severe electronic countermeasures (ECM). The operation of P-15 and (French-made) Giraffe radars of the SVK was also disturbed from 13.10 until 13.55hrs. Meanwhile, the strikers approached and, immediately after 13.00hrs, the first eight unleashed their ordnance upon Udbina AB, followed by another 14 at 13.40hrs. Their first target was the SA-6 half-battery deployed in nearby Visuća about ten days earlier. This was attacked by two F/A-18Ds, which fired two AGM-88 HARM missiles from a range of 21km: both missed the SURN fire-control radar of the Serb SA-6 half-battery but its vehicles were then targeted by a combination of AGM-65E Maverick guided missiles. Finally, several volleys of Mk.82 and Mk.83 'dumb' bombs destroyed the vehicles carrying the command post and power generators, and one of the two TELs was set on fire, causing its load of three missiles to explode. Elsewhere, F/A-18Ds targeted the SA-2 SAM site of the 1st Missile Battalion of the RV i PVO at Šamarice and destroyed its main radar cabin and one of the power generators.

The second target was the Light Anti-Aircraft Defence Battalion deployed on either side of the runway and in a forest near Udbina AB. At 13.03hrs, its Giraffe radar was attacked by two AGM-88s and about a dozen GBU-12 laser-guided bombs. This strike not only knocked out the radar but also killed the commander of the battalion and seriously injured two of his personnel. The Man Portable Air Defence (MANPAD) teams of the battalion fired a total of 10 Strela-2Ms, but all of these missed. Moreover, after emptying his magazine of 40mm

A total of six F-15E Strike Eagles belonging to the 492nd FS from Lakenheath Air Base took part in the airstrike against Udbina Air Base. They used GBU-10s against the runway and GBU-12s against the Kub-M battery. (NAC/DoD)

A line-up of armed RNLAF F-16s at Villafranca. The Dutch contingent took part in the Udbina airstrike with two F-16s armed with Mk-84 bombs to hit the taxiways, while two other RF-16As were used for a Battle Damage Assessment mission after the strike. (Author's collection)

rounds, a Bofors-gunner grabbed another SA-7 and attempted to fire, before being killed by gunfire from a NATO aircraft. Eventually, two Bofors guns were damaged, and two more of their gunners wounded. With Serb air defences out of action, the NATO strikers then concentrated on targeting the runway: this was attacked by Jaguars, F-16As, and Mirage 2000N-K2s, which plastered the runway with a total of 80 Mk.84s and CBU-87 CBUs. The results were unavoidable: the runway was cratered in six spots, at a distance of 500 metres from each other; both junctions of the taxiway and the runway were cratered, too, while remaining bombs demolished the ammunition and fuel depots, and other major facilities of the base. The NATO aircraft did not target – and thus did not hit – any of the aircraft parked on the ground: thus, only one Utva-75 and two helicopters were slightly damaged. Two Serb airmen were killed and five wounded. Post-strike reconnaissance was flown by French Mirage F.1CRs, RAF Jaguars, and Dutch F-16A(R)s.[73]

Overall, the airstrike on Udbina AB was carried out in classic formation, almost 'by the book': the strikers were supported by electronic warfare aircraft and HARM-shooters, selected points along the runway were targeted by F-15Es and F-16Cs using LANTIRN targeting pods and laser-guided bombs, while other facilities were bombed with conventional, free-fall bombs. The damage caused was sufficient to render the target non-operational for several months.

SEAD Strikes

The Provisional Tactical Air Defence Group of the V i PVO was located in the wider area of Mount Grmeč, east of Bihać. It consisted of one SA-2 SAM site, one SA-6 half-battery and a single SA-13 SAM battery of the 474th Light Anti-Aircraft Defence Regiment.[74] On the morning of 22 November, a patrol of Sea Harriers from NAS 800 was fired at by three SA-2s. There was no hit, but the NATO aviation immediately disengaged. At 11:20 General Rose was contacted by General de La

Presle who informed Rose that he and Admiral Smith had approved airstrikes against Serb air defence targets since it was impossible to accurately locate the positions of the SA-2 missiles: the Serb missile battalion had moved to another firing position after leaving a single missile on its launch rail and a decoy mimicking radar illumination at its previous position.[75] The HQ of 5 ATAF ordered the first Suppression of Enemy Air Defences (SEAD) strike package against the Serbian air defence position. This included one EF-111A and two HARM-armed EA-6Bs, supported by F-15Es and F/A-18C/Ds. After neutralising Udbina AB, the NATO commanders now intended to knock out the Serbian air defences, too.

Regardless of the bad weather, the strike was launched on 23 November, when – starting from 10.00hrs – a total of 24 aircraft targeted the Serbian positions in the area between Krupa and Otok (according to General Novak, they targeted positions in the 'Jasenica area'). The second wave was flown between 14.30 and 16.00hrs by 32 aircraft, and the third between 19.00 and 22.00hrs, when air defences outside Ripač, Krupa, Drvar and Petrovac were bombed.

One SA-6 half-battery fired several missiles at the aircraft, but without success: in return, its fire-control radar was hit by a single AGM-88. Surprisingly enough, the missile knocked the radar antenna off its axle, but caused no other damage. Indeed, the crew was unaware of receiving a direct hit until it exited the vehicle. The SA-2 SAM site was effectively jammed and thus remained inactive, while its original position – which now acted as a decoy site – was destroyed.[76]

On 24 November, Serb forces fired missiles at two British Tornado F.Mk 3 aircraft. NATO reacted by scrambling another SEAD package, but after two hours of orbiting, sent everybody back to their bases in Italy. On the next day, Serb forces fired at two NATO F-16s, yet there was no response. Moreover, the 1st Battery of the V i PVO then fired a single SA-6 missile from a position between Donji Vakuf and Bugojno, on 26 September, once again without a NATO reaction. The reason was that the VRS simultaneously took dozens of UNPROFOR troops as hostages, and demonstratively chained many of these to the possible targets of airstrikes. Thus, instead of intensifying its SEAD operations, NATO suspended all flights into BiH airspace from 2 December 1994.[77]

The High Point and the End of the Air Bridge to Sarajevo

The five-month long NATO 'mini-offensive' on the Bosnian Serb air force and air defences in BiH proved highly counterproductive. Indeed, through this period not only the war in Bosnia and Herzegovina, and the resulting mass-suffering of the population, but even the position of UNPROFOR worsened to a level where multiple foreign governments were seriously considering a withdrawal of their peacekeeping contingents. The air attacks on Serb air defence positions had failed to de-escalate the air war in Bosnia: they only prompted the Serbs into making use of a more robust missile systems than the usual MANPADS. They had deployed Volhov and Kub-M (SA-2 and SA-6) units which threatened NATO aviation during the airstrikes and in the usual Deny Flight CAP missions. The practice of two-ship fighter patrols had to be abandoned. Now more ECM platforms had to be deployed to jam the air defence systems, and SEAD aircraft were needed to cover the missions. It increased the costs of air patrolling and burdened the limited capacities of the air contingents in NATO's Italian air bases.[78] The Serb V i PVO HQ noted in late 1994, that

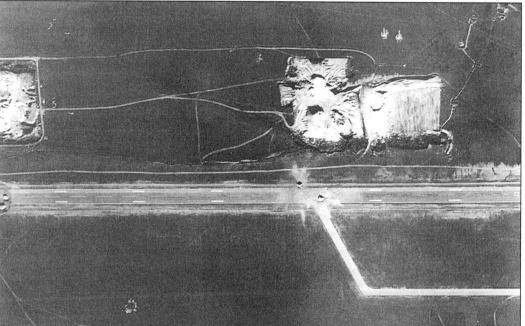

RNLAF aerial footage of direct hits on Udbina's runway and taxiway. (Wim Lutgert en Rolf de Winter, *Check the Horizon, De Koninklijke Luchtmacht en het conflict in voormalig Joegoslavie* 1991-1995)

The TV footage of the damage caused to Udbina runway. (Youtube.com/ watch?v=IFisruwAwIY)

Étendards at Risk

One of the most-overlooked aspects of NATO's activities over Bosnia in 1993-1995 were reconnaissance operations flown by Dassault Étendard IVP reconnaissance jets of the French Naval Aviation (Aéronavale). Based on a specification for a light fighter issued after Western experiences from the Korean War and French experiences in Indochina, Dassault developed the Étendard as a light and affordable striker capable of operations under relatively primitive conditions, as sought for by several NATO air forces in the 1950s. While Germany and Italy eventually selected the Fiat G.91 instead, and other NATO allies looked the other way, the French navy decided to acquire the type as a carrier-based ground attack aircraft for two light aircraft carriers under construction at the time: *Clemanceau* (R98) and *Foch* (R99). The first Étendard IVM thus entered service in 1961, at the same time as the first of two carriers, and served with several squadrons of the Aéronavale until replaced by the improved Super Étendard in the 1980s. However, while the last fighter-bombers were withdrawn from service in 1991, and because there was no dedicated reconnaissance variant of the new model, the single-seat photo-reconnaissance variant – the Étendard IVP – remained in service with the Flotille 16F squadron for a while longer. Indeed, because only 21 such aircraft were ever manufactured, and 11 of these written off between 1964 and 1977, several Étendard IVMs (serial numbers 153, 162, 163, 166) were meanwhile rebuilt into the photo-reconnaissance variant (IVPM). This is how it came to be that such aircraft not only flew dozens of reconnaissance sorties over Bosnia and Herzegovina in the 1993-1995 period, but two of them were also hit by Serbian air defences.

On 15 April 1994, Étendard IVP serial 115 piloted by Capitain de Vaisseau Clary (CO of Flotille 16F) was hit by a MANPAD while making a low-altitude reconnaissance pass over the town of Goražde in eastern Bosnia. Despite extensive damage to the tailpipe, elevators, and the fin, Clary managed to land back on board *Clemanceau*. On 17 December 1994, Lieutenant de Vaisseau Demeinex flew his 15th mission over Bosnia. When passing above Donji Vakuf, about 60km north of Sarajevo, the rear of his Étendard IVPM No. 163 was hit by a MANPAD. The aircraft remained operational and, because he could not lower his flaps, Demeinex decided to land back at the Gioia del Colle AB, in Italy, escorted by his wingman.

Damaged French Navy Étendard IV (No 115) managed to return safely to its aircraft carrier *Clemenceau*, after being hit by Serb MANPADS over Goražde, on 15 April 1993. (Marine Nationale)

NATO aviation, while on patrol, started to avoid the areas where there were estimated to be Serb SAM sites.

The other outcome of improved Serb air defences was a growing conflict between General Rose and Admiral Smith. The American Admiral asked for more NATO strikes against Serb air defence assets, as they were conducted against Iraq in the 1991 Gulf War. The opinion of General Rose was that such missions did not have any relation to peacekeeping and support for his UNPROFOR forces – it would just be an expansion of the war. The responsibilities of UNPROFOR for the events in Bosnia slowly slid out if its hands, concluded Rose. As he earlier explained to the *New York Times*, 'Hitting one tank is peacekeeping. Hitting infrastructure, command and control, logistic, that is war.' Simply, General Rose did not have same view of the use of airpower as did the senior US airmen in NATO.[79]

The frustration among the US commanders at the inadequate usage of airpower was growing. But, from September 1994, Admiral Smith had another important advocate of the usage of airpower against the Serbs: it was General Michael Ryan, the new commander of the 16th Air Force USAFE and Allied Air Forces in South Europe.

Post-strike footage of the Volhov (SA-2) Missile Battalion of the 155th Air Defence Brigade at Otoka. (250th Missile Brigade VJ)

3
PARALLEL AIR WARS 1995

After the airstrikes on Udbina Air Base and on the VRS Air Defence positions in November 1994, both Serb air forces assessed that NATO was now openly involved in the Bosnian War, and that it was completely belligerent to the Serb side. Moreover, intensive reconnaissance activity of the HRZ's unmanned aerial vehicles (UAVs) led the Serbian authorities in Croatia to be concerned about a possible general offensive by the Croat Army. Correspondingly, in February 1995 an agreement between Banja Luka and Knin was reached according to which the forces of the two Serbian entities were to operate jointly – especially in the event of a Croat attack on the 'Srpska Krajina'. Meanwhile, elements of both the RV i PVO and of the V i PVO were busy repairing the runway of Udbina AB, to enable renewed operations. However, instead of flying additional airstrikes, the two Serb air forces concentrated on interrupting the air bridge run between Croatia and the Bihać Pocket. The night sorties were a real challenge to the Serb air forces. Such operations were not only providing the Armija BiH with weaponry, supplies, and the ability to evacuate its wounded, but became a question of pride for the respective air defences of the VRS and the V i PVO.[1] The Serb Krajina RV i PVO radars identified ten night-sorties of Armija BiH helicopters between 24 January and 11 March and all of them were conducted during nights with low visibility, using the terrain to avoid the Serb air defences. It was also noted that the flights were occasionally covered with ECM and jamming of communications from unidentified sources.[2] Correspondingly, during early March 1995, the two Serb air forces launched Operation Sprečiti Dotur (Prevent Delivery): for this they redeployed the mass of their air defence systems – including SA-6 SAMs, MANPADs and light artillery – roughly along the route connecting Zagreb with Ćoralići, with the aim of intercepting the aircraft or helicopters involved. The enterprise was unsuccessful however and the Croat and Bosniak pilots managed to avoid all of the ambushes. In turn, their missions continued, causing suspicion and increasing tensions with the SVK and the VRS, as the respective commanders had no doubts that there was 'something behind' these sorties, even more so since their air defences had proved unable to deal with such 'easy' targets.[3]

Remaining stubborn, the Serbs kept on trying and were eventually successful. Around 01.32hrs of 28 May 1995, a Mi-8 took off from Zagreb to land at Ćoralići airfield at 02.07. The cargo was unloaded, the passengers embarked and at 02.40 the helicopter was airborne again. Shortly after, it was detected by the SVK's 2nd Battery – equipped with SA-6s. At 02.45, this unit fired a single missile from a range of 20km

and hit the helicopter as it was flying only 280 metres above the ground. The unlucky Mi-8 crashed near the village of Kremena, on the road connecting Slunj with Velika Kladuša, killing its combined Ukrainian and Bosniak crew and all passengers, amongst them the Foreign Minister of BiH, Irfan Ljubijankić. For the SVK, this was a major success, renewing the confidence of both the SVK and the VRS top brass.[4] Certainly enough, the air bridge to the Bihać Pocket was re-launched a few days later – and the Armija BiH later reported that 90 sorties were carried out between June 1994 and August 1995 (resulting in the loss of this Mi-8 and an An-2 transport) – but it never reached the same intensity or importance as before.

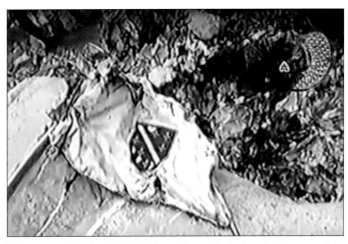

TV footage of the Armija BiH Mi-8 wreckage after being shot down on the night of 28 May 1995. The crash site was near the Slunj – Velika Kladuša road. The first to appear on the scene were wedding guests from a local village who picked-up the thousands of Deutsche Mark banknotes scattered out from the helicopter's wreckage. (www.youtube.com/watch?v=PXJ9a2apJ-c)

An SA-6 (Kub-M) TEL and, in the background, a fire-control radar in firing position. Responsible for shooting down a helicopter operated on behalf of the Armija BiH, in May 1995, this system was to represent the most advanced threat for the NATO aircraft involved in operations Deny Flight and Deliberate Force. (D. Vejnović)

Operation Bljesak: The Croatian Offensive in Western Slavonia

On 1 May 1995, the Croat armed forces launched Operation Bljesak (Flash), with the aim of eliminating the Serb-controlled 'pocket' in Western Slavonia, and thus a 558 square kilometre part of the 'Republika Srpska Krajina', centred on the town of Okučani. The area blocked the strategically important highway connecting Zagreb with eastern Croatia. This short but sharp offensive was quickly and successfully concluded, and thus served as a prelude to subsequent – yet much more massive – Croat operations to recover all of the Serb-controlled parts of the country and reintegrate these into their state. Already depleted by desertions and general war-weariness, the small SVK force deployed in the Okučani area quickly collapsed and withdrew – followed by thousands of civilians – over the Sava River into the Republika Srpska in BiH. Thus, Bljesak was over by 4 May, with a total defeat of the Serb forces.[5]

Certainly enough, the Serb-controlled pocket in Western Slavonia was geographically separated from the rest of the Srpska Krajina, and far away from Udbina AB, however, Banja Luka AB was only 30 kilometres away. Still, the Serbian leadership in Bosnia failed to react and never made a decision to counter the advancing Croat forces. The Serb combat aircraft thus remained parked on the ground, while air defences never attempted to challenge HRZ combat sorties: only the radar company at Mount Kozara monitored their activities. In turn, the Croats took care not to violate the airspace over the Republika Srpska in BiH. Nevertheless, the activities of the SVK and the RV i PVO during Operation Bljesak were little more than of 'symbolic' significance. Early on 1 May 1995, the commander of the 105th Air Brigade at Udbina AB ordered a pair of armed Gamas to support the

SVK forces in Western Slavonia. After an hour-long-flight, the two helicopters landed in Okučani to refuel, and then – separated from each other – went into action, starting at 13.00hrs. Unsurprisingly considering the local terrain, both were quickly detected and found themselves under near-constant ground fire. Although their crews managed to fire three Malyutka anti-tank guided missiles (ATGMs), no hits were scored. By the next day, the situation on the ground deteriorated to a level where there was no option but to withdraw both Gamas to Zalužani AB, outside Banja Luka, and then all the way back to Udbina AB.[6]

On the contrary, the HRZ played an important role in supporting the HV forces during Operation Bljesak. Both MiG-21 squadrons, as well as the Mi-24 unit (the latter operating from forward bases near Požega and Nabrđe) flew numerous airstrikes, amongst others targeting the HQ of the XVIII Corps SVK, and its units' positions in Stara Gradiška, Bogićevci, and Lamnica with a mix of 57mm S-5K and 240mm S-24B unguided rockets, and OFAB-250 bombs. Interestingly, they usually approached from the eastern side, over the Serb-controlled territory, while maintaining radio-silence. The Serb air defences managed to damage one Mi-24, but this returned safely back to Pleso Airport.[7]

On 2 May, the HRZ continued its operations from early morning. At 05:50 a pair of MiG-21s attacked targets in Stara Gradiška and the HQ of XVIII Corps SVK. Another pair which appeared on the scene ten minutes later used S-24B missiles against the bridge on the Sava and the HQ of XVIII Corps. But, between the two attacks the Serb ground forces from both sides of the River Sava organised themselves and opened AA artillery fire. The leading MiG (No 119) in the second pair, piloted by Lt Colonel Rudolf Perešin, commander of the 21st Squadron, was shot down. He managed to bail out but was obviously unconscious and fell into the river. His MiG was found two months later, and his body two years later in the woods that surround the Sava.[8] During the operation, the HRZ carried out a total of 71 missions. One MiG-21 was lost while another was damaged, as were two Mi-24 helicopters.

The bulk of SVK and VRS strike pilots were at Udbina Air Base during this period, conducting training flights with the available SVK Jastrebs and VRS Oraos, and a single G-4. During several of these sorties in April-June, NATO fighters intercepted the Serbian strikers even though this was not BiH airspace.[9] It was a sudden change but after visual inspection they would continue their CAP missions without further action. On 9 June 1995 four Serb aircraft from Udbina carried out strikes against advancing HV forces at Mount Dinara, that divided the Srpska Krajina from the Serb-controlled part of the BiH.

During Operation Flash against the SVK forces in Western Slavonia 1-2 May 1995, only two Gamas were deployed from Udbina, but without serious success. Here, Gazelle No 12658 is seen at Udbina. (M.D. Ristić)

Croatian Air Force Mi-24 attack helicopters supported the advance of its forces into Western Slavonia. (HRZ I PZO via Z. Despot)

They managed to surprise the Croatian forces, but there were no SVK ground forces to capitalise upon this attack. The UN peacekeepers reacted immediately and warned the Serbs not to use their aviation and violate the NFZ. Another evening sortie was cancelled as a large group of NATO fighters appeared over Udbina Air Base.[10]

The strikes against the wider Mount Dinara range continued with usage of SVK and VRS Gama helicopters during the rest of June and July. Moreover, the Dvina-equipped 1st Missile Battalion of the 44th Missile Brigade SVK moved from its position at Šamarice on 11 June and marched across Republika Srpska to the frontlines. From a firing position at Grahovo, which was on the edge of the current lines opposite the HV forces, the battalion fired two salvos with a total of eight Dvina missiles at the positions of the 4th Guards Brigade near Crni Lug in the first strike against ground forces by the SVK air defence missile unit. The battalion returned to Krajina on the same day: "The achieved effects were satisfying."[11]

New NATO strikes against the VRS

Spring of 1995 brought a renewal of the clashes on different sides of the Bosnian frontlines after the winter ceasefire. In the area of Sarajevo, the Muslim Armija BiH launched several offensives against the VRS forces. In response, the Serbs took their artillery and armour out of the UN-inspected locations and started shelling Armija BiH targets within the UN "Safe Zones". As a retaliation for these actions, the UN commander in BiH, requested NATO airstrikes.[12]

Another important change occurred: UNPROFOR (shortened to UNPF from March 1995) commanders were replaced in February 1995. The new commander of UN forces in the former Yugoslavia became French General Bernard Janvier, while the commander of UN forces in BiH became British General Rupert Smith – who had commanded 1st (UK) Armoured Division in Operation Desert Storm – with a "less parochial view of the conflict than that of his predecessor", as General Janvier explained to Colonel Bucknam later. The new UN commanders would show much more cooperation with NATO's Southern Flank commander, Admiral Smith, compared to General Rose in the previous period. It was another step closer to the NATO air campaign.[13]

Airstrikes were carried out on 25 and 26 May against stores and other facilities in Jahorinski Potok (Pale area), conducted by F-16Cs from 555th FS/31st FW and for the first time by Spanish Air Force F/A-18s using LGBs. The Spanish airmen reached Aviano in November 1994 with eight F/A-18s from Ala 15 and two KC-130 tankers from Ala 31.[14]

In retaliation, the Serbs took nearly 380 UN troops as hostage and placed them around different facilities as human shields to prevent further NATO air attacks. General Smith asked for the cessation of further airstrikes.[15] While the taking of UN troops as hostages prevented further air attacks it radicalised some of the European allies to became much more in favour of the air campaign against the Serbs than was the case before. The credibility of the UN, NATO and individual countries was at stake and soon, another unexpected event would especially fuel this notion: on 2 June the Serb air defences claimed a USAF F-16C. It was a huge surprise.

F-16 Down

Under the strategy of "Air Defence Attack", the Serb Kub-M batteries maintained ambushes in the wider area of Banja Luka and Western Bosnia, initially chasing Armija BiH helicopters and later against the aircraft participating in Deny Flight. In this period the Serbian SAM units changed their operational procedures. The air surveillance continued working and signalled the approach of enemy aviation over the 51st Air Surveillance Battalion Operations Centre to the SAM units. They did not illuminate targets until it was estimated that the target was close, at which point they would switch on their targeting radars and work in shortest possible time to launch missiles.

The 1st Battery of 172nd Regiment held the firing position at Bravsko, between Ključ and Petrovac, in combat readiness with missiles in firing position but without any illumination of radars, for some three days. On the afternoon of 2 June, a pair of F-16Cs belonging to the 555th FS/31st FW approached the position but using the constant ECM managed to jam the battery and continue over Mount Srnetica. The battery illuminated for only four seconds and then shut down the systems since targeting was impossible.

Some 15 minutes later the same pair of F-16s appeared again. In the meantime, the battery's radar had changed its working frequency. It was turned on and the target was "locked" at 18 kilometres. In the next moment a salvo of two missiles was launched and the first hit one of the F-16s at a distance of 15 kilometres and altitude of 5,500 metres. The second missile hit the falling debris of the aircraft. The missile battery turned off all of its equipment and hid. During the night it abandoned its firing positions and moved to a new one, some 100 kilometres away. The targeting radar had operated for just 26 seconds.[16]

The pilot managed to eject and landed some six kilometres from the place where most of his F-16 had crashed. The crashed F-16C, serialed 89-2032, was piloted by Captain Scott O'Grady using call sign Basher 52. The other pilot was Captain Bob Wilbur Wright who, along with O'Grady had been involved in the shooting down of the Serb Jastrebs on 28 February 1994.

O'Grady hid in the field and evaded capture by Serb forces until 8 June, during which time some 400 sorties were

Spanish F/A-18s of Ala 15 flew their first attack mission on 25-26 May 1995 using LGBs against the VRS facilities at Jahorinski Potok. (NAC/DoD)

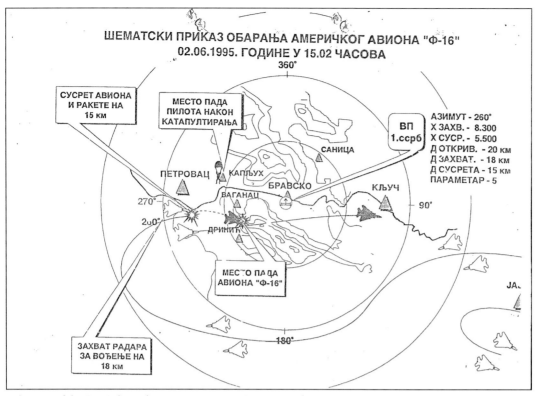

ШЕМАТСКИ ПРИКАЗ ОБАРАЊА АМЕРИЧКОГ АВИОНА "Ф-16"
02.06.1995. ГОДИНЕ У 15.02 ЧАСОВА

СУСРЕТ АВИОНА И РАКЕТЕ НА 15 км

МЕСТО ПАДА ПИЛОТА НАКОН КАТАПУЛТИРАЊА

ВП 1.ссрб

АЗИМУТ - 260°
Х ЗАХВ. - 8.300
Х СУСР. - 5.500
Д ОТКРИВ. - 20 км
Д ЗАХВАТ. - 18 км
Д СУСРЕТА - 15 км
ПАРАМЕТАР - 5

САНИЦА
ПЕТРОВАЦ
КАПЉУХ
БРАВСКО
КЉУЧ
ВАГАНАЦ
ДРИНИЋ

МЕСТО ПАДА АВИОНА "Ф-16"

ЗАХВАТ РАДАРА ЗА ВОЂЕЊЕ НА 18 км

A diagram of the F-16C shoot-down on 2 June 1995. (Gen B. Novak)

The wreckage of Captain O'Grady's F-16C (89-032) at the crash site south-east from Bosanski Petrovac. (R. Ćuković)

Captain Scott O'Grady at the press briefing after being rescued and returned to his squadron in Aviano. (NAC/DoD)

flown in an effort to locate him. Eventually a CSAR mission was launched after the pilot's signals were finally identified at 02:10 on 8 June by an AC-130 gunship. USS *Kearsarge* was mainly responsible for the following rescue mission. At 05:00 a fleet of four McDonnell Douglas AV-8B Harriers, three Bell AH-1W Cobras and two Sikorsky CH-53E Super Stallions was launched. Since the mission was deep in Serbian territory, Super Stallions were used instead of standard SAR Boeing Vertol CH-46 helicopters. After 06:00 the party was joined by EF-111 and EA-6B ECM platforms. F-15Es and F-16Cs were also in the air, making a total of up to 40 US aircraft involved. At 06:20 the pilot's position was identified and the helicopters with Marines aboard continued to the rendezvous point. Finally, at 06:44 O'Grady appeared from the woods and in the next minute boarded one of the Sea Stallions while two AH-1W Cobras and two AV-8B Harriers secured the rescue zone. The whole landing and taking off took about five minutes. At 07:07 a single MANPADS was launched at the formation but caused no damage. The rescue party continued over Serb Krajina and back to USS *Kearsarge*. The pilot was rescued.[17] O'Grady later described his exploits in a best-seller titled *Basher Five-Two*.

General Ryan commented at the press conference in Aviano following O'Grady's rescue:

It has always been dangerous flying over the top of Bosnia-Hercegovina and that is not changed as the result of anything that happened over the last week.… In the case of Scott O'Grady's shoot-down, they were in an area where we did not expect that they had SAM systems. So, in my personal opinion, they intentionally set a trap and sprung it and we have lots of indications that that was the case.[18]

The shoot-down of a USAFE F-16C by a Serb Kub-M missile system was a massive turning point in the planning of suppression or destruction of Serb air defence, later known as Operation Dead Eye. It was now obvious that the air campaign could not be carried out without the neutralisation of Serb air defences and highlighted to Western political leaders the dangers to NATO airmen posed by the Serb air defences. AFSOUTH commanders were now able to acquire the material resources and broader political support for their plans. This event also influenced improvements in the ROE in following years: SEAD aviation became mandatory in securing the strike packages, strict low altitude limits were introduced in combat sorties, and the SAR concept was improved with forces deployed much closer to the combat zone. ECM equipment to jam the Kub-M system, such as AN/ALE 50 towed decoy system, was introduced and used in the later Operation Allied Force.

All of these events also influenced Great Britain and France to create a heavily armed Rapid Reaction Force (RRF) tasked to support UN forces and Security Council Resolution 998 issued on 15 June enabled their deployment to Bosnia. These consisted of British, French and Dutch troops, with heavy artillery. There was also a helicopter fleet, based at the improvised heliport at Ploče Dockyard Camp in Croatia that consisted of eight French ALAT Gazelles and seven Pumas, nine British Army Air Corps (AAC) Lynxes and nine Gazelles, and six RAF Chinooks and six Pumas. The deployment of the RRF took the whole of July.[19]

Fall of Krajina: Joint Operations of VRS-SVK Air Forces

During the second half of July 1995, the Gama helicopters and SA-2 units of the two Serb air forces carried out limited air attacks on the HV forces advancing towards Mount Dinara in the territory of Western Bosnia but did not manage to halt the advancing Croat forces supported by the Mi-24 helicopters from No. 29 Squadron HRZ. Similarly, the small number of airstrikes undertaken by Serb jets from Udbina AB around 20 July, and again on 1-3 August, proved ineffective. On the other side, the HV made extensive use of UAVs to detect and monitor the positions and movements of SVK forces all over the Krajina. On other occasions, Croat MiG-21s were monitored flying reconnaissance along the

During the summer months of 1995, joint SVK-VRS strike aircraft were active in pre-emptive attempts to halt the advance of the Croatian Army against the Krajina. Here a Gazelle, a Jastreb and a Galeb G-4 are seen during the last SVK Vidovdan (St Vit) parade on 28 June 1995. (M.D. Ristić)

A line-up of the fleet of the 105th Air Brigade SVK at Udbina, summer 1995. Left to right: a G-2 Galeb, a J-21 Jastreb, a Utva 66 and a Gama. The Jastreb and Gama carry no national markings, just overpainted VJ roundels. (M.D. Ristić)

A scene from the abandoned Udbina Air Base after the entry of HV forces: two Jastrebs are seen near burnt-out portacabins. (Mario Raguž)

ceasefire lines and along the border with BiH. NATO aviation also flew intensively in Krajina: two to six sorties were registered daily, not counting the flights which continued into Bosnian airspace within Operation Deny Flight.

A Galeb G-2 without markings, and a Jastreb with Serb markings on the wings and a replacement tail section from No 24275 with VJ markings, found at Udbina Air Base after the entry of HV forces. (M. Raguž)

The tail section of a IJ-21 reconnaissance Jastreb, No 24407, sporting the Serb roundel and fin flash, at Udbina Air Base after the entry of HV forces. (M. Raguž)

smallest unit – the 45th Aerial Surveillance Battalion – found its old P-12 radar positioned outside Benkovac under attack by US Navy aircraft because it had apparently illuminated one of the NATO jets. From the Serb point of view, this was a clear indication of the Western alliance's support for the Croat offensive. Udbina AB was heavily shelled by Croat artillery, from early on 4 August, prompting the commanders of the 105th Air Brigade RV i PVO, and of the 92nd Brigade V i PVO, to launch several airstrikes as soon as the shelling slowed down at around 10.00hrs. The jets that took off shortly after primarily targeted HV forces on Mount Dinara, before redirecting their attention to the enemy columns near Teslingrad, Perušić, Mali Alan, Mount Velebit, and Gospić. Meanwhile, the 728th Helicopter Squadron redeployed its Gamas and Gazelles to Frkašić airfield outside Korenica, while between 11.00 and 16.00hrs two Mi-8s of the V i PVO ran an air bridge with the aim of evacuating over 100 wounded from the main hospital of Knin. By the morning of 5 August, the situation was critical to the point where a complete evacuation of Udbina AB was ordered. Loaded with whatever ordnance they could carry, the combat aircraft and helicopters were ferried to Banja Luka in several groups until 11:00. A non-airworthy Gazelle was ferried to Medeno Polje by a Mi-8. Shortly after, two Croat MiG-21bis appeared to hit the base in a low-altitude strike. Eventually, the ground personnel then sabotaged whatever installations were still intact, and withdrew with its vehicles to BiH, late on 5th and early on 6 August 1995.[20] A few other aircraft were left behind and captured by the Croat forces, which reached the ruined Udbine AB early on 7 August. These included two G-2 Galebs, three J-21 Jastrebs, three Utva-66s, and a Utva-75.

The beginning of August 1995 was marked by the large-scale Croatian Operation Oluja (Storm), the aim of which was to seize the 'Republika Srpska Krajina' and thus liberate most of the Croat territory controlled by the Serbs since 1991. The operation was launched at dawn of 4 August 1995, with simultaneous assaults from all sides of the territory in question, and in particular over Mount Dinara – from inside BiH. Regardless of some success during the early phase of this operation, the SVK was defeated during in the first two days of this operation and the capital of the Serbian-controlled area – Knin – was secured by the Croats on 5 August. As a consequence, the mass of the Serb population, about 200,000 civilians in total, fled to the Republika Srpska, and then continued all the way to the FRY, to avoid the revenge of the Croats. The 'Republika Srpska Krajina' thus ceased to exist, and the mass of its former citizens became homeless refugees.

Although operating only a few aircraft and helicopters during Operation Oluja, the RV i PVO carried out numerous missions – and many of these were hindered by NATO. Early on 4 August, its

At other locations, the Croats captured a single Piper Pawnee and two J-20 Kragujs. They also found a significant amount of equipment and other materials at the abandoned Serb air bases and airfields.[21]

In the following days VRS strike aircraft from Banja Luka carried out missions in low-level flight in formations up to three aircraft attacking the advancing HV forces at several locations at Lika or Banija. On 10 August, during one of these missions, one Orao was shot down by a friendly MANPADS at Malo Vrtoče near Drvar. The pilot was badly injured but survived the crash, despite Serb forces firing upon him from the ground.[22]

The VRS attacked HV positions at Mačkovac near Nova Gradiška, in Croatia, with cluster bombs, causing casualties among troops and civilians alike. On the following day, 6 August, two Orao strikers attacked a chemical plant at Kutina in the dusk. One Croatian MiG was on a CAP mission in the wider area was alerted and directed to Kutina to intercept the Serb intruders, but they managed to escape in low-level flight. Croatian Army sources counted around 30 Serb airstrikes on their forces, which fired 17 MANPADS but without success.[23]

Soon after the Croatian attack commenced units of the 44th Missile Air Defence Brigade carried out planned missions. Its 1st Battalion (Dvina/SA-2) was at a firing position in Šamarice at dawn on 4 August and at 05:05 it fired a volley of seven Dvina missiles against the HV forces at Sisak, Sunja and Nebojanski Džep. More strikes were carried out during the day. The battalion remained at its peace-time position until early 6 August and then withdraw into Republika Srpska with all of its equipment. It then took-up a firing position at Mount Kozara and fired more Dvinas against HV targets in Novska.

Three Kub-M batteries were at firing positions in Udbina, Padjene and Tepavci, though they were not active. During the early morning of 5 August, they were ordered to withdraw towards Srb and then into Republika Srpska and were followed by the brigade HQ and all mixed up with columns of fleeing Serb refugees. On 8 August the 2nd Battery was attacked by Croatian MiGs while mingled with the refugees on the road near Bravsko, Republika Srpska. They managed to avoid the attack, but a few civilian vehicles were hit causing eight killed and many wounded.[24]

All of the Krajina missile units reached Banja Luka a couple of days later and the personnel continued in coaches to FR Yugoslavia. The VRS took-over control of the equipment abandoned around the city. Three Kub batteries were introduced into the 172nd Regiment and sent to eastern parts of Republika Srpska. The Dvina-equipped 1st Missile Battalion, which actually had equipment for two battalions, became the 2nd Missile Battalion of the 155th Brigade, and was sent

Table 2: HRZ ORBAT, 4 August 1995		
Base	**Aircraft/Helicopters**	**Role**
91st Air Base, Pleso (Zagreb)	2 MiG-21bis & 11 MiG-21bis	air defence & strike
	1 Mi-24	anti-tank & ECR
	3 An-2 & 1 An-2	transport & ECR
92nd Air Base, Pula	4 MiG-21bis	strike
94th Air Base, Lučko	7 Mi-8	transport
95th Air Base, Split	2 MiG-21bis, 5 Mi-8, 1 An-2	air defence & transport
Požega helidrome	2 Mi-24	anti-tank

Cheerful members of the HRZ with General Anton Tus (former CO of the Yugoslav RV i PVO, 1986-91) near an intact Utva 66 (51109) at Udbina Air Base. (M. Raguž)

Croatian Mi-24s supported Operation Storm in anti-tank missions. (via D. Čanić)

immediately to the Petrovac area where it was used as a surface-to-surface missile unit until the end of the war.[25]

The Croatian HRZ in Operation Storm

The Croatian Air Force, the HRZ, conducted combat missions from 4 to 8 August supporting their troops in the advance and attacking important Serb targets in Krajina. As of the morning of 4 August 1995, the HRZ's ORBAT was as shown in Table 2.

The Croatian MiGs were active from early morning of 4 August and from 06:00 they attacked SVK communications sites at Ćelavac

A scene on the road near Petrovac after an attack by HRZ MiG-21s, 7 August 1995. (R. Ćuković)

and Magarčevac (Petrova Gora) and facilities in Golubić. They continued to attack the Serbian command posts at several locations during the day, operating in two or four-ship formations. One MiG was heavily damaged while three more were lightly damaged in these missions. Mi-8 helicopters were active ferrying wounded HV soldiers.

On the next day of the operation, 5 August, the HRZ continued its attacks. At 07:30 MiGs destroyed the communications site at Piramida Mount Zrinska Gora, which aggravated the command of SVK forces. Croatian MiGs attacked Serb positions and columns, mostly on-call in support of advancing HV units.

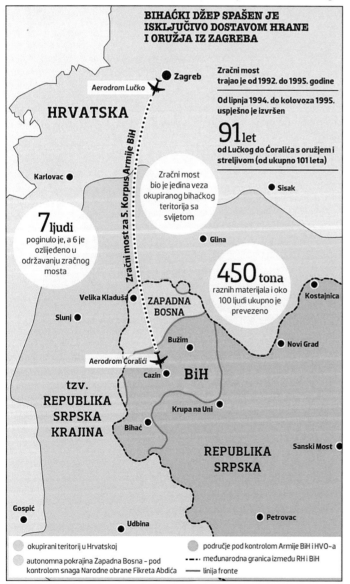

The air bridge between Zagreb (Croatia) and Ćoralići airfield near Cazin. (Author collection)

They also attacked a storage site at Stara straža near Knin and at around 11:45 attacked Udbina Air Base with cluster bombs. Most of the sorties were carried out before noon. Five MiGs suffered light damage from ground fire. Mi-24 helicopters attacked SVK motorised and armoured columns between 10:00 and 13:00, and Mi-8 helicopters continued to support HV troops in their advance and to evacuate the wounded.

On 6 August, Croatian MiGs carried out strikes in pairs against Serb armoured columns and positions at several locations, mostly around noon, and destroyed the single bridge at Mala Glina in the late afternoon. Mi-24s also conducted strikes in the late afternoon claiming two tanks north of Slunj. Two MiGs which maintained the CAP south of Zagreb failed to intercept VRS Oraos which carried out an attack on the chemical facilities in Kutina. The operations continued on 7 August attacking locations much deeper in Krajina territory as they followed the withdrawal of the SVK forces. The MiGs attacked a command post in Srb, an armoured column at Medeno Polje near Bosanski Petrovac (BiH), and a storage site at Lička Kaldrma. The last strikes occurred on the afternoon of 8 August on the territory of Republika Srpska (BiH): these were against tanks at Bosanski Novi railway station and a column at Svodna on the road to Prijedor. Two MiGs were slightly damaged.

During Operation Storm, the HRZ carried out sorties against strategic and important SVK targets, in CAS missions and upon the request of HV ground forces. These totalled 134 sorties with over 72 tonnes of ordnance dropped. Mi-24s conducted three anti-tank missions, while 50 missions were devoted to CAP patrols carried out from Pleso-Zagreb and Split air bases. Only seven missions were reconnaissance, carried out by Mi-24s, MiG-21s and AN-2s. There were 111 sorties by Mi-8s which ferried 485 persons, including wounded, and almost 85 tons of cargo.[26]

New Air Bridge by the Armija BiH

Reconciliation between the Armija BiH and HVO after the Washington Agreement in early spring of 1994 led to renewal of the air bridge between the Croatian helicopter base at Lučko and the airfield at Ćoralići near Cazin and the Bihać area. This was the key link for supplying the Armija BiH V Corps, which was separated from other Armija BiH units and surrounded by the SVK and VRS forces.

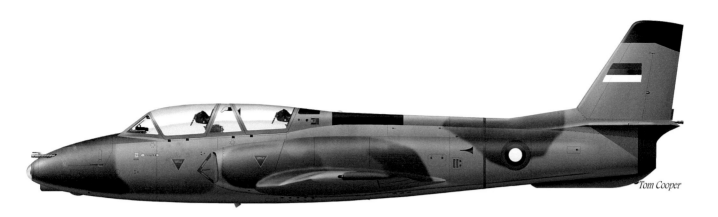

The G-2 Galeb was a two-seat jet trainer armed with two 12.7mm Browning AN/M3 machine guns and four underwing hardpoints with a capacity of 300kg. The first of two examples – serial number 23121 – was available to the 105th Brigade of the SVK, in the Serb-controlled part of Croatia. As usual for most domestically manufactured aircraft of the former Yugoslav Air Force, the aircraft originally received an RAF-influenced camouflage pattern in dark sea grey (BS381C/638) and dark green (BS381C/641) on top surfaces and sides, and PRU blue on undersurfaces. Top-side colours were quite worn out by 1994, and partially refreshed during its overhaul undertaken locally. The prominent large tactical number 121 was removed in late 1991, but it did receive a nickname 'Krajišnik', applied in black, low on the right side of the nose. This Galeb was eventually abandoned at Udbina and captured by Croat forces in August 1995. (Artwork by Tom Cooper)

While originally designed as a replacement for the G-2, the Galeb G-4 was also operated by dedicated fighter-bomber units of the former Yugoslav Air Force. The type proved precious enough that on the dissolution of Yugoslavia only one – serial number 23725 – was left with the V i PVO. In addition to serving as a continuation trainer for J-22 Orao pilots, it also flew combat sorties, frequently armed with US-designed Mk.82 bombs, as shown here. After suffering damage during a liaison flight to Belgrade in June 1992, it was repaired using the rear fuselage and tailfin from the G-4 serial number 23685, resulting in its look as depicted here. Notable is the application of a small No 249 Squadron insignia including a yellow disc and a cobra in black, white and red, low below the front part of the cockpit, the installation of a pod with 23mm GSh-23 gun under the centreline, and chaff and flare dispensers under the lower fuselage. (Artwork by Tom Cooper)

On its establishment in 1992, the 27th Fighter-Bomber Aviation Squadron of the 92nd Mixed Aviation Brigade, V i PVO was equipped with a total of 13 J-22 Orao fighter-bombers and NJ-22 Orao two-seat conversion trainers. At least two of J-22s – including the example illustrated here, serial number 25173 – were compatible with the most potent weapon in the arsenal of this type: US-made AGM-65B Maverick electro-optically guided missiles, one of which is illustrated as installed under the outboard underwing pylon. Other weaponry in the arsenal of the J-22 is illustrated at the bottom and included (from left to right) 200kg bombs of French design; FAB-250-270 bombs of Soviet design, L57-17MD pods for unguided 57mm rockets, and British-made Hunting BL.755 CBUs. As usual for the type, all aircraft were camouflaged in dark sea grey and dark green on top surfaces and sides, and PRU blue on undersurfaces: notable on the forward fuselage is the fresh coat of dark green used to cover the 'last three' of the serial number, applied in late 1991. (Artwork by Tom Cooper)

i

All the helicopters of the Serb Krajina in Croatia were operated by the 56th Helicopter Squadron SVK. This included about a dozen Gazelles and Gazelle Gamas. Because the unit was originally subordinated to the Ministry of the Interior of the Serb Krajina, and because some of the Gazelles were taken from the former police of Yugoslavia, these retained their white and blue livery, depicted here. Rather surprisingly, they also continued wearing the former Yugoslav flag on their fins. A notable addition was the insignia with the inscription 'Milicija Krajina' (Krajina Police) in Cyrillic letters, at the base of the boom. Although anything other than well camouflaged, the Gazelles served in this livery during many combat operations, starting with the Serb Operation Koridor 92. Illustrated is the SA.341 c/n 011, formerly RV i PVO 12619: another example, c/n 103, is known to have retained its full ex-Yugoslav serial, 12872, applied near the top of the fin. (Artwork by Tom Cooper)

Thanks to financial support from abroad, the government of Bosnia and Herzegovina in Sarajevo was quick in acquiring several Mil Mi-8MTV-1 transport helicopters for the Armija BiH. By March 1993, 12 of these were in operational service. While some were based at Tuzla, most were operated from Croatia, to and from which they ran several crucially important 'air bridges' to Bosniak-controlled parts of Bosnia and Herzegovina. All were originally left in the livery of their operators in the former USSR, such as Aeroflot. Some had only crudely overpainted serial numbers and national markings, and most received red crosses (indicating their deployment for medical purposes). Some received civilian registrations, such as T9-HAA in this case. Another known example was the former RA-27085, which did not receive any Bosnian markings, but did have a weather radar installed low on the front fuselage. (Artwork by Tom Cooper)

During 1992, Croatia 'acquired' its first three MiG-21bis through defections of pilots of the JRV i PVO. All retained their livery in 'air superiority grey' overall, but received prominent Croat insignia. As well as the national tri-colore (applied over that of Yugoslavia across the fin), they included the crest of No. 1 (later: No. 21) Squadron, HRZ. Serial numbers 102 and 103 also received 'personal names' in the form of crests of the towns of Dubrovnik (102) and Vukovar (illustrated here on 103), accompanied by the word 'Osvetnik' (Avenger). Furthermore, the small white insignia on the dielectric antenna-cover on the fin denoted the Zmaj Works: the facility at which this aircraft was last overhauled. Standard armament of early Croat MiG-21bis aircraft consisted of FAB-250M-54 bombs (illustrated here) and UB-16-57 pods for S-5K 57mm unguided rockets. A few BL.755 CBUs were obtained with the help of Bosniaks from former stocks of the JRV i PVO at Bihać AB. (Artwork by Tom Cooper)

In early 1994, the USAF Europe deployed elements of the 512th and 526th FS of the 86th TFW from Ramstein AB in West Germany to Aviano AB in northern Italy, where these were assigned to the 401st Operations Group (Provisional) as part of the NATO's Operation Deny Flight. On 28 February 1994, four F-16Cs intercepted six Bosnian Serb J-21s shortly after these attacked targets in the Novi Travnik area, and shot down five of them (though the USAF officially credited its pilots with four kills). The lead in the first section to open fire was the F-16C 89-2137, piloted by Captain Robert G Wright. The jet is illustrated in the configuration as during that mission, wearing the standard camouflage pattern in grays FS36320 and 36118 on top surfaces, and light ghost gray (FS35375) on undersurfaces, and with the red band of 526th FS near the tip of the fin. The aircraft went on to take part in Operation Deliberate Force, in September 1995, by when it wore three kill markings and several bomb markings. In April 1994, through combining all the 48 F-16C/D Block 40s of the 86th TFW with elements of the 301st FW and the 401st FW, the USAF created the 31st FW. Correspondingly, the 512th and 526th FS were reorganised as the 510th and 555th FS. (Artwork by Tom Cooper)

Aircraft of the British Royal Navy saw participation in both operations Deny Flight and Deliberate Force. HMS *Ark Royal* undertook an Adriatic Sea cruise with Sea Harrier FRS.Mk 1s of Naval Air Squadron (NAS) 801 aboard in 1993, and again in 1994. In July 1995, HMS *Invincible* arrived carrying the much upgraded Sea Harrier F/A.Mk 2s of NAS 800. This illustration shows a Sea Harrier FRS.Mk 1 from NAS 801 at the time it was shot down, on 15 April 1995. A veteran of the Falklands War, this jet was painted in dark sea grey (BS381C/638, FS16173) overall and, in addition to national insignia in six positions and the unit insignia on the fin, wore the tactical number 001 on the fairing forwards of the front jet nozzle, and the serial XZ498 on the ventral fin under the tail. Standard armament consisted of AIM-9M Sidewinder missiles carried on outboard underwing pylons: sometimes, a single 1,000lbs/454kg bomb was attached under the centreline. (Artwork by Tom Cooper)

On 21 July 1995, in support of NATO's operations in Bosnia, the German Luftwaffe deployed Einsatzgeschwader 1 (Task Force/Operational Wing 1) to Piacenza AB, in Italy. Consisting of up to 14 Tornado IDS and Tornado ECRs drawn from Jagdbombergeschwader 32 (Fighter-Bomber Wing 32) and Aufklärungsgeschwader 51 (Reconnaissance Wing 51), the unit had the task of protecting allied aircraft from Serbian radar-guided SAMs and flying reconnaissance. Depicted here is one of the Tornado ECRs of the EG.1, the insignia of which is visible on the side of the intake. The aircraft was painted in the then brand-new camouflage pattern 'Norm '95' consisting of three grey colours (FS35237, FS36320, and FS36375). The tip of the fin was painted in dark grey RAL 7012, and the radome in black. Barely visible on the fin is the low-visibility version of the JaBo 32's crest (the full colour version of which is shown inset). Primary armament consisted of two AGM-88 HARM anti-radar missiles, two AIM-9 Sidewinder missiles for self-defence, Cerberus ECM-pods (left outboard underwing pylon) and chaff and flare dispensers (right outboard underwing pylon). (Artwork by Tom Cooper)

On 30 August 1995, NATO suffered its sole loss of Operation Deliberate Force, when this Mirage 2000N-K2 was shot down by a 9K38 Igla MANPAD of the VRS over the Pale area, and both of its crewmembers were captured. The reasons for this loss were related to the French air force lacking aircraft with modern attack systems and precision-guided munitions: instead it was forced to deploy Mirage 2000Ns – originally developed for nuclear strike, but adapted to have a minimal conventional capability – for dive-bombing attacks with free-fall weapons. On 30 August 1995, this Mirage 2000N-K2 (serial 346/3-JD) of the 3e Escadre de Chasse was equipped as depicted here, with two Magic Mk 2 air-to-air missiles on outboard underwing pylons, four Mk.82 bombs on inboard underwing pylons and two massive, 1,500-litre drop tanks. Notable is the insignia of EC.2/3 Champagne on the fin. (Artwork by Tom Cooper)

While F-15s and F-16s of the USAF and European allies flew most of the sorties during Operation Deny Flight, and then played the dominant role during Operation Deliberate Force, F/A-18 Hornet-equipped units of the US Marine Corps and the Spanish Air Force also became involved. The VMFA(AW)-533 Hawks flew Deny Flight missions in 1993, followed by VMFA-251 Thunderbolts and VMFA(AW)-332 Polka Dots, in 1994 and 1995. By September 1995, it was the turn of VMFA(AW)-224 Bengals to deploy 12 of its jets at Aviano AB. One of these is depicted here, together with typical weapons load: this usually consisted of a single AGM-88 HARM under the left wing and one GBU-12 laser-guided bomb (inset, bottom left) under the right wing. Thanks to the AN/AAS-38 Nite Hawk Forward Looking Infra-Red and laser designator pod (inset, bottom centre), the aircraft could designate targets for its own weapons or those of other aircraft. (Artwork by Tom Cooper)

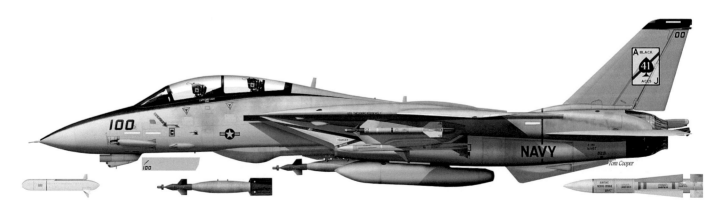

Originally designed as a highly manoeuvrable fighter-interceptor, adapted for the deployment of long-range AIM-54 Phoenix missiles (inset, lower right corner), the F-14 Tomcat was left without its primary opposition by the end of the Cold War. Correspondingly, during the early 1990s a small group of enthusiastic crews worked hard to adapt it for the deployment of laser-guided bombs. The modifications were ready by 1995, but VF-41 deployed without any of the LANTIRN targeting pods. Correspondingly, when the unit flew the first combat sorties in which GBU-16 laser-guided bombs were dropped from its F-14As, it depended on F/A-18s to mark targets. The first 'Bomcat' to release a pair of GBU-16s (shown inset centre) was this one, Modex AJ100, AerNo 161607. What is less well-known is that VF-41's F-14As and VF-102's F-14Bs released a number of ADM-141 TALD decoys (inset, lower left corner) – to further disturb the work of the Serbian air defences. Like most of VF-41's Tomcats, this jet was painted in light ghost gray (FS36375) overall, with large anti-glare panels and fin-tips in in flat black. (Artwork by Tom Cooper)

A J-22 Orao of the V i PVO, seen taxying for a strike sortie while armed with four British-made BL.755 CBUs, in September or October 1995. (D. Vejnović)

A nice study of J-22 Orao serial number 25119 of the V i PVO. Notable are the crudely overpainted tactical number on the forward fuselage, and chaff and flare dispensers installed at the bottom of the rear fuselage. This type was the most potent strike asset of the Bosnian Serbs. (D. Vejnović)

Although obsolete and much too slow, the J-21 formed the backbone of the V i PVO during the Bosnian air war of 1992-95. Clearly visible in this photograph of the example with serial number 24212 are not only the three heavy machine guns installed in the nose, but also hardpoints for bombs or containers for unguided rockets (inboard underwing pylons), attachments for rails for 127mm unguided rockets, and the installation of two chaff and flare dispensers at the bottom of the fuselage. (M Micevski)

An F-16C Block 40 of the 555th FS/31st FW taking off from Aviano AB while loaded with AIM-120 AMRAAM and AIM-9 Sidewinder air-to-air missiles, laser-guided bombs, and a LANTIRN pod under the intake. The aircraft was bound for the strike on Jahorinski Potok storage depot on 25 or 26 May 1995. (NAC/DoD)

Four MiG-21bis of the HRZ seen while underway at a relatively low altitude over central Croatia. Their disruptive camouflage patterns identify them as belonging to the aircraft acquired from Ukraine in 1994. Notable is the national insignia, the complete lack of serial numbers, and that only the front two aircraft have their unit insignia. (V. Šebrek via Z. Despot)

One of aircraft that proved of crucial importance for NATO's operations over Bosnia was the Grumman EF-111A Raven. Packed with electronic warfare systems, and operated by the 429th ECS from Aviano AB. The EF-111A supported all the major NATO air strikes starting with the attack on Udbina AB. (NAC/DoD)

Another frequently overlooked crucial component of NATO's ability to 'air police' the situation in Bosnia was the availability of big tanker aircraft, like this Boeing KC-135R of the Air National Guard, photographed while in-flight refuelling an EF-111A of the 429th ECS. Tankers enabled the allied aircraft not only to reach the operational zone over Bosnia, but also to patrol it or search for their targets over extended periods of time. (NAC/DoD)

Another crucially important combat-support aircraft of NATO during the operations over Bosnia was the Grumman EA-6B Prowler. During operations Deliberate Force and Dead Eye, elements from three different squadrons flying Prowlers were deployed at Aviano, one of each is visible in this photograph. Nearest to the camera is an example from VAQ-130 Zappers, to the left is an EA-6B from VAQ-141 Shadowhaws, and in the rear another is from VAQ-209 Star Warriors. (NAC/DoD)

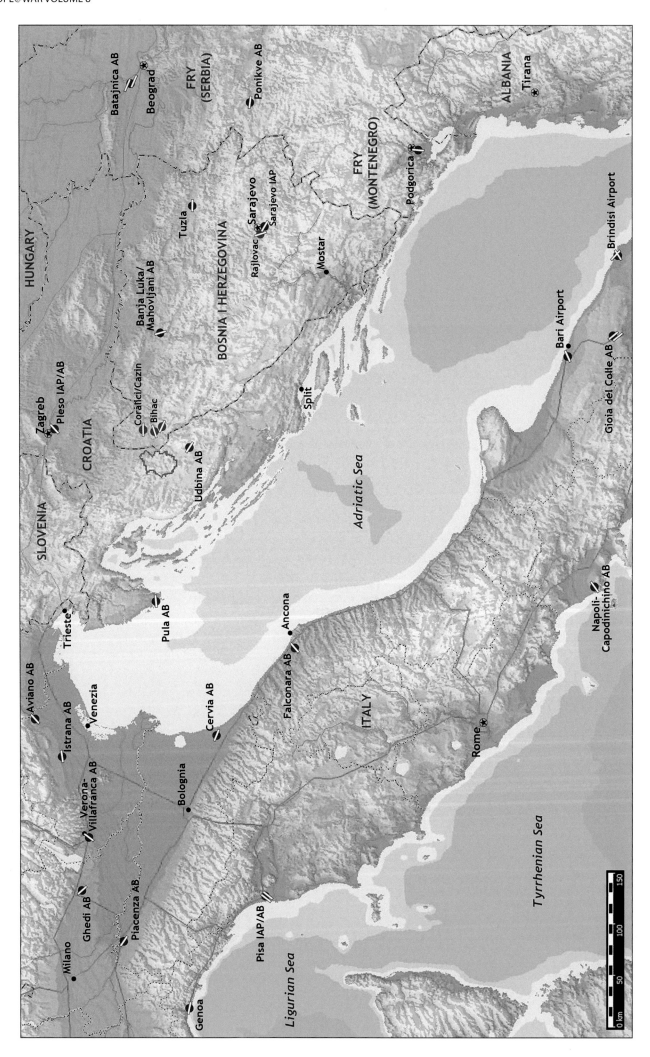

Table 3: Overview of the Armija BiH Helicopter Missions 1994-1995

Year	Month	Successful missions:	Unsuccessful missions:	In total:
1994	June	5	0	5
	July	2	1	3
	September	2	1	3
	October	0	2	2
	November	6	1	7
	December	15	2	17
1995	January	12	1	13
	February	9	0	9
	March	7	1	8
	April	13	1	14
	May	15	0	15
	July	3	0	3
	August	2	0	2
	Total of	91	10	101

A plan of the Armija BiH helicopter missions to Goražde, known as Operation Postman. (Bahto Hamid, *Sa braniocima Sarajeva i Goražda*)

The coordination was at the highest level between the two air forces (HRZ I PZO and RV i PVO ARBiH).

The helicopters operated from Lučko air base. Fixed wing CASA C-212 (T9-ABA) and Cessna C-550 (T9-BiH) transports operated from Zagreb-Pleso, Krk and Pula airports. Beside their own fleet Armija BiH leased transport aircraft and helicopters with crews, mostly from Ukraine. One such leased aircraft, an AN-26 registered as UR-26207, which ferried weapons obtained in Kazakhstan from Pula to Ćoralići, was shot down by the SVK on 1 August while on the nocturnal return leg of the mission. The crew members were Ukrainian and one Bosnian Muslim pilot.[27]

The supply missions were taken further by helicopters and CASA at the "regular" line between Lučko and Ćoralići. Despite pressure from VRS forces, the aircraft and helicopters landed at Ćoralići, even during the harsh fighting in mid-November 1994, and occasional VRS and SVK shelling with 130mm guns and Volhov missiles.

Another incident jeopardized this air bridge on the night of 3 December 1994. One of two Armija BiH helicopters (T9-HIA) which had landed previously at Lučko, crashed at 22:00 after taking off with a load of ammunition, rocket launchers and MANPADS, though the crew managed to bail out from the cockpit prior to it exploding. One Bosnian (T9-HIA) and one Croatian Mi-8 (H-209) caught fire and were destroyed and six members of ARBiH, HRZ and a Hungarian leased crew were badly injured. Brendan O'Shea from the EU Mission in Bihać, commented that the crashed helicopter was probably the personal helicopter of Alija Izetbegović and the HIA markings confirmed his comment.[28]

Ш Е М А
дејства ларв ПВО при уништењу
непријатељског хеликоптера
у рејону с.Мркаљи
09.05.1995. године у 02.30 часова

Кладањ

Олово

Хан Пијесак

В.Жеп

Мркаљи

Жепа

Цимрије

Деветак

Дрина

Соколац

Рогатица

Легенда:

- Ватрени положај ларв ПВО
- Процењени правац лета непријатељског хеликоптера
- Стварни правац лета критичног дана
- Ao   Тачка нишањења и гађања
- Ao   Тачка погађања хеликоптера
- Место обарања - пада хеликоптера

An illustration of the shooting down of an Armija BiH Mi-8 on the return leg from the Žepa enclave. (Gen. Božo Novak)

The air bridge flights between Lučko and Ćoralići were continued in 1995 with significant intensity which provoked the Serbs to maintain the constant "SAM-bushes". On 28 May 1995, an Armija BiH Mi-8 heading for Lučko was claimed at 02:45 at Kremena in the Slunj area. BiH foreign Minister Irfan Ljubijankić was killed alongside the Ukrainian and Bosnian Muslim crew, as previously mentioned.[29]

From September 1994, Armija BiH had established more-or-less secure air bridges with its enclaves in Eastern Bosnia in a daring effort flying loaded Mi-8s, with roaring engines, over the Serbian territories to the enclaves surrounded by belligerent troops with AA artillery.

Two attempts to reach Goražde were made: one on 23 April 1994 in which an Mi-8 was damaged by groundfire, and another one in September when the helicopter had returned to Zenica. Finally, in October Armija BiH helicopters managed to reach Goražde and establish communications in an operation coded "Postman". However, the night sorties were not easy and two more helicopters were heavy damaged in missions on 12 and 30 October.

In 1995 there were five successful missions to Goražde between 26 January and 21 April. Each of the missions carried three tons or more of armament or supplies and could ferry 10-20 persons out of the enclave. In the ninth mission, which was carried out on the night of 22-23 August 1995, a Mi-8 (T9-HAE) was lost with its Ukrainian crew and six passengers; the helicopter struck trees while landing, lost control and crashed. There were a few more missions before the end of the war; in one of them another helicopter was damaged by Serb AA fire, and remained in the enclave for over month, until it was repaired. Serb forces continued to maintain the AAA ambushes until November 1995.[30]

On 31 December 1994 an air bridge was renewed to Srebrenica and Žepa in support of 28th Division of the Armija BiH. There were nine successful ferry flights, shipping rockets and AT launchers, 60mm mortars and ammunition, supplies, cigarettes and salt. The last flight was carried on 7 May 1995 when Mi-8 (T9-HAC) took off at 02:30 but was soon ambushed by Serb AA artillery. Hit by 30mm shells, the helicopter continued the flight but soon crashed in the Žepa area. Nine persons among the 22 onboard were killed including the complete crew. The air bridge to Srebrenica and Žepa was not renewed since both enclaves were seized by VRS forces in July 1995.[31]

Reviewing the success of the Armija BiH helicopter air bridges at a ceremony held on 22 May 1996, its first commander Salko Begić, stressed the importance of those missions. The grand total of 7,000 sorties were carried out with 30,000 passengers, 3,000 wounded and 3,000 tons of material ferried. Those missions especially helped Western Bosnia (the Bihać pocket) avoid being seized by the Serb forces, and improved the situation in the Eastern Bosnian enclaves.[32]

4
OPERATION DELIBERATE FORCE

Planning the Operation

The planning process for Operation Deliberate Force was a long-lasting one. Mark Bucknam suggests that senior USAF officers "began planning in December 1992 for an air campaign in Balkans, and they initially modelled their plan on Gulf War air operations". The 1991 Gulf War had a big impact on debates over whether to use airpower in Bosnia. High-technology airpower had acquired an image as a near surgical instrument capable of destroying without killing and winning without risking, stresses Bucknam.[1] The first indication of the use of NATO airpower in the Bosnian War can be identified as Operation Deny Flight, begun in spring 1993. There were several studies which analysed this process in depth. Here, we shall outline the main cornerstones of planning which led to the execution of the operation in the late summer of 1995.

Planning

Once Operation Deny Flight started in spring 1993, the first drafts of plans to use airpower against the Serbs in Bosnia were outlined. The first plan was approved by the NATO Council on 8 April 1993 and anticipated just the enforcement of a No Fly Zone.[2] After the Bosnian Serbs rejected the Vance-Owen Plan on a new territorial division in Bosnia on 6 May 1993, President Clinton and other US officials intensified the idea of using airpower and they discussed the possibility of using large-scale strikes to coerce the Serbs into acceptance. Several studies and the research of USAF historians indicate that the State Department decided to use airpower against the Serb side in the Bosnian war as an act of punishment for Serb "aggression". In June 1993, partly in response to pressure from the United States, the Security Council passed Resolution 836 which authorised NATO forces to provide close air support for UN forces upon request.[3] The procedure to request air support was quite complicated, as it involved the "dual key" of both UN and NATO approval. UN approval required contact with the United Nations headquarters in New York City, making effective coordination nearly impossible given the difference in time zones. The UN approval process was later somewhat streamlined when UN Secretary-General Boutros Boutros Ghali delegated the authority to authorise airstrikes to his special representative in Bosnia, Yasushi Akashi. On 13 August 1993, the Deny Flight plan (CINCSOUTH OPLAN 40101 Deny Flight) was approved with the important addition of CAS to the UN troops on the ground. At that point, three "options" emerged for the attack of targets on the ground. Those targets included:

On 10 July 1995, a detachment of EC-130E Hercules from the 42nd Airborne Command and Control Squadron, Davis-Monthan Air Force Base arrived at Aviano Air Base and took-over the ABCCC missions. (NAC/DoD)

- those who directly attack the UN forces or violate the UN decisions and resolutions;
- military targets and engaged troops deployed against the Safe Zones;
- important/strategic targets which were out of the Safe Zones;

Such division of targets and 'options' would remain until, and during, Operation Deliberate Force in the late summer of 1995.[4]

Although NATO deployed sizeable air contingents in Italy and used them over the Balkans, their weak influence on the conflict and the neutralisation of the fire power superiority of the VRS frustrated many American military leaders in the Alliance. Nearly all of the posts in the chain of command from SHAPE to NATO's Southern European flank were held by US officers. In the earliest phases of the plaining there was some concern among the highest circles of the US military, to avoid "Americanization" of such an air campaign. Soon, some of the new personalities in the higher tiers of NATO came to match the standpoint of the political circles in the US that opted for the use of airpower. The American political belief that war in Bosnia could be stopped through an air campaign against the Serbs became a step closer within USAF circles. This was in total contrast to most senior European political and military figures, who were cautious and opted for a political solution through the negotiation process. To some of the key US figures such an approach seemed endless and without vision and having their forces already in the region at Aviano and other air bases, as well as aboard the aircraft carriers, they continued planning a decisive air campaign against the Serbs in Bosnia.

Still, the exact plan for carrying out the air campaign, or annexes to existing operations over Bosnia, were not outlined. The early phase was gathering the facts and figures from the ground on possible targets, starting in August 1993, and expanded to include Serbian air defence in late 1994. The earliest list of targets of all three warring parties reached the number of 444. Later in 1995, a revision took place at the level of COMAIRSOUTH, CAOC, AOC and NATO representatives and the list was downsized. Around 300 Serb targets were removed, due to the fear of civilian casualties. A master plan with a total of 151

targets was passed to CINCSOUTH and UNPF for approval and after the meeting of North Atlantic Council (NAC) on 25-26 July 1995 the target list was approved. Of these, only 56 were targeted during Operation Deliberate Force.[5]

In his book *To End a War*, Richard Holbrooke explained that the plan was created by Admiral Leighton Smith and General Michael Ryan, while the targets had already been selected. Holbrooke revealed that he had visited Smith's HQ in the hills above Naples where he had a chance to see the vast aerial footage material with hundreds of potential targets from simple bunkers to sophisticated SAM missile systems. The US Special Envoy concluded that when the order came, Ryan and Smith carried out the mission skilfully and impressively successfully. Plan 40-104 was outlined with the intention to withdraw UNPROFOR forces from Bosnia with US military assistance. The existence of this plan assured Holbrooke that the United States could not avoid their military involvement in Bosnia.[6]

Fall of Srebrenica and Žepa

It is obvious that the key role in planning and preparation of the air campaign was that of the Americans, although within the formal chain of NATO command structure. But, by the beginning of summer 1995, some of the European allies started to approve the idea of the use of airpower against the Serbs in Bosnia. This change came after the Serbs took UN troops hostage to protect them from air attacks after the shooting down of a USAFE F-16, and finally, after the fall of two "Safe Zones" in Eastern Bosnia.

After several raids by Armija BiH forces in mid-June from the Safe Zone of Srebrenica – one of which nearly reached the VRS HQ in Han Pijesak – the VRS Main Staff decided to launch an attack on the city's Muslim enclave. The operation was codenamed "Krivaja", after the river in Bosnia. The Drinski Corps was tasked to carry out the operation, supported by elements of Main Staff military police and reconnaissance units and Ministry of Interior Special Purpose Brigade. There were no connections or any liaison with FRY forces or authorities during the operation which was launched at dawn on 6 July 1995. The operation was commanded by General Živanović, who commanded the Drinski Corps, but on the morning of 11 July, General Mladić arrived and took-over the command and took part in the last stage of the operation, when the VRS forces had already started to enter Srebrenica. The town was empty and most of the civilians

A pair of RNLAF F-16s carried out a symbolic attack on VRS forces advancing into Srebrenica on 11 July 1995. This photograph shows J-063, which became famous when its pilot claimed an FRY MiG-29 at the beginning of Operation Allied Force on 24 March 1999. (NAC/DoD)

Ground crew prepare the AAMs and an LGB under the wing of an F-16C of 31st FW. After being fired upon from the ground and unable to find their targets, two pairs of F-16Cs withdrew from a strike in the vicinity of Srebrenica on 11 July 1995. (NAC/DoD)

a request from the battalion commander. The strike package included 18 aircraft, including six strikers. Two Dutch F-16s attacked the VRS positions with standard bombs, while four USAF F-16s were unable to locate their targets and withdrew after being fired upon from the ground. The influence upon the situation was minor and did not halt the Serb advance: it only enraged General Mladić who triumphantly entered the town.[7]

As the VRS offensive continued against another Muslim enclave in Žepa, south-east of Srebrenica, NATO carried out two additional 'limited airstrikes', on 16 and 20 July, targeting the VRS positions in the wider area of Žepa. Serb military sources concluded that those two airstrikes "significantly changed the ratio of forces and meant military support to Muslims".[8] In Žepa, the VRS forces acted differently when compared to Srebrenica and simply let the Armija BiH's 285th Brigade abandon the enclave and cross to Serbia/FRY were its men remained in internment until the end of war.

The VRS's seizing of the two UN Safe Zones of Srebrenica and Žepa in Eastern Bosnia during July were not taken as the pretext or 'trigger event' for launching the airstrikes against the Republika Srpska, since there was no information on the fate of the Armija BiH forces and the later massacre. Still, one would expect NATO – if really concerned about the fate of the Bosniaks in the besieged

gathered around the UN base in the nearby village of Potočari, while the forces of the 28th Division Armija BiH retreated during the early morning some 40-50 kilometres north-west of the enclave. In the following days, almost half of the retreating column was captured by VRS and the local police. After being held for a few days in captivity, several thousand of them were summarily executed. Regardless of ICTY trials and wider public accusations, no specific reason, motive or order for this atrocity has been identified. The Srebrenica massacre became regarded as the worst atrocity in Europe since the Second World War.

During the final stage of clashes around, 14:30 on 11 July, RNLAF F-16s carried out a strike mission in support of the UN Dutch Battalion on the outskirts of the enclave. The mission was approved by the UN Secretary-General's Representative Akashi and General Janvier, after

enclaves – to launch an all-out attack on the VRS, at least in that area. The cold fact is that it did not do so. Instead of acting, as the two Smiths had demanded, NATO set up a conference to discuss what to do should this happen again. The meeting in question was held in London on 21 July 1995: representatives of the 16 NATO members met to consider new options for Bosnia. It was agreed that if the Serb forces launched an offensive against the remaining Muslim enclave at Goražde in Eastern Bosnia, then the airstrikes would be launched, exclusively at NATO's discretion and without further consultation with the UN. The two main figures in the chain of command with responsibility for launching the air campaign were General Janvier (UNPF) and General Ryan (AFSOUTH). The North Atlantic Council and the UN also agreed to use NATO airstrikes in response to attacks on any of the other safe areas in Bosnia. The participants at the conference also agreed in principle to use large-scale NATO airstrikes in response to future acts of Serb aggression. This was an important step among the NATO allies towards the expected air campaign against the Republika Srpska.[9]

Target Selection

The plan for the air campaign was expanded in July 1995 to include strikes against the Serbian radar and missile sites. Initial work had already been conducted in the CAOC, by its new director General Hornburg in mid-December 1994. It seems that General Ryan baptised the plan as 'Dead Eye'. This sub-part of the general plan for the air campaign was created not to support the UN troops, but with the intention to completely neutralise the Serb air defences.[10] In August 1995, NATO planners estimated the strength of the Serbian air defence as seven SA-2 SAM sites, six SA-6 sites, 12 SA-9 sites, an unknown number of MANPAD teams, and nearly 1,100 anti-aircraft guns of 20-76mm calibre. Furthermore, it was estimated that the VRS air defences could rely on information and resources from the FRY's air defences.[11] While some confusion on the side of the Western alliance could be expected, simply because the VRS had by then been reinforced with some of the equipment that the SVK had withdrawn from Croatia, this indicates that even two years after the start of NATO's involvement in the Bosnian War, its intelligence still lacked precise information about the strength of the Bosnian Serbs.

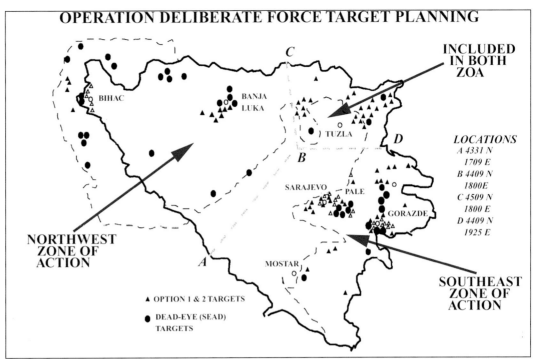

The initial plan for Operation Deliberate Force, including the sub-operation Dead Eye against the Serb air defences. (Mark A. Bucknam, *Responsiblity of Command, How UN and NATO Commanders Influenced Airpower over Bosnia*)

An aerial photograph of a target, with KLU designating those for the RNLAF. (W. Lutgert and R. de Winter, *Check the Horizon*)

In the first half of August 1995, the forthcoming air campaign was given the title Operation Deliberate Force. The Deliberate Force air campaign plan eventually reflected several elements of OPLAN 40101 but also differed from it in many ways.[12] The intention was readable in the operation's title: it would be the intentional use of airpower. But the operation had to have some pretext for its launch: some kind of "trigger" event was required. It was concluded that this could be: the killing UN hostages, an attack on UN personnel, the concentration of VRS forces against the protected Safe Zones, or the shelling of civilians out of the Safe Zones. This also defined the "Bosnian Serbs" as aggressors, that there would be no opposition from Croatia, that

Serbia (FRY) would remain neutral in all military matters, and that robust attack on the VRS was the only possibility to change the balance of power in the Bosnian theatre.[13]

The UN and NATO Joint Targeting Board held a meeting on 14 August 1995 and the list of targets was redefined and downsized from 151 to 87 targets to be attacked in Operation Deliberate Force. The targets were organised into Option 1 and Option 2. Option 3 included strikes on Serb infrastructure. Airstrikes against the Serb's integrated air defences were the main contents of Operation Dead Eye, and it had two sub-operations: "North-west" and "South-east."[14] On 14 August General Ryan presented a detailed briefing on his concept of operation to General Janvier and Admiral Smith. The military objective was to destroy everything that gave the VRS superiority over its adversaries. Under this plan, agreed on 25 August, General Janvier was ready to "turn the key" and order that airstrikes commence. An exercise titled "Vulcan" was planned to be conducted between 29 August and 1 September, with the intention of checking out the chain of command, reactions and approved targets.[15]

The key planners of the air campaign, Admiral Smith and General Ryan, had two main problems in preparing the air campaign: weather conditions and eventual civilian casualties. They were clear in the standpoint that the operation had to be as short as possible and to minimize civilian casualties, to avoid the pressure of public opinion. On the other hand, Richard Holbrooke was satisfied that the expectations for the use of airpower within the political circles in the United States would be achieved. But before the operation could be launched, a trigger event was needed; a violent action by the Bosnian Serbs.[16]

A dummy Kub-M (SA-6) seen at Udbina Air Base. Some of these mock-ups helped the Serbs to preserve their air defence assets from destruction during the airstrikes in Operation Dead Eye/Deliberate Force. (M.D. Ristić)

The VRS Intelligence on Possible Airstrikes

By the beginning of July the VRS Main Staff was aware that some kind of international military action could be taken to enforce the peace negotiation process. VRS intelligence reports had some information on this, but the course of action was not predictable other than that Western public opinion was prepared for a military intervention. The deployment of the Rapid Reaction Force and presence of German Luftwaffe assets attracted much attention from Serb military intelligence. The Luftwaffe deployed 14 Tornados from its Einsatzgeschwader 1 to San Domiano-Piacenza AB in Italy on 21 July 1995. This was the first time since the Second World War that Germany provided combat aircraft to support an air operation. The engagement of the Luftwaffe had a mostly psychological impact on the Serbian Main Staff, drawing a parallel with the Luftwaffe of the Second World War, rather than the contingent's actual role and strength. These would be used in reconnaissance missions over Bosnia from 7 August.[17]

The American intention to destroy the Serb air defences "without prior warning, in a single, strong and systematic operation" became known to Main Staff VRS in a report on 4 July report and was repeated in a 27 July report that also stated "the cause is what is needed, which they can easily create on the ground".[18]

Looking at the preserved intelligence reports, the VRS military intelligence did not note the change of NATO attitudes in the London conference held on 21 July. They estimated that no important decisions were made which could influence the role of the Western states in the war in Bosnia and that no unity was shown among the NATO allies. On 24 July, upon analysing Western media, there was a change in estimations: 'a substantial air campaign' was possible, including airstrikes on air defences and V i PVO infrastructure, armoured units, stores, communications sites, command posts, etc.' Four days later, it was reported that three variants of airstrikes to protect Safe Zones existed. Serbian intelligence interpreted these as:

a) close air support strikes around Safe Zones;

b) limited strikes around Goražde and other Safe Zones;

c) massive strikes at the wider territory of Republika Srpska.

Serbian intelligence found out about Operational Plan 40104, which was developed for the event that the UN decided to withdraw UNPROFOR, and was confirmed in the session of the NATO Military Committee on 30 July 1995.[19]

The Serbian V i PVO analyses from this period estimated: "respective NATO forces were prepared and trained to act upon the VRS forces and objects, and they are practically non-stop over our territory and without any limitations. Time to their reaction was shortened so that the commander of the UN forces for ex BiH can order the attack upon one of the objects in real time." Those objects (targets) were "the subject of reconnaissance" and that "strikes on them were trained for". The V i PVO believed that "no matter how large NATO forces are, they are sensitive to losses. It is [our] estimation that the loss of four aircraft means the suspension of the air campaign for a long time".[20]

It is interesting that a VRS intelligence report, dated on 14 August, almost predicted the events which were going to happen just two weeks later: '…the cause for the engagement of the RRF and NATO aviation shall be staged by alleged massacre of civilians or attack on the UN forces'.[21]

NATO forces deployed for the Air Campaign

Sizeable NATO contingents had been present in Italy since spring of 1993, while others conducted their missions from homeland bases. For the execution of the planned campaign, additional forces had to be deployed to the theatre.

The 31st Fighter Wing was the core USAFE unit to receive and welcome many USAF, USN, USMC and NATO units, which soon gathered in its home base at Aviano. Under the USAFE orders of 1 July 1995, the 7490th Wing (Provisional) was formed to facilitate all of these units and was commanded by 31st FW commander Colonel (later General) Charles Wald. His staff eventually had to bed down a total of 140 aircraft, including 52 F-16s, 16 CH-47s, 12 US Marine Corps F/A-18s, 12 A-10s, three British E-3Ds, 10 Spanish EF-18s, 10 F-15Es, 10 EA-6Bs from the carrier USS *Theodore Roosevelt*, nine C-130s of various types, and six EF-111s. Of these, 114 were in place when Deliberate Force opened on the night of 29-30 August. Nevertheless,

The Luftwaffe deployed 14 Tornados on 21 July 1995 from Einsatzgeschwader 1 to Piacenza. They were engaged in SEAD and reconnaissance missions during Operation Deliberate Force. (Author's collection)

An unusual guest lands in Aviano, July 1995. A US Navy C-130 Hercules, most likely in support of the USN units deployed for Operation Deliberate Force. (NAC/DoD)

to 'recover' about 70-75% of the radar picture.[24]

The Trigger Event

The case for "turning the key" against Republika Srpska and its forces came unexpectedly soon. The explosion mortar shells at Markale market in Sarajevo on 28 August, killed 38 and wounded many more civilians. The worldwide media, which immediately aired TV reports from the scene, promptly accused the Serb side of responsibility for the attack.[25] It was stated that the mortar shells had been fired from VRS positions around Sarajevo. Protests from the Serbian political and military leadership were in vain. The "trigger event" for launching air campaign was there.

Holbrooke, a great advocate of the usage of airpower against the Serbs, finally had the chance to make this notion into reality. While talking that afternoon with the special advisor to the Secretary of State, Strobe Talbott, he stressed that the cruelty of the Bosnian Serbs provided an unexpected chance to do what needed to be done. He advocated the air campaign against the Serbs as the most important test of the American leading role after the Cold War, and that the shelling of Markale

as commander of the 7490th Wing (Provisional), Colonel Wald did not exercise command authority over the non-USAF units.[22]

In mid-July two EC-130H Compass Calls arrived at Aviano with the task of identifying and monitoring the daily work of the Serbian air defences. The strengthening of the SEAD component was necessary for planned Dead Eye operation. On 13 August, aircraft carrier CVN-71 USS *Theodore Roosevelt* entered the Adriatic. Five days later, on 18 August COMAIR SOUTH asked the allies to provide additional contingents to Italy. Part of them were sent to Italy during September while part of them remained on alert at their home bases.[23]

In spite of the disruption caused by losing the radar site at Plješevica, the 51st Air Surveillance Battalion intensively monitored NATO aviation operations in mid and late August. Jamming of their radars increased as Operation Deliberate Force came closer and closer. Beside the airborne platforms which jammed the Serbian radars orbiting out of BiH (RS) airspace, there was also jamming from the ships in the Adriatic and from the formations which patrolled the skies above BiH (RS). Saša Ratković, who was at that time one of youngest lieutenants in the 51st Air Surveillance Battalion stressed that the British-made S-600 radars were not fully jammed, since they had a 'Q-anti-jamming device', the use of which enabled the operator

market was a direct humiliation of the United States. Holbrooke describes that this event finally silenced opposition in the State Department and among the Europeans on using airpower against the Serbs. Now, within the State Department, there was a feeling that this was the point which could not be allowed to pass. President Clinton became determined that an air campaign against the Serbs was necessary and the recommendation of the US negotiation team was that air campaign should start, no matter its eventual influence on the negotiation process. The Europeans, who had their troops on the ground in Bosnia, and thus a different perspective and interests, were silenced now and there was no initial European opposition to air campaign as had previously been the case.[26]

The next day, the contact group for Bosnia and Herzegovina, which was responsible for political issues, announced the decision that there would be a 'military response to a massacre in Sarajevo'. General Rupert Smith believed that Serbs fired the mortar shells at the Sarajevo market. In a telephone conversation during the night of 28-29 August he confirmed his belief to Admiral Leyton Smith and that "turning the key" for the airstrike was necessary. The British general asked his American namesake not to launch the operation for 24 hours, until his superior, General Janvier, returned from Paris,

Table 4: NATO ORBAT, Operation Deliberate Force, August-September 1995			
Nationality/Unit	**Aircraft**	**Base**	**Notes**
Canada			
No. 405/407/415 Sqns	2 CC-140	Sigonella	
-	CC-130	Ancona	
France			
EB.1/91 & 2/91	Mirage IVP	Cazaux & Mont de Marsan	Reconnaissance
EC.1/3	4 Mirage 2000D	Cervia	
EC.2/3	3 Mirage 2000N-K2	Cervia	
EC.3/5	6 Mirage 2000C	Cervia	
EC.3/11	8 Jaguar A	Istrana	
EC.2/33	5 Mirage F.1CR	Istrana	
ED.36	1 E-3F	Avord, Trapani	AWACS
EE.51	1 DC-8 Sarigue		
EET.11/54	C.160G	Istrana, Metz, Orleans/Briei	
ERV.93	KC-135FR	Istres	Tanker
ET.2/61	1 C-130H/H-30	Ancona	
EH.67	3 SA.330 Puma	Brindisi	
Germany			
LTG.61	1 C.160D	Ancona	Luftwaffe
AKG.51	6 Tornado IDS	Piacenza	Luftwaffe
JbG.32	8 Tornado ECR	Piacenza	Luftwaffe
MFG.2	2 Atlantic Peace Peach	Nordholz	Marineflieger; SIGINT
MFG.3	Atlantic	Sigonella/Elmas	Marineflieger, MPA
Italy			
6 Stormo	8 Tornado IDS	Ghedi	
36 Stormo	8 Tornado IDS	Gioia del Cole	
48 Brigada	4 G.222, 1 C-130	Pisa	
51 Stormo	6 AMX	Istrana	
NATO			
NAEWF	8 E-3A	Geilenkirchen/Trapani/Previza	AWACS
Netherlands			
No. 306 Sqn	5 F-16A(R)	Villafranca	
No. 320/321 Sqn	P-3C	Sigonella	
No. 322 Sqn	13 F-16A	Villafranca	
No. 334 Sqn	F.27	Rimini	
No. 336 Sqn	C-130H/H-30	Rimini	
Portugal			
No. 601 Sqn	1 P-3F	Sigonella	
Spain			
12/15 Ala	8 EF-18A+	Aviano	
No. 37 Sqn	1 CASA.212	Vicenza	
No. 221 Sqn	1 P-3B	Sigonella	MPA
No. 311 Sqn	2 KC-130H	Aviano	Tanker
Turkey			
191. Filo	18 F-16C	Ghedi	
UK			
No. 1 PRU	1 Canberra PR.Mk 9	Gioia del Colle	
No. 4 Sqn	12 Harrier GR.Mk 7	Gioia del Colle	
No. 8 Sqn	2 E-3D	Aviano	AWACS

No. 10 Sqn	2 VC.10 C.Mk 1	Palermo	Tanker
No. 39 Sqn	1 Canberra PR.Mk 9	Marham	
No. 47 Sqn	1 Hercules HC.Mk 1P	Ancona	
No. 51 Sqn	2 Nimrod MR.Mk 2P & R.Mk 2P	Sigonella & Pratica di Mare	MPA
No. 54 Sqn	2 Jaguar GR.Mk 1	Gioia del Colle	
No. 111 Sqn	6 Tornado F.Mk 3	Gioia del Colle	
No. 216 Sqn	2 TriStar	Palermo	Tanker
NAS 800	6 Sea Harrrier F/A.Mk 2	HMS *Invincible*	Aug 1995 – Sep 1995
NAS 814	7 Sea King HAS.Mk 6	HMS *Invincible*	
NAS 849	3 Sea King AEW.Mk 2	HMS *Invincible*	
USA			
7490th Wing (Provisional)		Aviano	
9th RW (Det.)	3-4 U-2R	Fairford, Akrotiri	USAF
55th RW (Det.)	2 EC-135W	Mildenhall	
23rd FS	8 F-16C HTS	Aviano	USAF
42nd ACCS	4 EC-130E ABCCC	Aviano	USAF
43rd ECS	3 EC-130H Compass Call	Aviano	USAF
104th FG	12 O/A-10A	Aviano	USAF
303rd FS	12 A-10A	Aviano	USAF/ANG
429th ECS	6 EF-111A	Aviano	USAF
494th FS	8 F-15E	Aviano	USAF, 48th FW
510th FS	24 F-16C	Aviano	USAF, 31st FW
555th FS	24 F-16C	Aviano	USAF, 31st FW
VAQ-130/141/209	2-6 EA-6B	Aviano	USN; Aug-Oct 1995
VFMA(AW)-224	12 F/A-18D	Aviano	USMC; Sep-Nov 1995
VFMA(AW)-544	12 F/A-18D	Aviano	USMC; Jul-Sep 1995
VMAQ-1/3	2-6 EA-6B	Aviano	USMC; Aug-Oct 1995
9th ARS	5 KC-10A	Genoa	USAF, 100th ARW; Aug-Oct 1995
91st ARS	6 KC-135R	Pisa	USAF, 100th ARW
99th ARS	6 KC-135R	Istres	USAF, 100th ARW; from 1 Sep 1995
351st ARS	9 KC-135R	Mildenhall	
712th ARS	6 KC-135R	Istres	USAF, 100th ARW; to 31 Aug 1995
16th SOS	4 AC-130H	Brindisi	
19th/67th SOS	4 HC-130P	Brindisi	
20th/21st SOS	7 MH-53J	Brindisi	
VP-6	8 P-3C	Sigonella	MPA
VQ-2	5 EP-3E-II Aries II	Rota	COMINT/ELINT/SIGINT
CVW-8 (AJ)		USS Theodore Roosevelt (CVN-71)	to 12 Sep 1995
VF-41	F-14A		
VFA-15	F/A-18C		
VFA-87	F/A-18C		
VMFA-312	F/A-18C		
VAW-124	E-2C		

HS-3	SH-60F/HH-60H		
VAQ-141	EA-6B		
VS-24	S-3B		
VQ-6 (Det.)	ES-3B		
CVW-1 (AB)		USS America (CV-66)	from 9 Sep 1995
VF-102	F-14B		
VMFA-251	F/A-18C		
VFA-82	F/A-18C		
VFA-86	F/A-18C		
VAW-123	E-2C		
HS-11	SH-60F/HH-60H		
VMAQ-3	EA-6B		
VS-32	S-3B		
VQ-6 (Det.)	ES-3B		

and approved the list of targets. Smith also stressed that this time delay was needed so that the UNPF forces deployed all over Bosnia could take up safer positions and move away from the targets or VRS forces. After General Janvier arrived at his Zagreb HQ, Admiral Smith phoned him to say: "My pilots are showing up in the ready rooms, and they don't know which targets to go hit. So, I've got to have your answer now because you're endangering the lives of my pilots and I won't put up with that!" Janvier approved first ten of 13 targets which were suggested by Admiral Leyton Smith and General Ryan, but he refused to approve three targets that had the word "barracks" in their title.[27]

The preparations were ongoing. During the take-off from Fairford AB for a mission over Bosnia, a U-2R (serial 68-10338) of the 9th RW crashed and the pilot was killed.[28] On 29 August 1995, the Serb military intelligence provided the Main Staff VRS with fairly accurate information, stressing that several of its sources indicated that during a meeting between Admiral Leyton Smith and General Rupert Smith:

...A plan was approved for air and artillery strikes against the vital elements of the VRS. NATO air strikes and RRF artillery fire was coordinated to start at agreed time and locations. The immediate cause was an orchestrated crime, committed in Sarajevo, for which the Serbian side was accused. Air strikes could be expected to commence momentaly. Most likely, against the air defence systems on the whole territory of Republika Srpska, then command posts, storages of ammunition, equipment and the artillery positions around Sarajevo.[29]

General Ryan flew to CAOC in Vicenza on 29 August and ordered that Operation Deliberate Force should commence on the following night. The crews that were flying CAP or other daily missions over Bosnia and Herzegovina were ordered to abandon its airspace.[30] The jamming of the Serbian radars lasted throughout the whole day, and an intelligence report arrived at the Serbian air defence units advising that the attack should be expected in a matter of hours.[31] What had

A fully loaded F-15E of the 494th FS takes off from Aviano, during the first day of Operation Deliberate Force, 30 August 1995. (NAC/DoD)

F-16Cs of 31st FW being prepared for strike missions with LGBs and LANTIRN pods, 30 August 1995. (NAC/DoD)

been expected by many actors in the Bosnian war for almost three years was now about to happen.

Operation Deliberate Force

Operation Deliberate Force was initiated shortly after midnight of 30 August 1995. Prior to the start of the operation, the ABCCC – call sign Bookshelf – had a mechanic failure, and it returned to base. But the CAOC had no doubts: the operation had to start – even if its initial phase would take place with the ABCCC-support provided only by the reserve aircraft after dawn. The strike packages which took off from Aviano or USS *Theodore Roosevelt*, gathered over the Adriatic Sea and at 01:40 entered BiH (RS) airspace.[32]

Logically, the first target of the NATO operation was the air defence system of the V i PVO, which consisted of the eight firing units when Operation Deliberate Force was initiated:

- three SA-2 SAM sites (two equipped with Volkhovs and one with Dvinas),
- five SA-6 SAM batteries (including two in eastern part of the Republika Srpska),
- several MANPAD and light anti-aircraft artillery units.

The V i PVO HQ decided that the 155th Regiment, equipped with Volkhov missiles, should hide its assets to preserve them until the intentions of NATO could be discovered. NATO estimated that most of the SAM systems were kept around Banja Luka, however missile systems had been moved deeper into BiH territory and were kept in ambushes on the corridors expected to be used by NATO aviation. With the exception of the Kub battery at Čavarine near Sokolac, as detailed below, no other unit was targeted.

The first AGM-88 anti-radar missiles hit the Serbian air defence positions around, and to the east of Sarajevo at 02.00hrs on 31 August 1995.[33] They were launched within the framework of Operation Dead Eye, the aim of which was the destruction of the Serbian air defences.

There were 25 targets in this sub-operation, plus 15 more that were targeted by the artillery assets of the RRF. These targets included the communications centres at Jahorina – also an important V i PVO surveillance facility – and Han Pijesak, and the Kub battery at Sokolac. "At 02:15 all telephone and radio communications were cut off. Radio communication between the units (172nd Air Defence Regiment) and radar surveillance as well. First strike wave lasted around 40 minutes." A radar site at Košuta height was destroyed, as was a communication facility at Ravna (Object No 7) where all seven of its personnel were killed. Other communications facilities, Ojbects Nos 5 and 6, were also damaged.[34] The first strike package comprised of 43 strike and 14 SEAD aircraft backed by electronic and radar jamming carried out by EF-111A Raven and EC-130H Compass Call platforms.

At 04:30 a new strike package attacked the positions of the VRS forces and other important military and civilian facilities around Sarajevo. NATO aircraft continued the Dead Eye operation, hammering the same V i PVO targets on Mount Jahorina and Sokolac, conducting the strikes from lower altitudes. This strike lasted around 50 minutes.[35]

During these attacks, 2nd Battery/172nd Air Defence Regiment was discovered at Čavarine near Sokolac. The battery had reached this firing position on the previous afternoon, and remained uncamouflaged, repairing some of its systems in the open. NATO aviation used LGBs to destroy the battery's radar and one of its TELs. Just a few moments prior to attack, battery personnel managed to abandon the vehicles, hide in the nearby forest, and avoid any casualties. Captain Bogdanović, who commanded the battery, had already survived a

The EC-130F ABCCCs of the 42nd ACCS at Aviano played a vital role in coordination of the missions during Operation Deliberate Force. (NAC/DoD)

EA-6B Prowlers were vital in "opening the windows" inside the Serb air defence. Here Prowlers from VAQ-141 USN are seen during the loading of AGM-88 HARM missiles at Aviano Air Base. (NAC/DoD)

A destroyed launch vehicle and R-StON radar of the Kub-M-equipped 2nd Battery/172nd Air Defence Regiment at Čavarine above Sokolac, which was attacked on the first night of Operation Deliberate Force. (Gen Milan Torbica)

A ground crew prepares the ordnance for a nighttime SEAD mission by F-16C-HTS of the 23rd FS at Aviano. (NAC/DoD)

HARM attack on the Volhov unit that he commanded at Mount Grmeč in November 1994. The neighbouring 1st Battery was hidden in the woods near Sokolac: it remained undiscovered throughout Deliberate Force by changing its position every second or third day.[36]

During these nocturnal strikes, the Pretis factory and its depot in Vogošća were hit, and storage depots at Toplo, Lukavica, Toplik and Žunovica near Hadžići and VRS positions at Gabrića Brdo were targeted. Armija BiH sources confirmed that the Serbian light AA artillery was active from nearly all positions around Sarajevo but caused no interruption to the ongoing airstrikes.[37] Two more attacks were carried out in the morning at 07:00 and 10:00 in the wider area of the eastern part of Republika Srpska, ranging from Herzegovina to north-eastern Bosnia. These included communications sites at Mount Majevica, Stražnica near Čajniče, Kraljica at Ozren, Kmur near Foča, stores at Ustikolina near Goražde and facilities near Nevesinje and Bileća.[38]

There were a total of five strike packages, referred to "Alpha" to "Echo", on the first day of the operation.[39] Serbian ELINT counted a total of 209 sorties, of which 166 were combat sorties. NATO insisted on the use of laser-guided munitions to assure precision and avoid collateral damage. The RRF artillery fired around 2,000 artillery rounds at VRS positions and facilities in the wider Sarajevo area. The strike packages and the UN/RRF TACPs on the ground were coordinated with an EC-130H belonging to 42nd ACC Squadron USAF acting as an ABCCC. Occasionally they would redirect the strike aircraft to other targets, if the previous targets had already been hit.[40]

The F-15E Strike Eagles of the 494th FS were the backbone of the assets which attacked the most important VRS targets or infrastructure. (NAC/DoD)

Effects upon the Serb Air Defences

Serbian infrastructure was badly hit during the first day of the operation. Thanks to effective ELINT assets, the numbers of NATO fighter/strike aircraft were known, along with their expected targets. There was no surprise. Knowing that NATO had established almost complete control over BiH airspace, and identified all the assets and static positions, V i PVO HQ ordered that radars should not be active during the NATO strikes.[41]

The V i PVO Operations Centre was moved into to civilian building in Banja Luka downtown where it remained until the end of 1995. The ELINT centre was also moved out of the barracks into the city of Banja Luka and apart from the day after the telecommunication site at Stolice was destroyed, remained operational for the whole duration of Deliberate Force.[42]

The V i PVO radar network of the 51st Air Surveillance Battalion was partly disrupted. Due to a Croat offensive in the first week of August 1995 a radar company at Mount Plješevica was forced to partially destroy its equipment and abandon its crucial position, before withdrawing to Banja Luka. As replacement, an independent platoon with S-605H radar was deployed to Mount Klekovača to enable radar coverage of the airspace west of Republika Srpska. In turn, in mid-September 1995, this unit was forced to withdraw to Mount Manjača, south of Banja Luka, by further Croat advances: it was to remain in that area until the end of the war, though making slight changes in its positions.[43]

Before Deliberate Force was initiated, the V i PVO HQ decided to withdraw a radar company from its site at Bukvica near Nevesinje in Herzegovina, since it was estimated that it would be immediately targeted. It was at the immediate south of RS territory, in a position which was difficult to camouflage. Some dummy equipment was set in position and the radar was evacuated. During the first night of Operation Deliberate Force, the Bukvica radar site was bombed with six projectiles and the remaining 15 gunners with triple-barrelled 20mm AA guns and MANPADS were evacuated. The following day, everything that was still useful was collected and the radar site was abandoned. In the following night, the site was again targeted with LGBs, and twice more before the end of Deliberate Force.[44]

As deputy CO of the 51st Battalion Major Petko Rašević, recalled: 'The most difficult moment was the break in communications after the first attack. Radio and telephone silence was maintained while we were waiting to receive the information on the fate of the personnel at radar sites which were attacked.'[45]

On 31 August, at the Forward Command Post of the VRS Main Staff at Kula, the Air Surveillance Centre was formed to support General Mladić's staff with information on the situation in the airspace.[46] It is interesting to note that the radar site at Kozara – where the 2nd Radar Company with S-600 radar was located – was not targeted and it remained operational until 9 September, in spite of jamming, to provide a valuable radar picture to superior HQs.

Armée de l'Air's Mirage 2000

The Serbian air defences remained inactive during the first day of the operation, except for the light AA artillery and MANPADS. Light AA batteries of the 172nd Regiment launched missiles twice in the morning of 30 September; at 09:35 at pair of F-16s; and around 11:00 at an A-10, but without success. The main problem was a lack of vehicles and fuel so the MANPADS teams were not able to manoeuvre and increase their effectiveness. In the afternoon Sergeant Aleksandar Studen, a platoon leader in the MANPADS Battery of the 172nd Regiment, managed to shoot down a French Mirage 2000 from Donji Pribanj in the wider Sarajevo area.[47] Coincidentally, Sergeant Studen was a nephew of pilot Uroš Studen who had been shot down in a Jastreb on 28 February 1994 by USAF F-16s. His report stated:

At 16:00 a low and middle altitude strike started, targeting Koran barracks, Famos factory, Jahorinski Potok storage and transmitter at Mount Ravna. In one of the first overflies, a F-18 hit the transmitter from an altitude of around 1,200 metres and pulled out heading towards my position. I had wrongly estimated and launch the missile at the distance of 5,000 metres. The missile was correctly guided to the target. But there was no hit. The target did not enter my launching zone. Bombing continued at 17:05. Two Mirage 2000s approached at 1,500 metres altitude. I choose one of them and after setting the parameters launched the missile. It was guided correctly to the target. The missile managed to overtake the Mirage and hit in the middle. Previously this aircraft dropped four bombs which hit the Famos factory. The aircraft caught fire and both pilots ejected. The Mirage crashed some eight kilometres from Pale."[48]

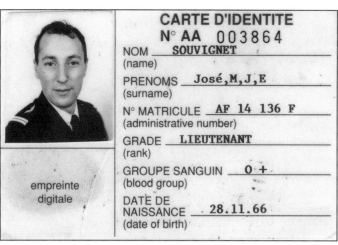

The identity card of Lieutenant Jose Souvignet, one of the two Armée de l'Air pilots shot down over Pale on 30 August 1995 and captured by the VRS forces. (Gen M. Torbica)

Television footage of the Mirage 2000 crash on 30 August 1995. (www. youtube.com /watch?v=zsNY9B7M1yk)

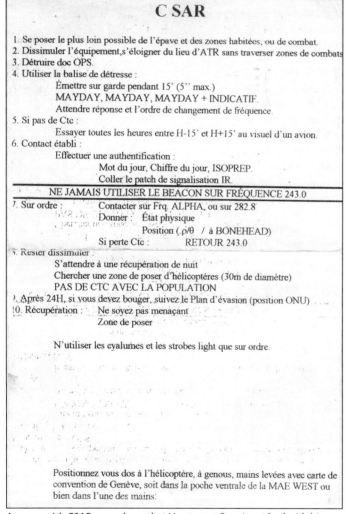

A paper with CSAR procedures that Lieutenant Souvignet had with him when captured by VRS forces. (Gen M Torbica)

Sergeant Studen finished his report explaining that bombing was stopped, and that NATO aviation started to carry out reconnaissance and observation missions with UAVs and A-10s until darkness.[49] At 17:15 NATO had lost its first and only combat aircraft during the operation. It was a Mirage 2000NK-2, belonging to 3/2 EC, coded 3-JA, No. 346 with callsign EBRO 33. Two-member crew: Jose Souvignet and Frederic Chiffot were captured by an armed villager who took them to the nearest VRS unit and later to a military hospital in Sokolac. General Mladić ordered that the fate of the two French pilots had to remain secret pending his following orders.[50]

After the Mirage was shot down, a single EF-111 (callsign Nikon 24) which was the nearest to the crash site was ordered to remain and jam the Serbian radars. An AWACS ordered a single F-15E into the area to cover any eventual SAR mission. Two MH-53 helicopters from the Adriatic and a single HC-130 Hercules conducted SAR for the downed pilots but without success. In the forthcoming days there were several attempts to find and evacuate the French pilots, all without success and CNN reported that in a rescue attempt on 7 September, two US servicemen were wounded. In a press conference held on 9 September, a spokesman for NATO's Southern Flank declined to comment on the claim.[51]

Much later, after Deliberate Force, Admiral Leighton Smith revealed more details on three unsuccessful attempts to rescue the French pilots. Based upon the gathered aerial imagery, in the early morning of 6 September, a group of HH-60 helicopters from USS Theodore Roosevelt and an MH-53 from Brindisi Air Base, covered by other combat and support aviation, tried to enter the area. Apparently, the attempt failed because of bad weather, and a helicopter was damaged by fire from the ground. The whole rescue party managed to land safely back on the carrier. On the following day, 7 September, a group of MH-53J helicopters, backed by other types of combat aviation tried to enter the area where the French pilots had been downed, and this time an AC-130 gunship was supporting the mission. Due to bad weather over the area and fire from the ground, this party also withdrew without success. The most dramatic attempt was the third one, carried out on 8 September. A group of CSAR helicopters took off from Brindisi and managed to land in the zone where the French pilots were supposed to be. After 30 minutes of flying over the area, they were fired upon by the Serbian forces on the ground, two crew members were wounded, and the helicopters were ordered to withdraw from the area. The US helicopters twice came under friendly fire; first, from its own CSAR party consisting of A-10s of 104th FG and F/A-18s, and secondly from the fire of an AC-130 gunship. This demonstrated that landing in the area of Pale was hazardous and that there was no trace of the French pilots, and so further SAR missions were cancelled.[52]

The search for the downed French pilots was continued on political grounds for three months. General Mladić was pressured to release the pilots by the French military leadership, Serbian President Milosevic, his head of State Security and Chief of General Staff, Russian political and military representatives, and even some French writers who had previously sided with General Mladić. Finally, after the war was over, General Mladić decided with heavy-heart to release the French pilots and on 12 December 1995, in a hotel near Zvornik they were turned over to the joint FR Yugoslavia/French military delegation and ferried back to France.[53]

NATO Air Attacks continue

Despite the interruption caused by the downing of the French Mirage 2000, the operation continued on the following night of 31 August. There were three strike packages (though Serbian sources counted four of them). Numerous targets were hit that night: Pale, Sokolac, Han Pijesak, communication sites at Mount Jahorina and stores in Jahorinski Potok, VRS positions at Kalauzović and Mount Ozren, a radar site at Nevesinje, and facilities at Čajniče. The RRF artillery shelled Blagovac and the Pretis factory. On that night, the first Serbian civilian casualties were recorded. It was obvious that NATO was still targeting the radar network, communication sites, HQs and other command posts and stores.[54] A report from Sergeant Studen explained:

> On the following day (and later), the bombardment continued, but from rather higher altitudes. The aircraft occasionally entered in our launching zone, but we did not fire upon them, since it was forbidden by the higher military leaders. On five or six occasions we were placed into combat readiness No 1 and given the clearance to launch the missiles. But we were ordered not to open fire prior to their attack or lower altitude reconnaissance.[55]

Deliberate Force and its airstrikes continued into the night of 1 September. It was the first night when the German air force joined the missions. The targets were of the same kind as on the two previous days. Factories and repair plants at Vogošća and Hadžići, communications Object No 5 at Jahorina (targeted for the third time and finally destroyed by a penetration munition), and the radar site at Košuta-Jahorina. While returning to their Italian bases, some of the strike packages targeted bridges on a number of different roads.[56] The air attacks were halted at 05:00 that morning. This break, at political request, was intended to see if the Serbian side would withdraw heavy artillery from positions around Sarajevo. NATO aviation continued flying sorties, but without using ordnance.

For the first three days of Operation Deliberate Force, the CAOC counted a total of 635 sorties, among them 318 were

CAS or Battlefield Air Interdiction (BAI). It was difficult to estimate the exact outcome of these missions, but CAOC judged through after-strike reconnaissance that most of the targets were out of action. It was stressed that Serbian military infrastructure had been damaged, and the factory at Vogošća was cited as an example. But, as the facts gathered from ELINT and SIGINT showed, the Serbian air defence was "heavily damaged" but still functional. The same could be said for the 172nd Air Defence Missile Regiment with Kub missiles at Sokolac: that it had suffered considerable damage, but that the airstrikes did not make it "impotent".[57]

The practice of the Serbian air defence to not illuminate its radars, and thus avoid becoming the target of AGM-88 HARM missiles was noted. The Serbs judged that any "illumination" would be suicidal; no one "tipped them off" and there was no "sympathizer somewhere with phone number and makes call", as General Hornburg later explained, claiming that someone in NATO had warned the Serbs.[58] It was a simple estimation that it was better to remain under the radar. Soon, it was discovered that most of the stores had been dispersed prior to Operation Deliberate Force, or immediately after the initial strikes.

Pair of F-16s of 510th FS "Buzzards", loaded with LGBs, prepares for another mission over Bosnia, 6 September 1995. (NAC/DoD)

A Spanish F/A-18 from Ala 12, armed with an AGM-88 HARM takes off from Aviano, 6 September 1995. (NAC/DoD)

An A-10 belonging to the 104th FG Massachusetts ANG taxies while equipped with AGM-65s and an AN/ALQ-131 ECM pod, at Aviano during Operation Deliberate Force. (NAC/DoD)

However, the three-day break in Operation Deliberate Force did not bring about any political agreement. The Serbian side, the VRS in particular, accused the international forces of misinterpretation of those negotiations.[59] The strikes resumed after 23:00 on 4 September, with an attack on targets in Vogošća. This area was shelled by the RRF artillery from 13:00 the next day, with the explanation that the VRS forces had moved their heavy weapons inside the "exclusion zone".[60]

On 5 September 1995, air attacks continued, focussing on Serbian targets around and in the wider area of Sarajevo. Shortly after dawn on 5 September, when UAVs confirmed Admiral Smith's suspicions that the Serbs were not pulling back their heavy weapons, he told General Janvier that "there's no intent being demonstrated. Let's get on with it." There were four strike packages between 13:00 and 18:00:

- first, with F-16Cs of 555th FS targeting stores at Jahorina and Hadžići
- second, command and communications centre in Han Pijesak (aircraft and squadron unknown)
- third, with F-15Es of 494th FS armed with CBU-12s also targets in Han Pijesak, and
- fourth, the largest one, with F/A-18s of VMFA-533, F-16Cs of 510th FS and F-15s of 48th FW targeting several communications sites with varying success.[61]

Serbian sources added that Lukavica, Kasindol, Novo Sarajevo and Pale were also targeted. NATO aviation also hit another important target: the TV and radio transmitter at Stolice, Mount Majevica in north-eastern Bosnia (RS). It was hit at 14:24 and caused the disruption of all communication between the Eastern and Western parts of Republika Srpska.[62]

During the continuation of Deliberate Force, there were usually around seven strike packages per day. The US Navy used F-14A fighters ("Bombcats") for the first time in the ground attack role, using LGBs against targets which were designated by F/A-18s.

On 5 September, General Ryan requested the use of Tomahawk land attack missiles (TLAMs) against air defence targets near the Serb stronghold of Banja Luka. Because the general and his staff recognised the danger that Serb air defences posed to NATO aircraft in this area, he wanted to soften-up the area before sending in manned aircraft in large numbers, as Lt. Colonel Conversino later described.[63]

On the night of 6 September, there were six strike packages which attacked the targets in the wider territory of Republika Srpska: Lukavica, Ozren, Nevesinje, Čajniče and Foča. During daylight there were no sorties as there was bad weather over most of the theatre of operations. On 7 September, there were attacks on Jahorina, Han Pijesak, Višegrad, Pale, Kalinovik, and an attack on Doboj caused 17 civilian casualties.[64] In Han Pijesak, the barracks were targeted just as the leadership of Republika Srpska entered to participate in a regular meeting. There were a total of eight strike packages on 7 September.[65]

In a later analysis of Operation Deliberate Force, it was noted that on 7 September General Ryan registered the two problems in carrying out the Operation. The first was the difficulties with the meteorological conditions over Bosnia. The other problem was even more serious: the list of targets approved on 14 August was nearly exhausted and this led to repeated strikes against already damaged targets, leading to their

AC-130 Hercules Gunships were used in several reconnaissance missions around Sarajevo during Deliberate Force. An AN/ALQ-184 ECM pod can be seen here fitted under the wing of one of the AC-130s. (NAC/DoD)

USAFE armourers preparing ordnance for 494th FS Strike Eagles. The bombs were covered with various messages to the Serbs such as: *Serb Slayer II* and *Have you ever danced with the devil?* (NAC/DoD)

The Serb radar position at Mount Kozara seen in 1994. The 2nd Company of the 51st Air Surveillance Battalion VRS was attacked here and the site was heavily damaged on 9 September 1995. (D. Vejnović)

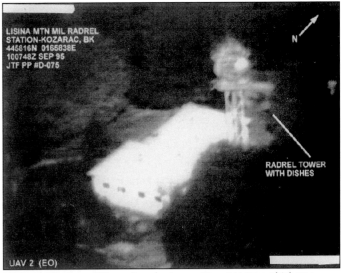

UAV aerial footage of the radio-relay transmitter at Lisinac which was targeted by a TLAM on 10 September 1995. Eventually, imagery of the Lisinac targets became available on the afternoon of 7 September, which permitted Navy targeters to complete the full mission plans required. (Author's collection)

total destruction. The aim, however, was to keep the operation going until its expected political outcome could be achieved.[66]

On 8 September, there were four strike packages. Of these, the first was cancelled due to bad weather over Bosnia. In other attacks, three bridges were destroyed, and in attacks in wider area of Mostar, 11 civilians were killed. The toll among Serb civilians started to rise. Contrarty to this trend, General Ryan and his aides stressed that they wanted to minimize the Serb civilian casualties.[67]

In the regular daily NATO press briefings, officials denied allegations that airstrikes had caused larger collateral damage and victims among civilians. After a week of airstrikes, several journalists questioned the core reason for the operation, mainly due to the attacks on civilian targets, infrastructure, and the rising number of casualties. It was difficult for NATO spokesmen to relate the relationship between these attacks and the aims of the military operation. NATO representatives explained that the reason for the strikes against the civilian targets was to decrease the mobility of the VRS forces and hamper its supply network. But the journalists had many questions: was NATO expanding on the initial list of 25 targets? Why was Operation Deliberate Force taking so long? Why were munitions with almost expired dates used? Were the weather conditions a problem or were the pilots missing the targets? NATO representatives replied that the caution in the attacks was the outcome of focussing on military targets and avoiding collateral damage. They also tried to explain that the operation had a slow pace, and its intensity was growing step by step.

From 9 September, Operation Deliberate Force was expanded to include the western parts of Republika Srpska, into Bosanska Krajina and in the wider area of Banja Luka. The initial intention was to supress the Serbian air defence, as a continuation of the Dead Eye sub-operation. There were five strike packages ordered for that day. The first two were unable to drop their ordnance over the targets due to bad weather. Three other strike packages waited for a few hours for weather conditions to improve. One of them, comprised of around 30 aircraft, was a SEAD-tasked strike package and fired a total of 33 AGM-88 HARM missiles against seven Serb missile positions near Majkić, Donji Vakuf, Šipovo and Kolonija "with less than optimal results".[68] It is possible that in one of these strikes, a dummy Volohov firing position was destroyed. Another target was a set of transmitters located at Mount Kozara, west of Banja Luka, most of them belonging to the television or postal service. Other targets included military targets in Kneževo, Kotor Varoš, Ključ, Sanica, as well as the previously struck targets around Sarajevo (Hadžići and Lukavica).[69]

The radar site at Mount Kozara operated by 2nd Company/51st Battalion was not targeted until 9 September. The site regularly

suffered daily jamming of its radar and communication devices. Because the site was a distance from the main targets around Sarajevo and eastern Bosnia this minimized the effects of jamming, reducing the picture by about 30%. However, if the jammer platform was at a distance of less than 50 kilometres from the radar site, the degradation of the "radar picture" would rise to 50-60%. This radar site provided almost continuous information to V i PVO and VRS top brass from the beginning of the air campaign.[70]

In the early morning of 9 September, the Kozara radar site was attacked: first with HARM missiles, then with PGMs. As the strike occurred, a watch changeover was taking place just in front of the surveillance radar and two soldiers were killed and an NCO heavily wounded. The crew of the surveillance radar were in the cab, while the rest of personnel outside the perimeter when the HARM missiles hit the radar and other equipment. The HARM missiles damaged the radar and stopped it working but caused little other damage. Being aware that this was just beginning of an attack, the radar company withdrew from the site to the village of Lamovita at the foot of Kozara. The AA platoon remained at the site with its triple-barrelled 20mm guns and Strela-2M MANPADS. The radar site was attacked twice on following day: 10 September in morning and evening: the remaining concrete facilities at site were destroyed with cruise missiles.[71]

Cruise Missiles against Serbian Air Defences
On the next day, 10 September, Dead Eye continued with 13 TLAM cruise missiles launched by USS Normandy in the Adriatic at air defence positions in the wider region of Banja Luka and western parts of Republika Srpska. The TLAMs proved to be remarkably accurate; seven of them hit the radar site at Kozara. Three more TLAMs fired later put the radar site totally out of service, destroying the antennas of surveillance and altitude radars. TLAMs were also fired at a radio-relay communication site on a nearby hill in the vicinity of Lisinac. Another radio-relay communication site and TV transmitter located on Lisinac were not targeted.[73]

Usage of TLAM cruise missiles against the Serbian air defence position at Mount Kozara could be regarded as the confirmation of the Serbian air defence's combat capability. Estimations most likely showed that sending a regular strike package over territory with an unknow number of deployed SAM units, and where O'Grady's F-16 had been lost in June, was a risky task with loses expected among the

Blooding the Bombcats

Amid all the advanced assets deployed by NATO during Operation Deliberate Force was the VF-41 Black Aces: a unit of the US Navy equipped with 20-year-old Grumman F-14A Tomcat interceptors, recently modified to deploy precision-guided munitions. This unit was embarked aboard the aircraft carrier USS *Theodore Roosevelt* (CVN-71), which was actually on its way back to the USA towards the end of its six-month deployment in the Persian Gulf, when ordered to re-route to the Adriatic Sea. Once on station, the carrier began planning and running operations as part of Deliberate Force, but most of its airstrikes had to be aborted due to bad weather. However, on 5 September 1995, two F-14As – each loaded with one AIM-7M Sparrow, two AIM-9M Sidewinders, and one AIM-54C Phoenix air-to-air missile, and a pair of GBU-16 454kg (1,000lbs) laser-guided bombs – entered Bosnian airspace accompanied by a pair of F/A-18Cs, which were to designate their target. Commanding Officer of VF-41, Commander Bob Brauer, recalled what became the first air-to-ground sortie ever flown by Tomcats of the US Navy:

> On the day of the first strike the weather was a big factor, and it continued to be a factor into the winter

months. As we launched off the ship and headed in over the coast, it didn't look like the strike was going to go ahead because of an undercast. But, about ten miles out from the target the weather cleared, and we could see the target well out. We rolled in at a very steep angle, from high altitude, against some ammunition facilities. The F-14s dropped while the F/A-18s lased. We egressed the target area having achieved absolutely superb results from direct hits, and there were impressive secondary explosions.

In another mission, some of the most junior pilots of the squadron deployed Mk.82 'dumb' bombs – reportedly also with excellent results. Between 5 and 12 September 1995, F-14As of VF-41 delivered 10,886kg (24,000lbs) of ordnance on targets in Bosnia and Herzegovina.

About a week later, USS *Theodore Roosevelt* was replaced by USS *America* (CV-66). The latter carrier's air wing CVW-1 saw much action during the following days: however, while its F/A-18Cs expended additional LGBs and even SLAM-ER guided missiles, the F-14Bs of the squadron VF-102 were not tasked with any airstrikes: instead, they flew CAPs, forward air control missions and reconnaissance with TARPS pods.[72]

The F-14A Modex AJ101, assigned to the commander of VF-41, seen launching from USS *Theodore Roosevelt* while loaded with a pair of GBU-16s. (US Navy Photo)

NATO combat aircraft. Such estimation was confirmed by EU Special Envoy to Former Yugoslavia, Carl Bildt in his memoirs just two years after. He stressed that in Banja Luka, the Serbs had modern air defences, which shot down a USAF F-16 just three months before and had earned respect. Bildt stressed that there was no eagerness to fly over that area, even with the support of the different combat-support aircraft that a strike package consisted of.[74]

The formal US explanation to European politicians, who regarded usage of cruise missiles as a widening of the conflict, was that dealing with the Serb air defence in that area was too risky. Instead of the standard strike package, the cruise missiles would do the job, and the operation remained under the strict control and would not expand into a wider conflict.

General Mike Ryan was also aware of the danger of sending his pilots so deeply in the territory of Republika Srpska with the task of destroying its air defences. As mentioned earlier, on 5 September he had asked for the usage of the Tomahawk cruise missiles. At the meeting with Admiral Smith, it was decided that six Lockheed F-117A Nighthawk Stealth Fighters would be asked for from the Pentagon and deployed for performing the task. Two days later, the Secretary of Defence, William Perry, approved the deployment of six F-117A Nighthawks from the 9th Fighter Squadron/49th Fighter Wing at Holloman AFB. The duration of their deployment would be up to 30 October, and they would be based in Aviano.[75]

Unlike the TLAMs, the strike package of 30 SEAD and 18 strike aircraft achieved "modest success" while attacking the air defence targets around Prnjavor, Mrkonjić Grad and Mount Glamoč. On this

The moment of launching a TLAM Tomahawk cruise missile against the Serb targets around Banja Luka, 10 September 1995. (NAC/DoD)

During the same day, NATO carried out a close air support mission for the second time, in response to Serb shelling of Tuzla Air Base in which neighbouring VRS positions fired 14 shots at UNRPROFOR forces. One Pakistani soldier was wounded, and the Nordic battalion was allegedly attacked. Alerted through the UN chain of command, a group of F/A-18s from USS *America* and RAF GR.7 Harriers were sent into action. Around 15:15, they attacked Serbian artillery positions at Vis and Vukovine, and Zeline near Kalesija. The Hornets used CBU-16 cluster bombs, but the NATO aircraft did not manage to destroy the Serbian artillery positions. The patrolling in the area continued for more two hours, until the local UN commander received assurance that the VRS would not shell the Tuzla Air Base or UN positions. Following this event, UNPF HQ requested that NATO establish a system of "boxes" over three "safe areas" of Tuzla, Goražde and Sarajevo for the protection of its forces. It was proposed that NATO fighters should be continually present and if UNPF forces should be attacked again by the VRS these aircraft would provide close air support. Since Operation Deliberate Force ceased on 14 September, however, this system was not introduced.[77] After 17:00 NATO a strike package again attacked the transmitter on Stolice, at Mount Majevica and this time completely destroyed it. A couple of hours later, a detachment of four fighters destroyed the auxiliary transmitter on Mount Majevica.[78]

Finally, at 21:30, at Cerovljani, a Kub radar antenna of the 1st Battery was hit by a HARM missile while another one missed its target. As General Milan Torbica, chief of the Air Defence Department in the V i PVO HQ in 1993-95 explained, this Kub battery was moving between positions at Dubica and Gradiška below Mount Kozara. The battery's CO had strict orders not to illuminate his radar for more than two rotations of the antenna, however he remained active longer, tracking a NATO aircraft at a distance of 35 kilometres. The radar was detected by NATO SEAD aircraft, which the Kub crew was unaware of due to ECM signals. The SEAD aircraft fired two HARM missiles, one of which hit a transmission line in the vicinity of the radar and detonated above it, spraying the firing position of the battery with shrapnel and leaving one soldier wounded. The position of the 2nd Battery, also equipped with Kub missiles, was targeted without success.[79] It was estimated that three strike packages later that day were successful in their performance.

occasion, the Lakenheath F-15Es launched three GBU-15 glide bombs for the first time. One of them hit a radio-relay communications transmitter at Mount Svinjar near Prnjavor. In another attack, against targets at Glamoč, F/A-18s fired AGM-84E SLAMs (Stand-off Land Attack Missiles) for the first time in combat. However, the USAF analytics in CAOC, estimated that the SLAMs showed disappointing results. All seven of the SLAMs fired at Glamoč, plus two at Kozara-Lisinac, had technical problems and all of them missed their targets.[76]

It is interesting that the V i PVO air base Mahovljani/Laktaši north of Banja Luka was not targeted in the course of the Deliberate Force attacks. The passivity of the Serbian combat aviation, air defence assets and the distance made this place safe during Deliberate Force.

Destruction of the radar site at Mount Kozara was a serious blow to the V i PVO air defence. On the same day, a replacement had to be introduced. The oldest radar in service, a Soviet P-12 surveillance radar, was activated in the vicinity of Banja Luka. There was also a platoon with an S-600, a replacement for the Plješevica unit, which had abandoned its position at Klekovača and was stationed at the Manjača highlands, south of Banja Luka, and operated occasionally. The radar picture

EA-111 Ravens from 429th ECS were part of the SEAD packages used during Operation Deliberate Force. (NAC/DoD)

A Tornado of Luftwaffe Einsatzgeshwader 1 in low-level flight returns from a mission during Operation Deliberate Force. (Author collection)

USS *Theodore Roosevelt* launches an F-14 of VFA-41 on a mission, while an F/A-18 of VFA-87 waits in the foreground. From 5 September they operated jointly: an F/A-18 would lase the targets, while the F-14 would deliver the LGBs. (NAC/DoD)

A taxiing A-10 belonging to the 104th FG Massachusetts ANG, equipped with AGM-65s and an AN/ALQ-131 ECM pod, at Aviano during Operation Deliberate Force. (NAC/DoD)

Vogošća, and VRS positions near Doboj and Višegrad. The radar and communications site at Jahorina was attacked for the eighth time since the start of the operation.[83]

Operation Deliberate Force led to the start of an offensive by Muslim and Croat forces in the west of BiH. On 12 September, a first report of renewed activity of Serbian combat aircraft in the Banja Luka area arrived at CAOC. During the day, a number of fighters were switched from CAS to CAP missions and were sent to patrol the wider area from Banja Luka to Tuzla, using visual or radar methods, but no Serb aircraft were discovered.[84]

Bad weather conditions hampered most of the air activities on 13 September. The continuation of Dead Eye 3 was planned with targets at Lisinac: the radar site there had already been destroyed but the civil radio-relay and TV transmitter still remained intact. AGM-84E SLAM missiles were used that day, and now they were successful: targets were destroyed or severely damaged. Weather conditions started to hamper the continuation of the operations during the day and strikes against the Banja Luka, Ozren, Doboj and Sarajevo areas and the bad weather led to a drastic decline in the combat missions. That day was finished with 140 sorties, or just 40% of those planned. Among these, the first strike package was unable to find its targets, the second was cancelled, the third was postponed to the afternoon, while the fourth strike package consisting of eight aircraft attacked VRS positions around Sarajevo later that evening with mixed success. The only active combat aviation were SEAD teams and AC-130 Gunships which carried out combat reconnaissance sorties.[85]

The end of the Combat Operations in Deliberate Force

On 13 September, Serbian President Milosevic had a meeting with US Special Envoy Richard Holbrooke and General Wesley Clark at Dobanovci, a couple of kilometres north of Belgrade International Airport. After the meeting, General Mladić – who was summoned later – agreed to withdraw all of the VRS heavy weaponry around Sarajevo, open roads and air routes and to agree on details of ceasefire around the city.[86]

The success of the political negotiations in Belgrade led to the cessation of the combat sorties on the following day, 14 September. The 20 sorties that were carried out that day included tankers, AWACS and reconnaissance U-2s. Other combat strike or SEAD missions

was re-established, and the P-12 showed itself as a reliable asset between 10-15 September. It operated in "metric waves", had a limited radiation, which kept it much safer from HARM missiles than modern Marconi or Ericsson radars, and as it was inside a van-trailer it enabled movement no matter the situation in the air.[80]

On 11 September, Dead Eye continued with tasks carried out by three strike packages. The arrival and operational deployment of F-117A Stealth Fighters was expected, but the Italian government did not approve their deployment at Aviano on this date. Carl Bildt points out that the Americans had not counted on the refusal by Italian Defence Minister Susana Agnelli, described as of "strong principles and will." The Italian answer for the requested F-117A deployment was "no".[81] The night strike packages were cancelled, and they were re-planned for daytime. A SEAD strike package was engaged, as well as F-15Es with GBU-15 glide bombs, and a radio-relay system near Mrkonjić Grad was struck. Another strike package destroyed a TV transmitter at Kraljica at Ozren causing a number of casualties. Over 50 weapons hit the Technical Repair Plant in Hadžići, while the targets around Pale and VRS positions around Goražde were targeted again.[82]

On the morning of 12 September, NATO strike packages targeted several positions around Sarajevo, among them the Pretis factory in

A KC-135 of the 121st ARW, Ohio ANG took part in refuelling mission on TDY. (via Gen. Jovica Draganić)

Armourers unload GBU-10 munitions from an M989A1 Heavy Expanded Mobility Ammunition Trailer, at Aviano during Operation Deliberate Force. (NAC/DoD)

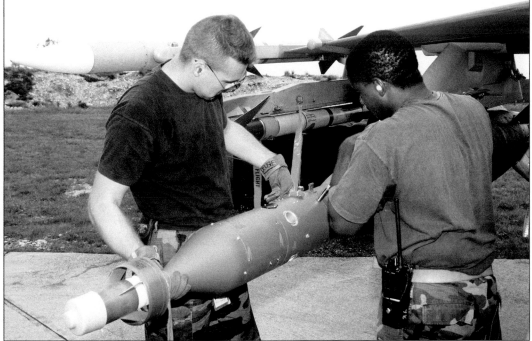

Armourers of the 555th FS load an F-16C with LGBs during Operation Deliberate Force. (NAC/DoD)

Sarajevo International Airport. First to land was an Armée de l'Air C-130H Hercules. Five days later, Admiral Leyton Smith and General Janvier arrived in Sarajevo where they inspected the withdrawal of Serbian heavy artillery and armoured units around the city and toured the downtown. Soon after, on 20 September, they announced that there was no need for the resumption of airstrikes. Deliberate Force was over.[88]

NATO aviation remained present over the Bosnian skies in the following weeks. Fighters which patrolled under the practice developed during Deny Flight now included SEAD and strike aviation and were tasked to react to any violation of the agreement or other threats, mainly from the Serbian side. In the first ten days of October there were two such reactions. In the first case, on 3 October Serbian radar illuminated a pair of EA-6Bs which then fired HARM missiles at the radar site. In the other case, on 9 October, a unit from UNPF was caught during clashes between the VRS and ARBiH and one peacekeeper was killed. At the request of the UN commander a detachment of F-16Cs from 555th FS carried out the strike on the VRS positions, while another F-16C from 510th FS acted as an airborne FAC. This was first mission carried out in this fashion by the Vipers of the 31st Fighter Wing. It was also the last combat mission conducted by NATO air forces from Aviano in this period.[89]

The aims of the operation that were set at the beginning were fulfilled: the withdrawal of the Serbian heavy weaponry from around Sarajevo and the prevention of alleged Serbian attacks on the city. The operation enabled the American shuttle diplomacy to make use of the resulting momentum which led

were cancelled or postponed. In the late evening of this day, at 22:20 Operation Deliberate Force was suspended.[87]

On 15 September, after a break of six months, transport aircraft with humanitarian aid coordinated by the UNHCR started to land at

to faster political solution. Through intensive strikes and bombardment the Serbian side was brought to political negotiations. It was regarded as one of the most important achievements of Operation Deliberate Force. The successful NATO engagement was accomplished at air and sea. The Serbian side suffered significant damage to the military and civil infrastructure, but with collateral damage and a number of civilian casualties as the outcome of the airstrikes. NATO lost only one combat aircraft with its two pilots, who remained in captivity until mid-December 1995.

At a press conference held on 26 September, General Mladić – the VRS commander – summarised the consequences of Deliberate Force for the Serbs in BiH. He stated that an important part of the military infrastructure was destroyed, the telecommunication system of Republika Srpska was disabled and major material damage had been caused to civilian institutions and citizens. Mladić did not mention VRS (V i PVO) casualties but stressed that a total of 152 civilians were killed and 273 wounded. With Operation Deliberate Force "NATO became the aggressor, since it openly sided with one of the parties in the war" concluded General Mladić.[90]

From the end of Operation Deliberate Force until the present day, Serbian casualties, treated as collateral damage, were regarded as low and numbered at around 30. Since spring of 1992, the Serbian side in the Bosnian War has been continually accused in the worldwide media of aggression, brutality, atrocities, genocide and systematic rape, with no sympathy demonstrated for their casualties.

The road to peace negotiations and the end of the war was laid, but not yet finished. The politically agreed ratio of territorial division 51:49 (Muslim/Croat Federation – Republic of Srpska) was not yet achieved. This led to another, always hidden objective of Operation Deliberate Force: assistance to the joint Croat/Muslim offensive in the west of Bosnia (RS) that downsized the percentage of territory that Serbs controlled. This nearly took them to edge of military defeat in the west, in Bosanska Krajina.

Joint Croat-Muslim offensive and renewed combat operations of the Serbian V i PVO

On 8 September, in the middle of the period of Operation Deliberate Force, a large Croatian-Muslim offensive was launched, consisting of the HV (supported by HVO) and Armija BiH forces. It started to break the VRS in nearly all of Bosanska Krajina and part of Mount Ozren. This can be regarded as direct effect of Operation Deliberate Force on the ground battle. Besides destroying VRS infrastructure, command and communications system and air defence, NATO aviation did not directly support the Croatian

Army or Army of BiH but it created a lot of difficulties for the VRS defence positions. Whenever possible, Croat or Muslim forces took advantage of the NATO airstrikes on VRS positions to improve their own frontlines or to launch attacks. In the last few days of Deliberate Force, Croat/Muslim forces helped NATO aviation by marking their positions against the VRS ones. Croatian forces conducted an operation titled Mistral (*Maestral*) in which its units managed to seize a large portion of the Serb-held territory. They defeated II Krajiški Corps and 30th Division VRS and took control of their former area of responsibility in Western Bosnia: including Drvar, Jajce, Šipovo, Mliništa and Mount Oštrelj.[91]

As NATO aviation secured the airspace there was no need for the Croatian Air Force to be engaged nor the possibility of the Serbian Air Force supporting its troops. Still, Croatian forces used some Mi-24 helicopter gunships to support their advance from 8 September. On that day they lost one Mi-24 (No. 309) at Čardak Polje near Mrkonjić Grad. The crew managed a forced landing and reached their own forces after trekking of some eight kilometres. The crew reported that the helicopter had been hit in the rear part, but they did not manage to observe from which side the missile had hit. Five days later, on 13 September, another HRZ Mi-24 was damaged by

Croatian Forces inspect the crashed HRZ Mi-24 near Čardak Polje. (M. Raguž)

A Volhov (SA-2) missile system in the firing position. During late September – October 1995 these were used as surface-to-surface missiles from positions south-west of Banja Luka against the advancing Armija BiH forces. (D. Vejnović)

groundfire. The gunner was badly wounded and the pilot returned the helicopter to base. On some occasions, helicopters attached to the RRF supported Croatian forces in their advance and one RAF CH-47 ferried its artillery to Mount Dimitor. The crashed Mi-24 previously mentioned was lifted and ferried from crash site by another CH-47. On many occasions, retreating VRS forces registered that UAVs were supporting advancing HV troops.[92]

On 13 September, the Muslim Armija BiH joined the offensive. Its V Corps, which controlled the so-called "Bihać pocket" from spring 1992, and VII Corps from Central Bosnia launched an offensive against VRS positions in an operation titled Sana 95. This was a serious blow for the VRS forces already pushed by the regular Croatian HV from the south. Between 13 and 17 September, Armija BiH took control over Donji Vakuf, Bosanski Petrovac, Ključ and Bosanska Krupa.[93] The VRS forces withdrew slowly, mixed with Serb civilians which fled towards Banja Luka and the situation became dramatic.

Moreover, the Croatian Army appeared on the river Una on 18 September and using the fleet of boats, pontoons and flat-bed ferries managed to carry elements of its forces to the Serb side. The intention of Operation Una 95 was to seize this portion of the territory and to attack Banja Luka from western side. This was a sudden and serious threat.[94]

Besides the tactical position on the front lines, the morale of the VRS was badly shaken, especially among territorially manned units which now turned into fleeing refugees. In this dramatic situation, VRS HQ ordered that V i PVO combat assets should be engaged, including the strike aircraft at Mahovljani. Dvina and Volhov (SA-2) surface-to-air missile units were to employ their weapons in the surface-to-surface role.

On 18 September, the first combat sorties by Serb Gazelles, Oraos and Jastrebs were carried out. The Serb armed Gazelles and later strike aircraft attacked the Croatian forces which had already crossed river Una around Dubica, operating as single-ships or in pairs. The unexpected appearance of the Serbian strike aircraft in the afternoon, and casualties, caused confusion and managed to stop the Croatian advance. On the following morning, the Croatian forces began to retreat. The appearance of Jastrebs from Banja Luka influenced the morale of VRS at this part of the front and there was no further retreat.[95]

As one of the pilots remembers, the Serbian Jastrebs took off from Banja Luka Air Base and followed a course above the clouds to Mount Kozara. After passing Kozara, they returned to low-level flight until the Una river, where they attacked Croatian forces with S-8-16 unguided rockets. The "low-low" model of sortie was generally used.[96]

The Serbian strikes continued on 19 and 20 September alongside the Una river at Novigrad. It was decisive moment in halting the unexpected Croatian offensive. Despite the clouds, Serbian aircraft continued the attacks. On 20 September, one of the two attacking Jastrebs was shot down by Croatian ground fire and due to the low altitude the pilot only just managed to eject. Incidentally, the same pilot had already been shot down by a USAF F-16 in February 1994 and this was his second ejection. Despite this loss, filmed by a Croatian VHS camera, the Serbian AF played a decisive role in stopping the Croatian Army offensive at Una.[97]

On the southern front, the situation was much more difficult. The Armija BiH and HV outnumbered and outgunned the retreating VRS forces. On 18 September, the VRS attacked Armija BiH concentrations with Dvina/Volhov missiles fired from positions at Manjača and near Sanski Most. The battalion with ex-Krajina Dvinas was especially active. On 19 September, armed Gazelles entered the action, and on 20 September fixed wing striker aircraft from Banja

VHS footage taken on 20 September 1995 by the Croatian 2nd Guards Brigade of the attack by two Serb Jastrebs on their positions near Dvor, and smoke after one was shot down in the vicinity. The pilot ejected safely. (via D. Čanić)

Luka followed. They attacked the positions of the Armija BiH's 5th Mixed Artillery Regiment at positions Kamičak, Koračnica and Ostrožnica with aviation on 20th and helicopters on 21 September. Larger concentrations of Armija BiH troops in the seized cities of Ključ and Bosanska Krupa were attacked on 20 September by helicopters and aircraft. At Ključ, on 21 September, a G-4 Super Galeb was hit by groundfire, but the pilot managed to return to base with a damaged tail section.[98]

Muslim officials complained that the Serbian air force was "very active despite flying being banned over Bosnia and Herzegovina and the presence of Western aviation which should prevent this practice".[99] At a press conference held on 22 September, Admiral Smith was asked to comment on Serbian activities even though the No Fly Zone was still active. The admiral explained that there were unconfirmed reports of such combat activities in the Banja Luka region. He stressed that such cases were investigated and that the NATO pilots were not in position to identify any targets and explained that violation of the No Fly Zone would be further investigated, though it seems that NATO turned a blind eye to those operations. Finally, the Serb pilots used low-level flying tactics and spent just the minimum necessary time in the air and especially over the targets.

The Armija BiH offensive was temporarily halted on 23 September in the direction of Prijedor, Bosanski Novi (Novi Grad) and Mrkonjić Grad. But between 23-28 September the V i PVO continued to attack the Muslim forces at the positions that they held at Ključ and towards Mrkonjić Grad. The intensity was tremendous – considering the situation – on 25 September there were five sorties by Serb strike aviation. On 28 September, a single Orao attacked the Armija BiH forces at Lanište at Grmeč, during the reloading of ammunition. The Orao was hit from the ground and with one working engine managed to return to Banja Luka.[100]

As the fighting continued in the first days of October, the V i PVO continued to carry out strike missions, helicopter attacks and the occasional launching of Dvina/Volhov missiles. NATO announced that on 3 October its aircraft launched missiles against the Serbian

Serb ground crew moving a J-22 Orao prior to its mission in late September/October 1995. (D. Vejnović)

Testing the Rolls-Royce Viper engine of Orao No 25119, between missions, late September/October 1995. (D. Vejnović)

An Orao with a typical load of four BL.755s, seen diving at Armija BiH positions near village of Krasulje in the wider area of Ključ, 9 October 1995. (R. Ćuković)

Suddenly, the air force of the Karadžić Serbs became active. Their combat Galebs took off from Banja Luka Air Base and attacked ours and Croat advancing columns. NATO did not react. The message was clear: there shall be no winner in [the] Bosnian War. Or: the Serbs should not be defeated completely. Which is the same.[102]

Prior to the beginning of the final phase of the joint Muslim/Croat offensive of 7-8 October, Serbian strike aviation and missiles targeted the Armija BiH positions at the Ključ -Mrkonjić Grad communication site, around Ključ, in the Drenovo-Tijesno area (4-6 October) and around Tešanj and Bosanska Krupa (8 October). After launching the final phase of attacking operations (Sana and Južni potez) Muslim forces captured Sanski Most and continued north, towards Prijedor, and Croatian forces entered Mrkonjić Grad and advanced further, towards Banja Luka. Croatian forces were backed by their Mi-24s on 11 October. Serbian aircraft were observed in flypast over Sanski Most on 10 October.[103]

At this part of the front, a detachment of Gamas were active and operated from Urije airfield near Prijedor. They supported the defending forces of the 10th Operational Group VRS primarily around Sanski Most, attacking advancing Armija BiH troops. As Major Janko Kecman explained, the practice was that Gazelles had four Malyutka ATGMs mounted on pylons and four more on the back seat. After the first four were fired at the targets, the helicopters which operated in pairs, would land and mount the other four missiles and continue chasing the targets, mainly combat vehicles.[104]

radar/air defence positions on three occasions: twice south of Banja Luka and once south of Sarajevo. It was explained that these zones were earlier bypassed which enabled the Serbian aircraft to operate. In the preceding few days, several of the Serbian aircraft were spotted on radars, but when NATO fighters were directed to intercept them, they would soon land or simply disappear from the radars.[101] Muslim Leader and Bosnian President Alija Izetbegović bitterly commented:

The Gamas used the stadium in Sanski Most just prior to entry of the Armija BiH forces. On following day, they continued in action upon the request of the 10th Operational Group and until Sanski Most fell into Armija BiH hands. Two Gamas took off and attacked an Armija BiH column of vehicles in the village of Usorci, in the direction of Prijedor. They fired first volley of eight Malyutkas, landed, mounted another eight missiles and fired another volley at their targets. They hit two Praga 2/30mm SPAA guns and a single tank. But more importantly they hit trailers with the ammunition for 107mm multiple rocket launchers, which the Armija BiH had borrowed from the Croatian Army with intention to target Prijedor.[105] The ammunition, some 150 rockets in all, was lost in an explosion, as Armija BiH sources also confirmed.[106] Prijedor was saved as a ceasefire soon started. The V i

PVO Chief of the Staff, General Novak, estimates that this was one of the decisive moments in this part of the theatre. Prijedor remained in Serbian hands. After the war, the four members of the Gama crews were proclaimed as honorary members of that city.[107]

A formal ceasefire started at 24:00 hours on 12 October. While the complete ceasefire in Bosnia and Herzegovina was agreed to start on 15 October. The war was over.

5
THE AFTERMATH OF THE NATO AIR CAMPAIGN

At the beginning of November 1995, the local political and national leaders were summoned by the Americans to Wright-Paterson AFB near Dayton for talks on a peace agreement. After 20 days of negotiations, finally the peace, and territorial division of Bosnia and Herzegovina were agreed. The Dayton Peace Accord led to the Paris peace conference on 14 December and a formal end to the war in Bosnia and Herzegovina. According to the agreement in Dayton, a NATO-led multinational force Implementation Force (IFOR) would be deployed into Bosnia and Herzegovina to "implement" the peace in the war-torn land. That meant new contingents of soldiers would arrive. UNPROFOR's mission was over along with operations Deny Flight and Provide Promise.[1]

Following the experiences of Deliberate Force, where Aviano housed ten times more aircraft and personnel than it was designed for, it was decided that this base should be expanded with more infrastructure. Still by the beginning of 1996, Aviano still housed far more personnel and aircraft than usual, which led to inadequate living conditions by American standards. In this period, the units which were on rotation (TDY) were part of the 4190th (Provisional) Wing, commanded by General Charles Wald – the commander of the 31st Fighter Wing, subordinated to 5 ATAF. Beside members of USAFE, there were ANG and AFRES units from CONUS and British, Canadian and Spanish

A considerable air contingent remained in theatre to monitor the deployment of IFOR forces in early 1996. Here, an A-10 of the 81st FS is seen on a taxiway at Aviano, while an interesting mix of types is visible in the background: an F-16C, a C-5 Galaxy and an E-3 AWACS. (NAC/DoD)

NATO Air Forces in Bosnia after the Dayton Peace Accord

The NATO combat aviation based in Italy in 1993-1995 remained present but was downsized. Their task was to support the IFOR forces and secure the BiH airspace from any violation. In practice, 5 ATAF and its deployed units became IFOR's air component. The IFOR forces were organised into three multinational divisions that covered BiH territory and were deployed during December 1995 and January 1996.

Important combat assets remained in Italy in this period and continued to carry out CAP and various other missions to control the implementation of Dayton Accord. Aviation units from ten NATO air forces remained and continued to operate from Italian air bases, mostly in Aviano. Others remained on standby in their home bases with the task of returning to Italy if necessary.

New USAF Boeing C-17 Globemaster III transporters took part in Operation Joint Endeavor in which they supported the deployment of US forces within the IFOR mission. (NAC/DoD)

United Nations forces unload the last pallet of relief supplies from a C-130 Hercules aircraft based at Ramstein, Germany, marking the end of the humanitarian airlift Operation Provide Promise, January 1996. (NAC/DoD)

From December 1995, C-130 Hercules aircraft from 37th AS, 86th AW, at Ramstein Air Base were deployed to Tuzla. In 1996 Tuzla was turned into the main hub for the deployment and support of US forces in Bosnia and Herzegovina, and for IFOR. (B. Dimitrijević)

which landed at Rhein-Main Air Base on 15 December 1995. These orbited in Hungarian and Croatian airspace and up until 14 February logged 50 missions, finishing the deployment with 95 consecutive operational sorties and more than 1,000 flight hours with a "98% mission effectiveness rate". Even though their success was underlined, it was very difficult to monitor ground movement in a typical European theatre, and especially terrain such as Bosnia.[3]

Predator UAVs were also active in monitoring the situation on the ground. They were moved from Gjader in Albania to Taszar in Hungary, from where they operated from December 1995 and into 1996. In a total of six months of operation they logged 128 missions. These were taken into the USAF inventory officially, as the Unmanned Aerial Vehicle RQ-1 Predator, on 3 September 1996. They remained in the region until 1999 using air bases in Tuzla (BiH) and Skopski Petrovac (Macedonia).

Operation Provide Promise ended on 9 January 1996, after two C-130 Hercules transporters

pilots with their aircraft. They all formed part of Operation Decisive Edge which was activated to control the airspace of BiH during its first peace-time year and the deployment of the multinational forces. During IFOR's deployment USS *George Washington* was present in the Adriatic to provide additional strength.[2]

The USAF organised an air bridge from December 1995 and into 1996 named Operation Joint Endeavor, in which a new transport aircraft, the C-17 Globemaster III, had its successful debut. In deploying the US forces into Bosnia as part of the IFOR mission, a fleet of C-5, C-130 and C-141 transports was engaged from Nos 62, 86, 314, 315, 433, 437, 439 and 512 Wings, and civil contractor Polar Air was used with Boeing 747s. Some missions were flown directly from CONUS, the others from Germany, using the Rhein-Main Air Base and Ramstein to a lesser extent. They initially landed at Tuzla or Taszar Air Base, though later flew only to Tuzla Air Base, where C-17s, C-130s and C-141s landed. The C-17 was especially praised in the conduct of the missions to and from Tuzla. One US Army contingent landed on 28 December 1995 with four C-17s at Belgrade International Airport before the contingent proceeded with its vehicles into Bosnia.

Another new system, the E-8 Joint STARS (Joint Surveillance Target Attack Radar System) had its debut during this period. This was a battle management, command and control platform based on Boeing 707-300 airframe, with a side looking airborne radar beneath the fuselage. These were tasked to monitor the IFOR deployment as part of Operation Joint Endeavor. Two platforms were engaged, one E-8A and another E-8C, belonging to 4500th J-STARS Squadron (Provisional)

– one French and another American – landed with humanitarian cargo in Sarajevo. It was announced that during the whole operation cargo aircraft were fired upon 93 times, and an Italian G-222 was lost. The UNHCR air bridge with humanitarian aid logged 12,951 sorties of which there were 2,828 sorties in which food supplies were dropped from the transporters to endangered areas.[4]

Until the end of the 1995, NATO conducted around 100,420 sorties over Bosnia and the wider region. Among them there were 23,021 CAP missions in Operation Deny Flight; there were 27,077 strike missions, 29,158 different support missions (including tanker, reconnaissance, AWACS, ELINT and jammers) and 21,164 training missions. The missions were carried out by 4,500 personnel from 12 NATO countries.[5]

The former RV i PVO air base at Tuzla was of special importance in this period, being the USAF hub for deployment and logistics. US European Command, EUCOM decided that Tuzla would be used for operations and to support the US forces in the region. The first to be deployed/stationed in Tuzla were the C-130 Hercules aircraft belonging to the Ramstein-based 37th AS (86th Wing). These landed on 6 December carrying the spearhead of the US forces that would become part of IFOR. 823rd RED HORSE Squadron was soon sent to Tuzla to create normal conditions for operations and daily life. Soon the provisional 4100th Air Base Group was created to control the operations in Tuzla. Later, it became part of the 16th AEW based in Aviano, which controlled such forward air bases in the region. Tuzla

Date (1995)	ATM Day	Scheduled	Added	Ground Aborted	Flown	Air Aborted	Penetrated
29-30 Aug	1	124	1	3	122	0	85
30-31 Aug	2	244	24	26	242	4	170
31 Aug – 1 Sep	3	237	52	16	273	23	202
1-2 Sept	4	206	5	32	179	6	118
2-3 Sept	5	272	2	91	183	8	103
3-4 Sept	6	183	11	5	189	10	122
4-5 Sept	7	185	20	19	186	3	122
5-6 Sept	8	191	84	10	265	3	176
6-7 Sept	9	193	119	25	287	43	213
7-8 Sept	10	245	103	54	294	0	232
8-9 Sept	11	226	42	11	257	17	171
9-10 Sept	12	229	13	31	211	10	145
10-11 Sep	13	223	25	26	222	1	152
11-12 Sep	14	216	48	9	255	5	180
12-13 Sep	15	162	54	6	210	0	151
13-14 Sep	16	178	44	82	140	14	81
14-15 Sep	17	171	0	151	20	1	0
TOTAL		3,485	647	597	3,535	148	2,423

Table 5: Deliberate Force Sorties Summary[8]

In addition to the figures given above, a further 20 missions were conducted on 15 September, after the operation had officially concluded.

collateral damage. Option 2 included targets which were in the vicinity of "safe zones" but included ammunition storage and air defence sites. It was believed that this option had a "medium" level of collateral damage. Option 3 included all other military and strategic targets of the VRS on the territory of Republika Srpska; above all communication, air defence and storage capacities. In reality, Operation Deliberate Force included strikes on the targets listed in Option 2 and 3.[7]

In the operation, according to the statistics, on average some 270 NATO aircraft were engaged each day, of which 43.2% were US assets (USAF, USN, USMC). Later figures show that during the 17 days of Deliberate Force, there were 3,515 sorties, including 1,372 strike and 785 SEAD missions.

The types of missions conducted by the NATO allies show the different capabilities of the American and European allies during the operation.

soon became the backbone for the US Army aviation assets: helicopters and light aviation which would use the base in the following years.[6]

Statistics of Operation Deliberate Force
During Operation Deliberate Force NATO focused on hitting the targets designated as Options 1, 2 and 3. Option 1 targets consisted of the VRS heavy artillery weaponry which shelled the UN Safe Zones. It was supposed that attacking those targets would produce minimal

CAP were conducted by:

- British Harrier GR Mk 7s: six at Gioia del Colle flew 68 missions. They did not operate in during the last two days of the campaign. Six more Royal Navy Sea Harrier FA-2s conducted 12 more missions operating from HMS *Illustrious*. In total the RAF and Fleet Air Arm flew 80 CAP sorties.
- Turkish TF-16Cs: 18 of them based at Ghedi flew a total of 70

An EA-6B Prowler belonging to VAQ 141, during its 56-day preventive maintenance inspection at Aviano, during Operation Deliberate Force, September 1995. (NAC/DoD)

missions.

- French Mirage 2000Cs: six based in Cervia and a number of others on-call from their bases in France, flew a total of 60 missions.
- Dutch NF-16As: six based in Villafranca, flew a total of 56 missions. They did not participate in the last two days of the operation.
- US Navy F-14As from USS *Theodore Roosevelt* with 16 missions carried on 30 August and 8-9 September.

SEAD missions were an important element of the tasks set in the Operation. These included:

- US Navy F/A-18Cs from USS *Theodore Roosevelt* from 29 August to 12 September and USS *America* on 13 September, with a total of 210 missions.
- US Navy and USMC EA-6Bs: 125 missions from Aviano (CAG 141/209) and a further 58 missions from USS *Theodore Roosevelt*; a total of 183 missions.
- USAFE F-16C-HTS (later known as F-16CJ), ten of which from 23rd FS/52nd FW flew 176 missions.
- USAFE EF-111A Ravens with 68 missions.
- USMC F/A-18Ds belonging to VMFA-533, based at Aviano with 66 missions.
- Spanish Air Force EF-18As, based in Aviano with 52 missions.
- German Luftwaffe Tornado ECRs, eight based in Piacenza flew 28 missions.
- US Navy S-3B Vikings aboard aircraft carriers flew 2 missions.

Out of 56 SEAD aircraft, 50 fired AGM-88 HARM missiles, 22 were ECM jammers, while 14 had the ability to jam the radars and fire HARMs. Usage of SEAD aviation was separately planned in the missions nicknamed as the 'windows' which were 'opened' inside the Serbian air defence for the other strike packages. A total of 56 HARM were fired, including two by Spanish crews.

Offensive or strike missions were of several different forms: these included strike missions, CAS and BAI. They were carried out by the following NATO aviation assets:

- USAFE 31st FW from Aviano, which maintained 12 ready aircraft on a daily basis, with total of 340 missions flown.
- Air National Guard 131st FS /104th FW with OA/A-10As at Aviano with 142 CAS and BAI missions flown.
- RAF Harrier GR.7s at Gioia del Colle with 126 strike missions conducted.

- USAFE 494th FS/48th FW with ten F-15Es at Aviano. A total of 94 missions were flown, mostly against key targets, infrastructure and bridges.
- USMC F/A-18Ds based at Aviano with 94 strike missions.
- Dutch RNLAF NF-16A based at Villafranca with 86 CAS missions.
- RAF Jaguars: six at Istrana with 63 missions.
- US Navy F-14As aboard USS *Theodore Roosevelt* with 47 strike and SEAD-related missions.
- Spanish EF-18As, based in Aviano, with 46 strike missions.
- French Mirage 2000N-K2s from Cervia, with a total of 45 missions. Among them 35 were carried out by the Ks and 10 other missions by D sub-versions.
- USAF 16th Special Operations Squadron/1st Special Operations Wing at Brindisi with four AC-130H gunships. They carried out 32 different missions including BAI, CAS, CSAR and reconnaissance. Gunships were used during the first week as reconnaissance platforms against the VRS troops in the wider Sarajevo area. On the fifth night of their engagement one AC-130 was nearly hit by the Serbian air defence and subsequently ordered to abandon the mission without further major incident.

The following missions were mainly reconnaissance:

- Royal Navy Sea Harriers from HMS *Illustrious* with 30 strike missions.
- Italian Air Force, AMI Tornado IDSs based at Ghedi with 26 strike missions.
- US Navy F/A-18Cs with 10 missions: four strike, four CAP and two reconnaissance.
- US Navy EA-6Bs with four missions.
- Turkish Air Force with TF-16Cs at Ghedi with four missions.
- German Luftwaffe Tornado ECRs based at Piacenza with three missions.

Further reconnaissance missions were carried by whole range of types:

- French Armée de l'Air, five Mirage F-1CRs based in Istrana, total of 66 tactical reconnaissance missions.
- Dutch RNLAF NF-16Rs, five of which at Villafranca flew 52 tactical reconnaissance missions.
- RAF, two Harrier GR.7s at Gioia del Colle which carried out 49 missions.
- German Luftwaffe, six Tornados based at Piacenza with total of

RAF Harrier GR.7 takes from Gioia del Colle. No 4 Squadron had 12 of these aircraft during Operation Deliberate Force. (British MoD)

Ground crew of the 555th Fighter Squadron, paint the Triple Nickel logo onto the munitions of an F-16C. (NAC/DoD)

- French DC-8 Sarigues with total of three missions.

ELINT and ECM jamming missions for SEAD aviation were carried out by the four EC-130H Hercules from USAF 43rd ECC Squadron with a total of 35 missions.

Airborne Early Warning missions were carried out by the aircraft widely known as "AWACS". Among them:

- USAF and NATO E-3A/D/ Fs, total of 104 missions. The As flew 74 missions, Ds 25 missions and Fs five missions.
- US Navy E-2C Hawkeyes, aboard USS *Theodore Roosevelt* and USS *America* total of 62 missions.

Airborne command posts or ABCCC carried out 32 missions, each of 12 hours, except for the last day of the operation, when the flying hours were shortened due to the cancelling of combat missions.

Combat Search and Rescue (CSAR) missions were carried out by:

- USAF, six MH-53J Pave Low III helicopters, based at Brindisi with 10 missions.
- USAF, four HC-130P Hercules with nine missions.

Air refuelling was carried out at two "stations" named Speedy and Sony over the Adriatic Sea. The tanker fleet included:

- USAF, total of 12 KC-135 E/Rs flying from different bases: Pisa and Sigonella (Italy), Istres (France) and Mildenhall (UK where 351st Sqn/100th ARW was located) with 108 missions.
- USAF, KC-10A Extenders, total of 45 missions starting from 2 September.
- RAF, two L-1011K TriStars based in Palermo with 32 missions.
- French CF-135R at Istres with 18 missions.
- Spanish Air Force, two KC-130Hs based at Aviano, with 17

36 missions, among them 32 tactical reconnaissance and four upon the request of the RRF.

- USAF U-2s based at Fairford and Alconbury with 44 missions for Operation Deliberate Force. Among them 13 reconnaissance and 10 ELINT regarded as successful, while 13 reconnaissance and five ELINT missions were unsuccessful. U-2s were also used, but operated to their own schedule.
- US Navy F-14As aboard aircraft carriers flew a total of 32 missions using the TARPS reconnaissance pods.
- Royal Navy Sea Harriers aboard HMS *Illustrious*, flew a total of 12 missions.
- French Mirage 2000Ds at Cervia with 12 tactical reconnaissance missions.
- US (CIA) Schweizer RG-8 based at Dezney, Turkey with nine missions and total of 52 hours of reconnaissance and observation.
- USAF Predator UAVs at Gjader, Albania. There were 17 launches with 15 sorties, and among them 12 completed missions totalling 150 flying hours.
- US (CIA) GNAT 750 based at Dezney, Turkey and undisclosed locations in Croatia with 12 completed missions. Seven of them regarded as successful.
- French Armée de l'Air Jaguar As based at Istrana with six tactical reconnaissance missions.
- USAF two F-16Cs, with two tactical reconnaissance missions.
- US Navy two F/A-18Cs with two tactical reconnaissance missions.

ELINT-gathering was carried out by the following NATO platforms:

- US Navy S-3B and ES-3A Vikings embarked aboard USS *Theodore Roosevelt* and USS *America*: total of 71 missions (including 38 by ES-3As and 33 by S-3Bs).
- USAF RC-135Ws based at Mildenhall with 21 missions.
- US Navy EP-3E Orions based at Sigonella with 18 missions.
- RAF Nimrod R Mk Is with seven missions.
- French C.160NG Gabriels from Avord with four missions, and

Weapon loaders fix LGBs onto an F-15E Strike Eagle, prior to take-off during Operation Deliberate Force. (NAC/DoD)

Table 6: Number of NATO Aircraft Deployed, Operation Deliberate Force

Country	Fighter	CAS	Gunship	AEW	EW	Reconnaissance	Transport	Tanker	Support	Total	Percentage
US	18	44	2		21			15		100	41.8
France	16	9		1		5	1	1		33	13.8
German	14									14	5.9
Italy	6	6				2		1	5	20	8.4
Netherlands	9					3	2	1		15	6.3
Norway							2			2	0.84
Spain	8							2	1	11	4.6
Turkey	8									8	3.3
Great Britain	6	16		2		2		2		28	11.7
NAEWF				8						8	3.3
TOTAL	85	75	2	11	21	12	5	21	7	239	

Table 7: Number of Missions/Sorties During Operation Deliberate Force

Country	Number of Sorties	Percentage of Total
US	2,318	65.9
France	284	8.1
Germany	59	1.7
Italy	35	1.0
Netherlands	198	5.6
Spain	12	0.3
Turkey	78	2.2
Great Britain	326	9.3
NAEWF	96	2.7
Other Nato Members	109	3.1
Total	3,515	100

Table 8: Types of Mission, Operation Deliberate Force[10]

Type of Mission	Number of Missions	Percentage of Total
CAP	294	8.4
SEAD	785	22.3
CAS/BAI	1,372	39
Reconnaissance	316	9
Support	748	21.3
Total	3,515	100

Table 9: Delivered Ordnance, Operation Deliberate Force[11]

Country	Guided	Unguided	Agm-88 Harm
US	622	12	54
France	14	73	
Germany			
Italy		50	
Netherlands		136	
Spain	24		2
Turkey			
Great Britain	48	47	
Total	708	318	56

missions, and

- Italian Air Force, a single Boeing 707, which carried out six missions, only for Italian aircraft.

Transport missions were carried out by a wide variety of NATO transport aircraft types but were not counted in the review.[9]

As Operation Deliberate Force was primary a USAF "show", somehow the fact that US Navy F-14s were used as the strike platforms against the Serb targets has largely "slipped below the radar". The classic Cold War USN fighter had now become a potent striker, nicknamed the "Bombcat". Carrier-borne F-14s had been involved in the policing of the No-Fly Zones since April 1993 and during the second half of 1994 they were flying pre- and post-strike reconnaissance sorties with TARPS pods. The Tomcats were used from initial missions in Operation Deliberate Force on 30 August 1995. "When the first aircraft returned shortly after 02:00hrs … with its racks and rails empty, we could hardly contain our surprise and excitement", recalled one of the VF-41 crews. Once the CAOC was aware that Tomcats could indeed drop air-to-ground ordnance, they were sent on more missions after 5 September and the squadron delivered LGBs and free-fall Mk-82 bombs. The Tomcats did not carry the LANTIRN pod during Operation Deliberate Force, and thus they would drop their LGBs with a "buddy-lase" from F/A-18s to designate targets and guide weapons. The major advantages of the F-14s were twofold: they could carry their standard air-to-air missile load in addition to a pair of 1,000lb LGBs and unlike the F/A-18, Tomcats were able to bring their load back aboard if something prevented them from reaching their targets. Hornets, on the other hand, had to drop or jettison their bomb load before landing on a carrier. Tomcats also continued to fly other missions in support of the effort. Most notable were the TARPS reconnaissance missions. VF-41, which was the only F-14 squadron on USS *Theodore Roosevelt* during the operation, was "First to Strike" within the Tomcat community, delivering some 24,000lb of ordnance against Serb targets.[13]

Unmanned Aerial Vehicles or UAVs, had their operational debut in the war in Bosnia where they were used for tactical reconnaissance. The first UAVs that appeared in the Balkans were Gnat 750s operated by the CIA in the summer of 1994. These operated over Bosnia and Herzegovina, taking off from an improvised airfield on the Croatian island of Brač. After this became known and was an issue with Croatian public, they were transferred to Gjader Air Base, in Albania.[14]

Table 10: Types of Delivered Ordnance, Operation Deliberate Force[12]	
Types of Munition	Number
Laser-Guided, Total	708
LGBs Total	653
GBU-10	303
GBU-12	125
GBU-16	215
GBU-24	6
AS 30L	4
Electro-optical/IR-Guided Total	42
AGM-84E SLAM	10
GBU-15	9
AGM-65 Maverick	23
TLAM Tomahawk	13
Unguided, Total	318
Mk-82	175
Mk-83	99
Mk-84	42
CBU-87	2
Other Munitions	
30mm cannon (A-10A)	10,086
40 mm cannon (AC-130H)	50
105mm cannon (AC-130H)	350
2.75 in rockets (A-10A)	20
AGM-88 Harm	56

In 1995, Predator UAVs were introduced into the USAF inventory following the shooting down of an F-16 at by the beginning of June that year. Approval came on 16 June, and ten days later, on 26 June, the first missions were carried out over south-western Bosnia in the wider areas of Livno and Kupres. The information collected was dispatched to the Croatian Army, which gathered in this area in preparation for launching a large-scale offensive against Serbian Krajina. On 7 July, a Predator conducted a reconnaissance mission over Eastern and Western Bosnia (RS). The missions were continued on 10 July, when CIA tested them in missions over Croatia and already seized/liberated territory of Serbian Krajina, then over Herzegovina and Eastern Bosnia.

At the same time the Croatian Army had developed some indigenous reconnaissance drones and used them to monitor the movements of both Serbian armies (VRS, SVK). One such drone was shot down on 5 June 1995 south-west of Draževići.

Through the summer months Predators started to be widely present over the Bosnian scenery in Operation Nomad Vigil, based at Camp NOVA at Gjader in Albania, supported by the personnel of 86th Airlift Wing from Ramstein. These appeared during the conflict between the VRS and the RRF in the wider Sarajevo area, and soon started to cause trouble for the VRS forces.[15]

As First Class Captain Aleksić from 155th Air Defence Missile Brigade VRS stated: "UAVs were very slow and were easy prey. But since they flew above 4,000 metres our light AA artillery did not manage to claim them… UAVs played a key role in [the] precision of enemy fire and registered every movement of our units, and we were without effective way to stop them."[16]

Television image of the claimed UAV Predator, by the VRS units around Nevesinje in Herzegovina. (YouTube)

In August one UAV was spotted at 40 kilometres north-west of Banja Luka at 4,500-5,000 metres altitude. One Orao was scrambled and directed by the radar station at Kozara to intercept the UAV. The pilot was unable to visually identify it and soon landed without success.[17]

During Operation Deliberate Force, Predators were operational and up to November 1995 they carried out a total of 52 sorties, mostly pre-attack and Battle Damage Assessment (BDA) reconnaissance missions. However, two were lost: one was claimed by the Serbian forces around Nevesinje in Herzegovina on 5 September, while another one crashed due to a malfunction.

Statistics of the V i PVO for the whole duration of war
The Serbian Air Force and Air Defence (V i PVO) operated throughout the whole of the 1992-1995 wars. During the first part of the operations until the UN Resolution 781, when the flying was banned, V i PVO carried out the following missions:

- 1,243 sorties with 612.5 tons of ordnance dropped
- 111 sorties of the light strike aviation with 17 tons of ordnance dropped
- 1,413 sorties by combat helicopters which conducted 533 launching of ATGMs. 80% or 415 were regarded as successful
- 4,687 transport helicopter sorties where 11,522 wounded and passengers were ferried as well as 924 tons of cargo.

On average, its fighter-bomber pilots each flew 83 combat sorties with some 40 hours of flying and 40 tons of ordnance used. In the period after Resolution 781, the V i PVO used Udbina Air Base to carry out a total of 62 strike sorties against targets in the Bihać, Cazin, Novi Grad, Drvar, Dubica, Končanica and Plješevica areas and several light aviation sorties were undertaken against the Srebrenica enclave.[18] The exact number of sorties undertaken during the summer and autumn of 1995 remains unknown.

During the combat sorties the two of the V i PVO's *eskadril*as deployed following bombs:

- 170 KPT-150,
- 6,120 RAB-3,5,
- 2,624 RAB-16,
- 86 FAB-PRAB 50,
- 454 FAB and OFAB 100,
- 137 260lb RAB,
- 204 FAB and OFAB 250,
- 71 PRAB 250,
- 250 227kg Mk.82 Snekeye,

- 200 FAB-500lb,
- 32 PPAB (PLAB-250-120),
- 206 PLAB-200,
- 128 PLAB-350,
- 14 SAB-100,
- 441 BL.755 CBUs,
- 2 Durandal runway-penetration bombs,
- 328 S-8-16 unguided rockets,
- 7042 NRZ 57mm BR-1 unguided rockets,
- 100 BR-2 unguided rockets,
- 690 128mm unguided rockets,
- Six AGM 65B Mavericks,
- 55,000 rounds for GŠ-23 guns.[19]

Helicopters flew during the whole duration of the conflict and logged 11,879 sorties including combat and transport missions.

Armed Gazelle helicopters, known as Gamas, carried out a total of 663 sorties launching a total of 725 Malyutka ATGMs, of which 606 hit the targets (81%). A total of 11,216 transport/liaison missions were carried out transporting 2,411 wounded, 8,202 passengers and 418 tons of cargo.[20]

During the war, V i PVO VRS and RV i PVO SVK lost a total of 12 aircraft: six J-21 Jastrebs, four J-22 Oraos, one NJ-21 Jastreb two-seater and one NJ-22 Orao two-seater and 12 helicopters (eight Gazelles and four Mi-8s). A total of 34 pilots and airmen were lost. They claimed three Croatian MiG-21s, three Armija BiH Mi-8s and a single leased AN-26, and a Royal Navy Sea Harrier, an Armée de l'Air Mirage 2000, and a USAF F-16 and Predator UAV.

Due to a lack of surface-to-surface guided missiles and the inability to use combat aviation during most of the conflict, the Main Staff VRS approved the usage of Volhov and Dvina (SA-2) missiles against targets on the ground. They were used to support the units of I and II Krajiški, Istočno-bosanski Corps and Operational Group Doboj. A total of 166 missiles were launched, among them 150 successfully against ground targets. Six missiles suffered technical failure. We may presume that the other ten missiles may have been launched in regular surface-to-air mode against NATO aviation in late 1994. No matter the difficulties in estimation of the real results, the usage of those missiles had a mostly psychological effect; positive on VRS troops and negative on the opposite side.

The main support unit of the V i PVO, the 474th Air Base supported the air force not just at the two main bases north of Banja Luka: Mahovljani for aircraft and Zalužani for helicopters, but it provided smaller units to support helicopter operations all over the Republika Srpska territory. In autumn 1995, a battalion of the V i PVO was formed as a replacement unit and sent into combat south of Banja Luka.[21] This unit suffered over two dozen killed and missing in action from a total of 35 men. During Operation Deliberate Force, a total of 26 members of V i PVO were killed.

The V i PVO fired six AGM-65Bs against very important targets, such as Armija BiH armament factories. The example shown here is an inert USAF training round. (B. Dimitrijević)

This V i PVO Gama of the 89th Helicopter Squadron is seen at Mahovljani, Banja Luka, with its crew and typical load of Malyutka ATGMs. (B. Dimitrijević)

MEDIEVAC was an important task for the Serb Mi-8 transport fleet during the clashes in autumn 1994. (D Vejnović)

NATO and USAF Experiences of Operation Deliberate Force
Operation Deliberate Force was a robust 17-day air campaign conducted by eight participating NATO nations. Deliberate Force's multinational force composition included:

- over 5,000 personnel from 15 nations;
- over 400 aircraft (including 222 fighters) available at any one time;
- approximately 260 land-based aircraft – 40% based at Aviano AB, Italy;
- 18 air bases in five countries across Europe; and
- up to three aircraft carriers in the Adriatic Sea.

In the sense of the USAF, it conducted Deliberate Force with about two fighter wing-equivalent combat force and an appropriate support slice of reconnaissance, surveillance, electronic warfare, SEAD, airlift, and other aircraft.

There was nothing particularly militarily novel about Operation Deliberate Force, however there were number of "firsts" in this Operation:

- first deployment of German, Spanish and Italian air forces in combat since the Second World War;
- first deployment of Predator unmanned aerial vehicles;
- first combat deployment of the Tomahawk cruise missiles in Europe;
- deployment of GBU-10 (2,000lb) and GBU-12 (500lb) Paveway II laser-guided bombs in combat;
- deployment of GBU-15 (2,000 lb) glide bombs in combat, delivered by F-15Es;
- deployment of Matra 1,000lb and GBU-12 laser-guided bombs by AdA Mirage 2000N-K2s and Jaguar As;
- deployment of AN/ASQ-213 HARM targeting systems (HTS) on F-16Cs;
- bombing from above 15,000 ft and from slant range.

Finally, it was the first air campaign with large ratio of PGMs used (69%).[22]

The results of the use of precision-guided munitions were estimated with euphoria, as General Ryan did after the end of the campaign "precision munitions were absolutely vital to the success of the mission… I think precision munitions are not only here to stay, but they're … the wave of the future". General Ryan claimed that care to avoid collateral damage was underlined: he had to stop the attack if hitting the target may cause collateral damage. This "care" led to widespread use of PGMs in the campaign. Due to these ROEs, around 10% of PGMs were not delivered on targets, but were jettisoned into the Adriatic on return from the missions.

It is important to mention that the USAF A-10s used ammunition containing depleted uranium against the Technical Overhauling Plant in Hadžići and on VRS targets around Vozuća and on Mount Ozren. Such ammunition, the PGU-14/B API round fired by the GAU-8/A 30mm gun, had much more destructive power than traditional aircraft gun ammunition against hard targets. Usage of this ammunition was not mentioned during press conferences and there was no "care" as to its effects which were seen sometime later. Ammunition with depleted uranium has subsequent effects in leaving uncontrolled radiation in the area where it was delivered, at levels up to 900 times higher than the usual radiation in the air. By 1996, the effects of these munitions were seen on the people and cattle, and later through an increased percentage of cancer among the military or civilians that were in the vicinity of the targets hit by the A-10s' munitions.

The RAF analyses noted that they used Jaguar-Harrier GR.7 pairs in action. TIALD pods were used by Jaguars to mark the targets, which then would then be hit with Paveway LGBs delivered by Harriers. Harriers belonging to No.4 Squadron carried out 144 sorties, delivering 48 LGBs with TIALD guidance and thirty-two 1,000lb bombs. The French air force used AS-30L laser-guided air-to-ground missiles, and the Spanish used AGM-88 HARMs and GBU-16 LGBs. As noted previously, the Italian and German air forces participated in combat missions for the first time since

A detachment of three F-16Cs of the 510th FS, 31st FW, July 1995. (NAC/DoD)

The Spanish Ala 15 contingent poses on one of their F/A-18 Hornets equipped with an AGM-88 HARM for SEAD missions. (@AircraftTalking)

the Second World War, flying missions using their Tornados. AMI 6th and 36th Stormo logged their first combat missions, as well as the Luftwaffe's JBG 32 in SEAD missions, and AKG 51 in reconnaissance missions. The latter were part of Einsatzgeschwader 1, a unit specially created for this operation.

The analyses from Deliberate Force stressed that USAF and other NATO units maintained high morale, especially strengthened when there were no losses after the first day of operation. However, the campaign showed an increasing discrepancy in the US and NATO allies' airpower. The air contingents sent to Italy to take part in Deliberate Force were far smaller than those of USAF and the Europeans did not possess a range of types of combat and support aviation, nor strategic assets such as ABCCCs, strategic reconnaissance, UAVs or the up-to-date strike aircraft that the Americans had. Some of the types, such as air tankers, AWACS and ELINT, were possessed by the European

allies, but only a handful of them used by a few of the larger air forces. This technological gap between the US and European allies would emerge even more in the air campaign against Serbia in spring 1999.

Most of the sorties (66%) were carried by the Americans (USAF, USN, USMC). After them, in fairly equal numbers were the RAF, Armée de l'Air and RNLAF, which logged between six and nine percent of sorties each. The other allies each managed to log one to three percent of the total number of sorties carried out. The smaller European contingents mainly conducted CAP missions.

Serbian Experiences

Although Operation Deliberate Force was in US and NATO political and military circles marked as a complete success, the airstrikes did not degrade the combat capabilities of the VRS on the battlefield. It continued to counter the advancing Croat-Muslim forces, in one

The Lakenheath-based 48th Fighter Wing played an important role with deployment of its two squadrons (Nos 492 and 494) for operations against the Serbs in BiH in 1994 and 1995. (NAC/DoD)

A US Marine Cobra helicopter manoeuvres in the background while air crew members from 110th Air National Guard prepare their A-10 for a mission. (NAC/DoD)

Two Serb pilots, captains Gvozden and Gavrić, return from a mission in autumn 1995. (D. Vejnović)

Ironically, once Operation Deliberate Force was over, the Serbian V i PVO combat aviation suddenly had the opportunity to fly and carry out important strike missions against the Croat-Muslim offensive. Strike missions improved the strategic position of the VRS in several areas and managed to even halt the Croat advance from the Una river to Banja Luka, and to slow down the Armija BiH advance on Prijedor. Moreover, they destroyed a shipment of BM-21 MRL ammunition for the Armija BiH during the final hours before the ceasefire.

Serbian combat aviation used its Orao and Jastreb strike aircraft and Gama helicopters skilfully, mostly flying at extremely low altitudes. General Novak later explained that in the return leg, the Serbian air defence would turn its fire-control radars on, thus confusing NATO while enabling safe landing of its pilots.[24] Colonel Gostimir Popović, head of the V i PVO Intelligence Department explained that using its ELINT centre, it was able to estimate the location of NATO combat aircraft in the airspace, which then enable the Serbian pilots to use the gaps in their presence and to carry out missions against Muslim and Croat forces.[25]

Due to the short distances to the targets, the aircraft were loaded with maximum of ordnance and did not need to use additional fuel tanks. They operated upon the request of the higher ground forces HQs and occasionally in "free hunt" regime. During the four weeks of Operation Deliberate Force they managed to avoid any encounter with NATO aviation. A single Jastreb was lost, while a G-4 was damaged but repaired and returned to combat service. There was some minor damage but no serious problems in carrying out the missions.

period almost simultaneously with the airstrikes. The VRS forces operated as a 'coherent military force' which manoeuvred with the units of brigade-size even during the heaviest air attacks on its positions. CIA analysts marked that this, 'was a triumph of the VRS Main Staff's professionalism and skill', because the Serb forces remained able to continue combat operations against its Muslim and Croat opponents all through the aerial campaign.[23]

Even though targeted from the earliest minutes of Operation Deliberate Force, the Serb air defences managed to survive the NATO air campaign, even the specially tailored Dead Eye sub-operation. This does not mean that the V i PVO suffered no losses: on the contrary, it lost one SA-6 SAM site, the radar company at Mount Kozara, and communications facilities at Jahorina. However, the rest of the system remained intact. The decision not to illuminate NATO aircraft and to remain remained hidden, despite the airstrikes, saved the day.

Defeat of the Republika Srpska Krajina and the link-up between the Croatian Army and V Corps of Armija BiH and their later joint operation in September 1995, caused much more difficulties to the VRS than Deliberate Force. Carl Bildt notes well in his memoirs that the real impact of the air campaign was much more modest than was realised, but its moral effect was great. He adds that during this period, rumours circulated among the VRS that this or that part of the territory would be given to the other side in expected negotiations. In such atmosphere, morale deteriorated, since nobody wanted to die for something which would be given away at the diplomatic table to the enemies.[26]

The air campaign impressed the political leadership of Republika Srpska, so they were much more willing to accept negotiations and peace talks. But the key decision was taken before Deliberate Force even began: President of Serbia Slobodan Milošević was authorised to represent the political interests of Republika Srpska at peace talks, on the day when the operation was launched.

CONCLUSION

Whatever else may be said about it, Deliberate Force marked a turning point for both NATO and the course of events in Bosnia. The role of the airpower in the war in Bosnia between 1993-1995 was important but not decisive: Operation Deliberate Force changed this by having a tremendous impact on the negotiation process. NATO's operation led to a relatively swift political solution.

Contrary to earlier air operations over Bosnia in 1993-1995 which were mostly air patrolling and occasional attacks on the Serb forces, under the constraints of different ROEs, Operation Deliberate Force consisted of large-scale attacks. It was considered that an extended campaign would be a disaster for the credibility of NATO, the UN, and ultimately the United States, of course. That is why NATO-US analyses justified the severity of the air attacks in Deliberate Force as necessary. Planners and senior commanders in Operation Deliberate Force estimated that a slow campaign would undoubtedly lead to its devaluation and misperception of the enemy forces, the VRS, who would continue their operations. The usage of precision-guided munitions enabled the success of the operation, mostly in achieving necessary accuracy in targeting. Using PGMs also led to avoidance of collateral damage and massive loss of human life to such scale that amongst the international public there was no criticism related to the loss of life among Serbian civilians. As Colonel Owen concludes "precision-guided munitions made Deliberate Force possible."[27]

The aims of the operation that were set at the beginning were fulfilled: withdrawal of the Serbian heavy weaponry around Sarajevo and preventing of alleged Serbian attacks on the city.

Another important fact was that in these air operations, NATO – which was experiencing an identity crisis after the end of the Cold War and the collapse of Communism in Eastern Europe – achieved cohesion and self-confidence. As Richard Holbrooke stressed, Deliberate Force was the largest military action in the history of NATO up to Operation Allied Force in 1999.[28] Outwardly, Deliberate Force gave the appearance of a true coalition effort. But perceptions of just how much Deliberate Force was a coalition effort varied among the NATO allies. Many non-US NATO officers complained that the operation was little more than an American-run air campaign and that they were just along for the ride.[29]

Operation Deliberate Force was "highly politicized operation", as USAF Colonel Bucknam puts it.[30] Soon it started to be seen as the main reason for the military defeat of the Serbs in the 1992-1995 war. Even more, the use of airpower started to be perceived as the main tool to overcome difficulties in political negotiations. Even though it was a very expensive way of waging war, the use of airpower showed that the modern war could be conducted with minimal or even incidental losses on its own side. It assured the sympathies of domestic public opinion, which in earlier cases was harshly critical. This strengthened the notion, especially in the US administration, that use of airpower was decisive and to be welcomed in all future conflicts, no matter how difficult and complicated they might be.

The successes of Operation Deliberate Force – regarded as a success of US diplomacy in bringing the actors of the war in Bosnia to the negotiating table – hid most of its shortcomings: from political to technological. All of those deficiencies would appear in the same or even larger scale in the Operation Allied Force air campaign against FR Yugoslavia (Serbia) in 1999.

Bibliography

Archival Sources

HRVATSKI MEMORIJALNO DOKUMENTACIJSKI CENTER DOMOVINSKOG RATA, [Croatian Memorial-Documentation Center of Homeland War, Zagreb, Croaita] fund: Srpska Vojska Krajine RV i PVO [Serbian Army of Krajina] 1994-1995

INTERNATIONAL CRIMINAL TRIBUNAL FOR THE FORMER YUGOSLAVIA, Court Records, General Ratko Mladić handwritten notebooks 1991-1996

SAVEZNI SEKRETARIJAT ZA NARODNU ODBRANU [Federal Ministry of Defence, SFR Yugoslavia]-III uprava (1991-1992)

VOJSKA REPUBLIKE SRPSKE [Army of Republika Srpska], original documents:

Glavni Štab VRS, *Sektor za OBP, dnevne obaveštajne informacije 1995*

V i PVO (assorted documents)

Published Sources and Official Editions

Komanda V i PVO, *Iz smrti u besmrt* (Komanda V i PVO, BanjaLuka 1996).

Press Briefings NATO Operation Deliberate Force, Allied Forces Southern Europe Naples Italy.

Republika Hrvatska i domovinski rat 1990-1995, Dokumenti vojne provenijencije Republike srpske Krajine: volumes 3 to 17 (Hrvatski Memorijalno Dokumentacijski Centar Domovinskog Rata, Zagreb 2008-2015).

Zapisnik sa 16. sjednice Skupštine srpskog naroda u Bosni i Hercegovini, održane 12. maja 1992. u Banja Luci.

31 FW Support to Contingency Operations since 1994 (unclassified material).

Oral Sources

Zoran Dunović, Duško Četković, Janko Kecman, Milorad Milojčić, Zlatko Mikerević, Dragan Nakić, Živomir Ninković, Božo Novak, Gostimir Popović, Saša Ratković, Petko Rašević, Uroš Studen, Milan Torbica, Drago Vejnović and Miljan Vlačić (VRS), Ranko Dašić, Ratko Dopuđa, Nikola Dukić, Janko Kecman, Dušan Kosanović, Milan Menićanin, Uroš Studen, Duško Žarković (SVK) and Luka Kastratović, Milan Menićanin (JNA/VJ)

Written Statements

Unpublished: Janko Aleksić, Milan Barvalac, Vlado Krsmanović, Zoran Lukić, Boro Samardžić, Aleksandar Studen, Zdravko Zeljković (VRS);

Published: Senad Palić (ARBiH) and Josip Hrgović (HRZ).

Magazines

Air Forces Monthly, Narodna armija, Nova krila, Politika, Srpska vojska

Video Materials (Films) and Youtube clips

DOKUMENTARNI FILM OPERACIJA SANA 95: NEDOVRSENA POBJEDA, <https://www.youtube.com/watch?v=RohHZQC62u4>

GENERAL (RET) HAL HORNBURG TALKS ABOUT OPERATION DELIBERATE FORCE AT USAFA <https://www.youtube.com/watch?v=F2NR5mLwoJU&feature=youtu.be>

ITALY: US PILOT RESCUED IN BOSNIA WELCOMED AT AVIANO AIRBASE <https://www.youtube.com/watch?v=a5vxdToj7WM&feature=youtu.be>

ITALY/AVIANO – NATO JETS FLY SORTIES <https://www.youtube.com/watch?v=_I3Lko0ems8&t=15s>

PAD KRAJINE<*https://www.youtube.com/watch?v=XtR4Ip-aEQU*>

RV i PVOARMIJE RBIH,<https://www.youtube.com/watch?v=ZMjEDG6OU1Y>

ZAKLETVA, DOKUMENTARNI FILM O VOSJCI REPUBLIKE SRPSKE RTRS <https://www.youtube.com/watch?v=uykGCos9gks>

TV ZIVINICE – AERODROM DUBRAVE 24.05.1992 <https://www.youtube.com/watch?v=u9ZIs2kw0FI>

BOROVIĆ, SELAK, IVANDIĆ PREDAVANJE (ZAGREB, TEHNIČKI MUZEJ, 30.11.2012.) <https://www.youtube.com/watch?v=WcM4MRISrM0>

Articles

Grant, Rebbeca, 'The Carrier Myth', *Air Force Magazine,* March 1999, pp.26-31.

Hodžić, Šefko, 'Dvanaesta godišnjica rušenja helikoptera na Žepskoj planini, Udes koji je uticao na sudbinu Srebrenice' (<http://bhstring.net/tuzlaslikama/tuzlarije/viewnewnewsb.php?id=16553>)

Lamothe, Dan, 'This F-16 fighter jet in Afghanistan might be the Pentagon's most decorated', <(https://www.washingtonpost.com/news/checkpoint/wp/2015/10/29/this-f-16-fighter-jet-in-afghanistan-might-be-the-pentagons-most-decorated/>)

Owen, Col Robert C., 'The Balkans Air Campaign Study Part 1', *Airpower Journal*, Summer 1997, pp.4-25.

Owen, Col Robert C., 'The Balkans Air Campaign Study Part 2', *Airpower Journal*, Fall 1997, pp.6-27.

Raguž, Mario, 'Pobjegli na traktorima, avione ostavili', *VP magazin za vojnu povijest,* January 2012, pp.64-67.

Šajinović, Dejan, 'Zlatan Crnalić, pilot koji je preživio NATO: Ne ljutim se, oni su imali svoj zadatak, ja svoj' (<http://www.nezavisne.com/zivot-stil/zivot/Zlatan-Crnalic-pilot-koji-je-prezivio-NATO-Ne-ljutim-se-oni-su-imali-svoj-zadatak-ja-svoj-FOTO/334613>)

Tirpak, John, 'Deliberate Force', *Air Force Magazine*, October 1997, pp.36-43.

'Transkript Okruglog stola na temu Uloga vojnog sektora u odbrani Tuzle 1992-1995' Part 2 (Međunarodna galerija portreta, Tuzla, 20.10.2006).

Werhas, Mario, 'Operacija Oluja, akcije Hrvatskog ratnog zrakoplovstva', *VP magazin za vojnu povijest*, March 2012, pp.44-51.

Yost, David S., 'The NATO Capabilities Gap and the European Union', *The International Institute for Strategic Studies Journal*, Vol.42, No.4 Winter 2000-01, pp.97-128.

Monographs

1. gardijska brigada hrvatske vojske, Tigorvi (Zagreb, Despot Infinitus, 2015).

Aralica, Tomislav, Robert Čopec, Marko Jeras, Zdenko Kinjerovac & Tomislav Haraminčić, *Sto godina ratnog zrakoplovstva u Hrvatskoj* (Zagreb, Despot Infinitus, 2012).

Bahto, Hamid, *Sa braniocima Sarajeva i Goražda* (Sarajevo, Vijeće Kongresa Bošnjačkih Intelektualaca, 2008).

Beale, Michael, *Bombs Over Bosnia, The Role of Airpower in Bosnia Herzegovina* (Maxwell AFB, School of Advanced Airpower Studies Air University, June 1996).

Bilt, Karl, *Zadatak mir* (Beograd, Samizdat B92, 1999).

Borojević, Danko, Drago Ivić & Željko Ubović, *Orlovi sa Vrbasa* (Ruma, Autorsko izdanje, 2014).

Borojević, Danko, Drago Ivić & Željko Ubović, *Vazduhoplovne snage bivših republika SFRJ* (Ruma, Autorsko izdanje, 2016).

Borojević, Danko, Drago Ivić & Željko Ubović, *Vojska Republike Srpske 12. maj 1992 – 31. decembar 2005* (Beorgrad, Autorsko izdanje, 2014).

Bucknam, Mark A, Colonel USAF, *Responsibility of Command, How UN and NATO Commanders Influenced Airpower over Bosnia* (Maxwell AFB, Air University Press, March 2003).

Tato, Čelik Taib, *Diverzanti* (Sarajevo, Šahinpašić, 2004).

Central Intelligence Agency, *Balkan Battlegrounds, A Military History of the Yugoslav Conflict, 1990-1995, Volume I* (Washington DC., Central Intelligence Agency, Office of Russian and European Analysis, May 2002).

Chiffot, Jean Louis, *Portes disparus, 104 jours aux mains des Serbs* (Paris, Seuil, 1997).

Clark, Richard M., Lt. Col USAF, *Uninhabited* Combat Aerial Vehicles, Cadre Paper No.8 (Maxwell AFB, Air University Press, August 2000).

Delić, Dr Rasim, *Lice i naličje rata* (Sarajevo, Vijeće Kongresa Bošnjačkih Intelektualaca, 2005).

Deveta gardijska brigada Hrvatske vojske Vukovi (Zagreb, Ministarstvo obrane Republike Hrvatske, Glavni stožer Oružanih snaga RH, 2012).

Dimitrijević, Bojan *Jugoslovensko ratno vazduhoplovstvo 1942-1992* (Beograd, ISI, 2006).

Dimitrijević, Bojan & Jovica Draganić, *Vazdušni rat nad Srbijom 1999. godine* (Beograd, ISI, 2010).

Dimitrijević, Bojan & Milan Micevski,*117 lovački puk* (Beograd – Niš, Galaksija, 2015).

Dimitrijević, Bojan, *Vazdušni rat na Republikom Srpskom i Republikom Srpskom Krajinom* (Beograd, Društvo istoričara Srbije, 2017).

Druga gardijska brigada Hrvatske vojske Gromovi (Zagreb, Ministarstvo obrane Republike Hrvatske, Glavni stožer Oružanih snaga RH, 2012).

Đukić, Borislav, General, *Razbijanje Jugoslavije, mesto i uloga hrvatske* (Sremska Kamenica, Srpsko kulturno društvo Zora, 2008).

Duraković, Kemal, *Na Istočnom bedemu Bosne IV, Dnevnički zapis za 1995.godinu iz donjeg Podrinja* (Sarajevo, Dobra knjiga, 2009).

Felić, Bejdo, brigadir, *Peti korpus 1992.-1995* (Sarajevo, Ljiljan, 2002).

Franchet, Commandant, *Casque bleu pour rien, Ce que j'ai vraiment vu en Bosnie* (Paris, J.C. Lattes, 1995).

Gawne, Brian G., *Dual Key Command and Control in Operation Deny Flight: Paralyzed by Design* (Newport, Naval War College, November 1996).

Halberstam, David, *War in a Time of Peace: Bush, Clinton and the Generals* (London, Bloomsbury, 2001).

Hodžić, Šefko, *Vitezovi i Huni* (Sarajevo, OKO, 1996).

Holbruk, Ričard, *Put u Dejton, Od Sarajeva do Dejtona i posle* (Beograd, Dangraf, 1998).

Holmes, Tony (ed.), *Bombcat: The US Navy's Ultimate Precision Bomber* (*Air Forces Monthly* Magazine special volume, 2015)

Izetbegović, Alija, *Sjećanja, autobiografski zapis* (Sarajevo, OKO, 2001).

Jertz, Walter, *Im Dienste des Friedens*, 2. aktualisierte auflage (Bonn, Bernard und Graefe Verlag, 2000).

Jovičić, Mile, *Dva dana do mira, Dnevnik sa „Aerodroma Sarajevo", april-maj 1992* (Novi Sad, autorsko izdanje, 2004).

Kirste, Knut, *Final Report: German Contributions to NATO Peacekeeping and Out-of Area Operations: The Case of the Former Yugoslavia* (NATO Individual Research Fellowship, 1996/98).

Koljević, Nikola, *Stvaranje Republike Srpske, dnevnik 1993–1995* (Beograd, Službeni glasnik, 2008).

Kramlinger, George D., *Sustained Coercive Air Presence, Provide Comfort, Deny Flight, and the Future of Airpower in Peace Enforcement* (Maxwell AFB, Air University Press, February 2001).

Lomović, Boško, *Crvena nit Koridora, Brčko u ratu 1992-1993* (Beograd, Svet knjige, 1999).

Lutgert, Wim & Rolf de Winter *Check the Horizon, De Koninklijke Luchtmacht en het conflict in voormalig Joegoslavie 1991-1995* (den Haag, Sectie Luchtmachthistorie, Staf Bevelhebber der Luchtstrijdkrachten, 2001).

March, Peter R., *Freedom of the Skies, An illustrated History of Fifty Years of NATO Airpower* (London, Cassell, 1999).

Marijan, Davor, *Graničari, Prilog za ratni put 108. brigade Zbora narodne garde Republike Hrvatske* (Slavonski Brod, Hrvatski institute za povijest – Podružnica za povijest Slavonije, Srijema I Baranje, 2006).

Marijan, Davor, *Oluja* (Zagreb, Hrvatski Memorijalno Dokumentacijski Centar Domovinskog Rata, 2007).

Međović, Jovo, *Jahorina 1992-1996 Dnevnik* (Beograd, Svet knjige, 2001).

Miller, Kurt, *Deny Flight and Deliberate Force: an Effective use of Air Power?* (Fort Leavenworth, 1997, thesis).

Morillon, Phillipe, Genral, *Crire et Oser, Chronique de Sarajevo* (Paris, Bernard Grasset, 1993).

NATO protiv Srba, Ritam zločina (Sarajevo – Ilidža, Oslobodjenje, Oktobar 1995).

O'Grady, Scott with Michael French, *Basher Five-Two, The True Story of F-16 Fighter Pilot Captain Scott O'Grady* (New York, Bantam Doubleday, 1998).

O'Shea, Brendan, *Crisis at Bihać: Bosnia's Bloody Battlefield* (Stroud, Sutton Publishing, 1998).

Owen, Robert C. (ed.), *Deliberate Force, A Case Study in Effective Air Campaigning, Final Report of the Air University Balkans Air Campaign Study* (Maxwell AFB, Air University Press, January 2000).

Pandurević, Vinko, *Rat u Bosni i Hercegovini i stvaranje Vojske Republike Srpske* (Beograd, Igam, 2015).

Primorac, Branka, *Perešin, život i smrt, O Rudolfu ne samo pilotu...* (Cakovec, Zrinski, 2001).

Prva gardijska brigada Hrvatske vojske Tigrovi (Zagreb, Ministarstvo obrane Republike Hrvatske, Glavni stožer Oružanih snaga RH, 2012).

Prvi hrvatski gardijski zdrug Hrvatske vojske (Zagreb, Ministarstvo obrane Republike Hrvatske, Glavni stožer Oružanih snaga RH, 2012).

Radić, Aleksandar, *Orao pogled iz jugoslovenskog ugla* (Beograd, Medija centar Odbrana, 2012).

Raguž, Jakša, *Hrvatsko Poneretvlje u domovinskom ratu* (Zagreb, Ogranak Matice hrvatske Metković; Hrvatski institut za povijest Metković, 2004)

Rajtar, Vladimir, *Nebeski ratnici, uspomene hrvatskog pilota* (Zagreb, Vlastita naklada, 1995).

Ripley, Tim, *Air War Bosnia, UN and NATO Airpower* (Osceola, Motorbooks Intl, 1996).

Rouz, Majkl, *Misija u Bosni – borba za mir* (Beograd, Tetra GM, 2001).

Sarajlić, Tarik, *Ratni dnevnik Goražde 1992-1995* (Sarajevo, Smail Sarajlić, 1998).

Sekulić, Milisav, *Knin je pao u Beogradu* (Beograd, Nidda Verlag/ Novosti, 2000).

Simić, Novica, *Operacija Koridor 92* (Banja Luka, Boracka organizacija Republike Srpske, 2011).

Srdanović, Slobodan, *Pale ratne hronika* (Beograd, Svet knjige, 1998).

Srpska pobuna u Zapadnoj Slavonjii 1990-1995: nositelji, institucije, posljedice, Zbornik radova, ur. Ivica Miškulin i Mladen Barać

(Slavonski Brod-Zagreb, Hrvatski institut za povijest, Podružnica za povijest Slavonije, Srijema i Baranje, Zagreb: Hrvatski memorijalno-dokumentacijski centar Domovinskog rata, 2012).

Stanković, Miloš, *Krtica od poverenja* (Beograd, Knjiga komerc, 2002).

Treća gardijska brigada Hrvatske vojske Kune (Zagreb, Ministarstvov obrane Republike Hrvatske, Glavni stožer Oružanih snaga RH, 2012).

Vojska Republike Srpske u odbrambeno-otadžbinskom ratu, aspekti, organizacija, operacije, Zbornik radova 1 (Banja Luka, Republički centar za istraživanje ratnih zločina, Mart 2011).

Wiebes, Cees, *Intelligence and the War in Bosnia 1992-1995* (Munster, Lit Verlag, 2003).

Zovak, Jerko, *Rat u bosanskoj Posavini 1992* (Slavonski Brod, Posavska Hrvatska d.o.o., 2009).

Notes

Chapter 1

1 Dimitrijević, *Jugoslovensko ratno vazduhoplovstvo 1942-1992* (Beograd, ISI, 2006). For details of Bihać Air Base, see Dimitrijević et al, *Tito's Underground Air Base* (Warwick, Helion, 2020).

2 Dimitrijević et al, *117 lovački puk*; Interview with Colonel Milan Menićanin (CO 200th Air Base), Zemun 2015; General Luka Kastratović (CO 200th Air Defence Light AA Regiment). For details on Bihać Air Base, see Dimitrijević et al, *Tito's Underground Air Base*.

3 Načelnik Generalštaba Oružanih snaga SR Jugoslavije, s/pov.2088-1, 12. May 1992; Jakša Raguž, *Hrvatsko Poneretvlje u domovinskom ratu* (Zagreb: Ogranak Matice *hrvatske Metković*; *Hrvatski* institut za povijest Metković–Zagreb, 2004), p.461.

4 'Uništen vojni aerodrome Dubrave kod Tuzle', *Politika* (Belgrade, 19 May 1992); 'Poslednji put iz Tuzle', *Intervju* (29 May 1992); 'Air War over Bosna Herzegovina,'*Air Forces Monthly* (December 1992), pp.25–31.

5 'Air War over Bosna Herzegovina', *Air Forces Monthly* (December 1992), pp.25–31; Mark Nixon, 'Forged in War-Dedicated to Peace', *Air Forces Monthly* (January 2003), pp.52–57.

6 'Na teritoriji BiH nema više jedinica RV i PVO', *Politika* (19 May 1992).

7 *Zapisnik sa 16. sjednice Skupštine srpskog naroda u Bosni i Hercegovini, održane 12. Maja 1992. u Banja Luci*, pp.31–41.

8 Interview with General Živomir Ninković (Commander V i PVO) 2 and 16 February 2016, Belgrade; Interview with General Božo Novak (Chief of Staff V i PVO) 2-3 February and 2 March 2016, Belgrade.

9 *Vojska Republike Srpske u odbrambeno – otadžbinskom ratu, aspekti, organizacija, operacije*, Zbornik radova 1 (Republički centar za istraživanje ratnih zločina, Banja Luka, Mart 2011). p.35.

10 Savezni sekretarijat za narodnu odbranu, s/pov 2284–1, 30 August 1991; 'Ponovo krila nad Zalužanima', *Narodna armija* (Belgrade 14 August 1991), p.4; 'Novi vojni aerodrom RV i PVO kod Banja Luke', *Politika* (13 August 1991), p.8.

11 Savezni sekretarijat za narodnu odbrana, s/pov, 2944-1, 30. Oktobar 1991; 'Nova krila krajine', *Narodna armija* (23 October 1991), p.5.

12 Savezni sekretarijat za narodnu odbrana, s/pov, 2944-1, 30. Oktobar 1991.

13 'Ratni put Komande i jedinica 5. p VOJIN', 5. puk VOJIN, s/pov. 01/98-4, 19. February 1992, pp.26–27; Dimitrijević, *Jugoslovensko ratno vazduhoplovstvo 1942-1992*.

14 Komanda 155.rp PVO, str.pov. br 03/26-39, 12.06 1992.

15 Komanda V I PVO, "Pregled stanja popune mirnodopskih i mobilisanih jedinica sa stanjem na dan ___ 1992."; Vinko Pandurević, *Rat u Bosni i Hercegovini i stvaranje Vojske Republike Srpske* (Beograd, Igam, 2015), pp.140 and 164; Dimitrijević, *Vazdušni Rat* (Beograd, Društvo istoričara Srbije, 2017), pp.61-65.

16 Komanda V I PVO, sp br. 02/152-25, 29.10.1992.

17 'Transkript Okruglog stola na temu Uloga vojnog sektora u odbrani Tuzle 1992-1995', Drugi dio (Međunarodna galerija portreta, Tuzla, 20.10.2006).

18 Dimitrijević et al, *117 lovački puk*; Dimitrijević et al, *Tito's Underground Air Base*.

19 Bejdo Felić, brigadir, *Peti korpus 1992.-1995* (Sarajevo, Ljiljan, 2002), pp.19-23; Senad Palic, written statement, 11 April 2005.

20 Josip Hrgovic, written statement; Vladimir Rajtar, *Nebeski ratnici, uspomene hrvatskog pilota* (Zagreb, Vlastita naklada, 1995), pp.217-233; Aralica et al, *Sto Godina*, pp.366.

21 Senad Palic, written statement; Rajtar, *Nebeski ratnici, uspomene hrvatskog pilota*, pp.217-233.

22 Borojević et al, *Vazduhoplovne Snage*, pp.182-183; 'Transkript Okruglog stola na temu Uloga vojnog sektora u odbrani Tuzle 1992-1995'.

23 'Transkript Okruglog Stola na temu Uloga vojnog sektora u odbrani Tuzle 1992-1995.'

24 Rajtar, *Nebeski ratnici, uspomene hrvatskog pilota*, p.234.

25 Aralica, *Sto godina*,. p.362.

26 Josip Hrgovic, written statement, 7 May 2008; Rajtar, *Nebeski ratnici, uspomene hrvatskog pilota*, pp.217-233; Aralica et al, *Sto Godina*, pp.365-366.

27 Borojević et al, *Vazduhoplovne Snage*, pp.221-225; Aralica et al, *Sto Godina*, pp.366.

28 Aralica et al, *Sto Godina*, pp.366-367; Borojević et al, *Vazduhoplovne Snage*, pp.227-237.

29 Aralica et al, *Sto Godina*, pp.368.

30 Borojević et al, *Vazduhoplovne Snage*, p.187.

31 Glavni Štab VRS, *Sektor za OBP*, 'Dnevne obaveštajne informacije,' July 1995.

32 Operation Sharp Guard < https://en.wikipedia.org/wiki/Operation_Sharp_Guard>.

33 Borojević, Drago & Željko, *Orlovi sa Vrbasa* (Ruma, Autorsko izdanje, 2014), p.124.

34 Komanda V i PVO, *Iz smrti u besmrt* (Banja Luka, Komanda V i PVO, 1996).

35 Aralica et al, *Sto Godina*, pp.365.

36 Komanda V i PVO, *Iz smrti u besmrt*.

37 Simić, *Operacija Koridor 92* (Banja Luka, Boracka organizacija Republike Srpske, 2011).

38 Komanda V I PVO, 'Pregled realizacije vazduhoplovne podrske,' (courtesy of General Novak); *Analiza borbene gotovosti i aktivnosti VRS u 1992. godini*; Simić, *Operacija Koridor 92*.

39 Interview with Colonel Janko Kecman (Deputy CO of the 56th Helicopter Squadron), 11 April 2016, Banja Luka.

40 Dimitrijević, *Vazdušni Rat*, pp.70-75.

41 'Diskusija načelnika Uprave V I PVO puk Radoslava Panzdica na analizi b/g za 1996. godinu' (courtesy of General Milan Torbica).

42 Interview with Colonel Miljan Vlačić (CO, 28th Squadron), Banja Luka, 11 April 2016; Interview with Lt. Colonel Zlatko Mikerević (27th Squadron), 8 May 2016, Zemun.

43 International Criminal Tribunal for the Former Yugoslavia, Court Records, General Ratko Mladić notebook No. 40, p.40.

44 Resolution UN SC 781 at: http://unscr.com/en/resolutions/781; Commandant Franchet, *Casque bleu pour rien, Ce que j'ai vraiment vu en Bosnie* (Paris, J.C. Lattes, 1995), p.113.

45 Interviews with General Ninković and General Novak.

46 According to the documents, shown to author by General B. Novak.

47 'An-2 i Utva-75 dejstvuju po neprijatelju' <https://www.youtube.com/watch?v=X6iXhO9p_7M&t=8s >

48 Glavni štab VRS, Banja Luka, 08.12. 1992. g, *Pismo generala Mladića komandantu snaga UNPROFOR generalu Satiš Nambijaru*.

49 Ripley, *Air War Bosnia: UN and NATO Airpower* (Osceola, Motorbooks International, 1996), p.39; more details on: <https://en.wikipedia.org/wiki/Operation_Sky_Monitor>

Chapter 2

1 Ripley, *Air War Bosnia: UN and NATO Airpower*, p.9; Morillon, *Croireet Oser, Chronique de Sarajevo* (Paris, Bernard Grasset, 1993), pp.93–94.

2 The fact that the Croats opened fire upon the aircraft was quickly omitted from related press releases in the West, because it did not fit into the established public impression in which the Serbs were the 'sole villains' in this war.

3 Ripley, *Air War Bosnia: UN and NATO Airpower*, p.18.

4 Ripley, *Air War Bosnia: UN and NATO Airpower*, p.28.

5 Komanda V i PVO VRS, str.pov br. 02/2-6, 07.03 1993.

6 Bucknam, *Responsibility of Command, How UN and NATO Commanders Influenced Airpower over Bosnia* (Air University Press, Maxwell Air Force Base, Alabama, March 2003), p.173; Ripley, *Air War Bosnia: UN and NATO Airpower*, p.28.

7 Ripley, *Air War Bosnia: UN and NATO Airpower*, p.28.

8 Ripley, *Air War Bosnia: UN and NATO Airpower*, p.39.

9 O'Shea, *Crisis at Bihać Bosnia s Bloody Battlefield* (Stroud, Sutton Publishing, 1998), pp.157-159; Wiebes, *Intelligence and the War in Bosnia 1992-1995* (Munster, Lit Verlag, 2003).

10 Resolution UN SC 816 at <http://unscr.com/en/resolutions/816>

11 Ripley, *Air War Bosnia: UN and NATO Airpower*, pp.39–47.

12 Bucknam, *Responsibility of Command*, pp.81, 94-99.

13 Owen (ed.), *Deliberate Force, A Case Study in Effective Air Campaigning, Final Report of the Air University Balkans Air Campaign Study,* (Air University Press, Maxwell AFB, January 2000). pp.48-52.

14 *Srpska vojska*, br. 6 (26 March 1993), pp.10–11.

15 ICTY, General Ratko Mladić notebook No. 36, p.33; Komanda V I PVO, „Letovi aviona NATO iznad grada Banja Luke na visinama ispod 2000m" (courtesy of General Novak).

16 *Deliberate Force, A Case Study in Effective Air Campaigning,* p.65; Ripley, *Air War Bosnia: UN and NATO Airpower*, p.48.

17 Alport, 'Bosnia's on-going air war', *Air Forces Monthly*, June 1994, pp.22-26.

18 Lutgert & de Winter *Check the Horizon, De Koninklijke Luchtmacht en het conflict in voormalig Joegoslavie 1991-1995* (den Haag, Sectie Luchtmachthistorie, Staf Bevelhebber der Luchtstrijdkrachten, 2001).

19 Alport, 'Bosnia's on-going air war', pp.22-26.

20 Alport & Thouanel, 'Operations Crecerelle and Balbuzard', *Air Forces Monthly*, July 1994, pp.29-31.

21 Ripley, *Air War Bosnia: UN and NATO Airpower*, pp.46-47.

22 Komanda V i PVO, *Iz smrti u besmrt*.

23 Komanda 155.rp PVO, str.pov. br 03/26-39, 12.06.1992.

24 Komanda V i PVO VRS, str.pov br. 02/152-37, 29.12.1992; Interview with General Milan Torbica (Head of the Air Defence Department V I PVO HQs), 13 March, Zemun / 10 April, Banja Luka 2016.

25 Interview with General Torbica.

26 GS VRS, str.pov 25-17, 17.02 1994; GS VRS, str.pov 11/30-32 11.03.1994; Komanda V i PVO VRS, str.pov br.05/21-13, 24.02 1994; Komanda V i PVO VRS, str.pov br.05/21-14, 15.03 1994; Komanda V i PVO VRS, str. pov br.05/121-26, 18.04 1994.

27 Interview with General Novak.

28 R. Bošković, *Nebo na dlanu*, p.485; see Dimitrijević et al, *Tito's Underground Air Base*. The most important of the five major radar stations operated by the V i PVO was the 1st Radar Company at Mount Plješevica, which proved capable of monitoring NATO operations not only over Croatia and Hungary, but also all the way out over the Adriatic Sea and was feeding its radar picture to the HQ of the Serbian forces in Croatia. Unsurprisingly, all such stations were heavily fortified and well-protected – not a minute too late: the Jahorina station was attacked by Armija BiH twice (on 18 December 1992 and 3 July 1993), while the Nevesinje station came under attack in November 1994. In all cases, their garrisons were able to repel the assailants.

29 Komanda V i PVO, sp. br. 02/152-25, 29.10.1992; Komanda V i PVO VRS, str. pov br. 05/26-11, 16.06.1994; Bosković, *Nebo na dlanu, Vek vazdušnog osmatranja javljanja i navodjenja* (Beograd, autorsko izdanje, 2017), pp.484-486; Interview with Colonel Petko Rašević (Deputy CO 51st Air Surveillance Battalion), Novi Beograd, 5 May 2016.

30 Bošković, *Nebo na dlanu*, p.494.

31 Interview with Colonel Gostimir Popović (Head of Intel Department V I PVO HQs) Banja Luka, 11 April 2016.

32 ICTY, General Ratko Mladić notebook No. 36, pp.334-344 and 381-385.

33 *Republika Hrvatska i domovinski rat 1990-1995, Dokumenti vojne provenijencije Republike srpske Krajine*, volume 7, siječanj-lipanj 1993 (Hrvatski Memorijalno Dokumentacijski Centar Domovinskog Rata, Zagreb 2009) and interview with Colonel Kecman.

34 Interview with Colonel Dopudja.

35 *Deveta gardijska brigada Hrvatske vojske Vukovi* (Ministarstvo obrane Republike Hrvatske, Glavni stožer Oružanih snaga RH, Zagreb 2012).

36 Komanda V I PVO, VRS, str. pov. br. 02/2-26, 28.10.1993 and interviews with several veterans of the 2nd Battalion Princess Patricia's Canadian Light Infantry.

37 Hrvatski memorijalno dokumentacijski centar domovinskog rata Zagreb (HMDCDR): RV I PVO SVK: GS SVK, Organ RV I PVO, pov. Br 41-239, 23.03.94.

38 Interview with General Duško Žarković (CO of the 2nd SP AD Battery SVK), Zemun, 4 February 2016.

39 HMDCDR: RV I PVO SVK: GS SVK, Organ RV I PVO, pov. Br 41-239, 23.03.94.

40 Komanda V I PVO, VRS, str. pov. br. 02/2-26, 28.10.1993; ICTY, General Ratko Mladić notebook No. 36, pp.334-344, 381-385.

41 Borojević et al, *Orlovi sa Vrbasa*. p.147.

42 The following reconstruction is based on interviews with four of the pilots involved, the former commander of the V i PVO, and his contemporary Chief-of-Staff. While some of their recollections differ, the gist of the story is the same.

43 Interviews with Colonel MIljan Vlačić, Lt. Colonel Uros Studen 17 February 2016, Zemun, Lt. Colonel Zlatko Mikerević (pilots who took part in this mission), General Ninković and Novak.

44 ITALY/AVIANO – NATO JETS FLY SORTIES <https://www.youtube.com/watch?v=_I3Lko0ems8&t=15s>; Ripley, *Air War Bosnia: UN and NATO Airpower*, p.72.

45 Dejan Šajinović, 'ZlatanCrnalić, pilot koji je preživio NATO: Ne ljutim se, oni su imali svoj zadatak, ja svoj' <http://www.nezavisne.com/zivot-stil/zivot/Zlatan-Crnalic-pilot-koji-je-prezivio-NATO-Ne-ljutim-se-oni-su-imali-svoj-zadatak-ja-svoj-FOTO/334613)>

46 *Nova krila* (28 June 1994). pp.8-11.

47 Resolution UN SC 836 at < http://unscr.com/en/resolutions/836 >

48   Koljević, *Stvaranje Republike Srpske, dnevnik 1993–1995*, vol 1 (Beograd, Službeni glasnik, 2008). p.428, Bucknam, *Responsibility of Command*, pp.122-123.

49   Rouz, *Misija u Bosni – borba za mir* (Beograd, Tetra GM, 2001). p.137.

50   Ripley, *Air War Bosnia: UN and NATO Airpower*, p.70; Rouz, *Misija u Bosni*, pp.137-138.

51   Rouz, *Misija u Bosni*, pp.140-141; Alport, 'Bosnia's on-going air war', pp.22-26.

52   Dimitrijević, *Vazdušni Rat*, p.187-188.

53   Alport & Thouanel, 'Operations Crecerelle and Balbuzard', pp.29-31; Alport, 'Bosnia's on-going air war', pp.22-26.

54   Rouz, *Misija u Bosni*, p.147; Alport, 'Bosnia's on-going air war', pp.22-26.

55   Alport, 'Bosnia's on-going air war', pp.22-26.

56   Tarik Sarajlić, *Ratni dnevnik Goražde 1992-1995* (Sarajevo, Smail Sarajlić, 1998). p.305.

57   Rouz, *Misija u Bosni*, pp.147-148; Ripley, *Air War Bosnia: UN and NATO Airpower*, p.70.

58   Alport & Thouanel, 'Operations Crecerelle and Balbuzard', pp.29-31.

59   108 Rouz, *Misija u Bosni*, pp.147-148.

60   Rouz, *Misija u Bosni*, p.206; Stanković, *Krtica od poverenja* (Beograd, Knjiga komerc, 2002), p.370-371, Bucknam, *Responsiblity of Command*, pp.162 and 165.

61   Rouz, *Misija u Bosni*, pp.206-207.

62   Bucknam, *Responsiblity of Command*, p.1-63.

63   Rouz, *Misija u Bosni*, pp.224-225; Ripley, *Air War Bosnia: UN and NATO Airpower*, p.70; Koljevic, *Stvaranje Republike Srpske*, vol 1 p.667; Stankovic, *Krtica od poverenja*, pp.370-377; Bucknam, *Responsibility of Command*, pp.165-167.

64   Interviews with General Novak, and Colonel Ranko Dašić (CO of the 44th Air Defence Missile Brigade SVK), Belgrade, 5 February 2016.

65   Felić, *Peti korpus 1992.-1995*, pp.309 – 343; HMDCDR: VRS: K-da Drugog krajiškog korpusa, str. pov. br. 13–454, 14. novembar 1994.

66   Felić, *Peti korpus 1992.-1995*, pp.306, 360, 372-375; Dimitrijević, Vazdušni Rat, pp.192-193.

67   Komanda V i PVO VRS, str.pov. br. 02/2-19, 18.11.1994; *Balkan Battlegrounds, A Military History of the Yugoslav Conflict, 1990-1995, volume I* (Central Intelligence Agency, Office of Russian and European Analysis Washington D.C., May 2002). p.249; Felić, *Peti korpus 1992.-1995*, pp.377-378.

68   O'Shea, *Crisis at Bihać: Bosnia's Bloody Battlefield*, p.107.

69   Resolution UN SC 958 at <http://unscr.com/en/resolutions/958>

70   Bucknam, *Responsibility of Command*, pp.176-177; Rouz, *Misija u Bosni*, pp.252-253.

71   Interview with Colonel Dopudja.

72   Lutgert & de Winter, *Check the Horizon*, p.316; Ripley, *Air War Bosnia: UN and NATO Airpower*, p.70.

73   Dimitrijević, Vazdušni Rat, pp.195-198 and Lutgert & de Winter, *Check the Horizon*, pp.313-315.

74   Interviews with General Torbica and General Novak.

75   Rouz, *Misija u Bosni*, p.255; Ripley, *Air War Bosnia: UN and NATO Airpower* pp.70-71, Stankovic, *Krtica od poverenja*, p.421; Komanda V I PVO, 'Postupci avijacije NATO pre napada (21.11.1994)' courtesy of General Novak.

76   O'Shea, *Crisis at Bihać: Bosnia's Bloody Battlefield*, pp.111-112.

77   Bucknam, *Responsibility of Command*, pp.183-184; 'Sema borbenog dejstva 1. ssrb PVO 26.11.1994' courtesy of General Novak.

78   Rouz, *Misija u Bosni*, pp.252-253, Bucknam, *Responsiblity of Command*, pp.184-189.

79   Bucknam, *Responsiblity of Command*, p.115; Rouz, *Misija u Bosni*, pp.252-253, Stankovic, *Krtica od poverenja*, p.370.

Chapter 3

1   Komanda V i PVO VRS, str.pov. br. 02/2-20, 30.11.1994.

2   HMDCDR: RV i PVO SVK: GS SVK, Organ RV i PVO, pov. Br 5/1-52, 13.03.95.

3   HMDCDR: RV i PVO SVK: GS SVK, Organ RV i PVO, pov. Br 5/1-52, 13.03.95.

4   Armija OS R BiH Komanda Vazduhoplovne grupe Bihac, str.pov. broj 01/280/1, 29.05 1995; Interview with General Žarković,

5   *Srpska pobuna u Zapadnoj Slavonjii 1990-1995: nositelji, institucije, posljedice*, Zbornik radova, ur. Ivica Miškulin i Mladen Barać (Hrvatski institut za povijest, Podružnica za povijest Slavonije, Srijema i Baranje; Hrvatski memorijalno-dokumentacijski centar Domovinskog rata, Slavonski Brod-Zagreb 2012).

6   HMDCDR: RVIPVOSVK: Komanda 728. mhe, pov br. 56145-7, 04.05.1995.

7   Aralica et al, *Sto Godina*. p.371-372; Borojević et al, *Orlovi sa Vrbasa*. pp.156-160.

8   Primorac, *Perešin, život i smrt, O Rudolfu ne samo pilotu...* (Cakovec, Zrinski, 2001); Borojević et al, *Orlovi sa Vrbasa*, p.160

9   HMDCDR: RVIPVOSVK: Komanda 105.vbr,str. pov. Br 01/11-14, 26.04.1995 and str. pov. Br 01/11-23, 02.06.1995; Dimitrijević, Vazdušni Rat,pp.249-254.

10   HMDCDR: RV I PVO SVK: GS SVK, Organ RV I PVO, pov. Br 5/1-98, 12.06.1995. Dimitrijević, Vazdušni Rat, pp.249-254.

11   Komanda V I PVO VRS, str.pov. 02/2-16, 13/06 1995.

12   Ripley, *Air War Bosnia: UN and NATO Airpower*, p.82.

13   Bucknam, *Responsibility of Command*, p.207.

14   Ripley, *Air War Bosnia: UN and NATO Airpower*, p.82.

15   Bucknam, *Responsibility of Command*, p.216.

16   Komanda V I PVO, 'Šematski prikaz obaranja američkog aviona F-16, 02 .06 1995.godine u 15.02 časova' (courtesy of General Novak).

17   O'Grady with French, *Basher Five-Two: The True Story of F-16 Fighter Pilot Captain Scott O'Grady* (Bantam Doubleday, New York, 1998).

18   ITALY: US PILOT RESCUED IN BOSNIA WELCOMED AT AVIANO AIRBASE
<https://www.youtube.com/watch?v=a5vxdToj7WM&feature=youtu.be>

19   Establishment of a Rapid-Reaction Force within the UN Protection Force, <http://unscr.com/en/resolutions/998>; Ripley, *Air War Bosnia: UN and NATO Airpower*, p.82.

20   *Republika Hrvatska i domovinski rat 1990-1995, Dokumenti vojne provenijencije Republike srpske Krajine*: volume 17, svibanj-listopad 1995 (Hrvatski Memorijalno Dokumentacijski Centar Domovinskog Rata, Zagreb, 2015).

21   Raguž, 'Pobjegli na traktorima, avione ostavili', *VP magazin za vojnu povijest*, January 2012, pp.64-67.

22   Interview with Colonel Vlačić.

23   *Treća gardijska brigada Hrvatske vojske Kune* (Ministarstvo obrane Republike Hrvatske, Glavni stožer Oružanih snaga RH, Zagreb 2012);

24   GŠ VRS, Sektor za OBP, strogo pov br. 12/45-1024, 07.08.1995, 'obaveštajna informacija'.

25   Interviews with Colonel Dašić and General Žarković.

26   Werhas, 'Operacija Oluja, akcije Hrvatskog ratnog zrakoplovstva', *VP magazin za vojnu povijest*, March 2012, pp.44-51; Marijan, *Oluja* (Hrvatski Memorijalno Dokumentacijski Centar Domovinskog Rata, Zagreb 2007).

27   Senad Palic, written statement.

28   O'Shea, *Crisis at Bihać: Bosnia's Bloody Battlefield*, p.156.

29   Senad Palic, written statement.

30   GŠ VRS, Sektor za OBP, strogo pov br. 12/45-1126, 24.08.1995; Bahto Hamid, *Sa braniocima Sarajeva i Goražda* (Vijeće Kongresa Bošnjačkih Intelektualaca, Sarajevo, 2008)

31   'Transkript Okruglog stola na temu Uloga vojnog sektora u odbrani Tuzle 1992-1995', Drugi dio (Međunarodna galerija portreta, Tuzla, 20.10.2006); Komanda V I PVO, 'Sema desjtva larv PVO pri unistenju neprijateljskog helikoptera u rejonu s. Mrkalji, 09. 05. 1995 godine u 02.30 casova' (courtesy of General Novak); Šefko Hodžić, 'Dvanaesta godišnjica rušenja helikoptera na Žepskoj planini, Udes koji je uticao na sudbinu

Srebrenice', <http://bhstring.net/tuzlauslikama/tuzlarije/viewnewnewsb. php?id=16553>

32 'Transkript Okruglog stola na temu Uloga vojnog sektora u odbrani Tuzle 1992-1995', Drugi dio (Međunarodna galerija portreta, Tuzla, 20.10.2006); Interview: 'Salko Begić, Sarajevo, Rujan 2005, Razgovor i snimka cuvaju se u Sredisnjem vojnom arhivu MORH-a."

Chapter 4

1 Bucknam, *Responsibility of Command*, pp.59 and 66.

2 *Deliberate Force, A Case Study in Effective Air Campaigning*, p.470.

3 Resolution UN SC at 836 < http://unscr.com/en/resolutions/836>

4 *Deliberate Force, A Case Study in Effective Air Campaigning*, pp.95-100 and 470; Bucknam, *Responsibility of Command*, pp.81-87.

5 *Deliberate Force, A Case Study in Effective Air Campaigning*, pp.107-108, 280-295.

6 Holbruk, *Put u Dejton, Od Sarajeva do Dejtona i posle* (Beograd, Dangraf, 1998), pp.70-71.

7 Lutgert & de Winter, *Check the Horizon*; Bucknam, *Responsibility of Command*, p.248.

8 GŠ VRS, Sektor za OBP, strogo pov br. 12/45-882, 16.07.1995, 'obaveštajna informacija' and 12/45-900, 20.07.1995 'obaveštajna informacija'.

9 *Deliberate Force, A Case Study in Effective Air Campaigning*, p.477-478; Bucknam, *Responsibility of Command*, pp.251-255.

10 *Deliberate Force, A Case Study in Effective Air Campaigning*, pp.101; Bucknam, *Responsibility of Command*, p.204.

11 *Deliberate Force, A Case Study in Effective Air Campaigning*, pp.135.

12 *Deliberate Force, A Case Study in Effective Air Campaigning*, pp.98; Bucknam, *Responsibility of Command*, p.204.

13 *Deliberate Force, A Case Study in Effective Air Campaigning*, pp.107.

14 *Deliberate Force, A Case Study in Effective Air Campaigning*, pp.57.

15 Owen, 'The Balkans Air Campaign Study, Part 1', *Airpower Journal*, Summer 1997, pp.4-25; Owen, 'The Balkans Air Campaign Study Part 2', *Airpower Journal*, Fall 1997, pp.6-27; Bucknam, *Responsibility of Command*, p.262.

16 Holbruk, *Put u Dejton*, pp.95–97.

17 Walter, *Im Dienste des Friedens*, 2. aktualisierte auflage (Bonn, Bernard und Graefe Verlag, 2000).

18 GŠ VRS, Sektor za OBP, strogo pov br. 12/45-922, 24.07.1995'obaveštajna informacija' and strogo pov br. 12/45-954, 27.07.1995.

19 GŠ VRS, Sektor za OBP, strogo pov br. 12/45-922, 24.07.1995'obaveštajna informacija' and strogo pov br. 12/45-954, 27.07.1995.

20 Dimitrijević, *Vazdušni Rat*, p.279.

21 GŠVRS, Sektor za OBP, strogo pov br. 12/45-1057, 14 August 1995 'Obaveštajna informacija'.

22 *Deliberate Force, A Case Study in Effective Air Campaigning*, pp.52-54, 134, 202.

23 *Deliberate Force, A Case Study in Effective Air Campaigning*, p.201.

24 Interview with Lt Colonel Sasa Ratković (member of 2/51st Air Surveillance Battalion VRS) Belgrade, 4 August 2016.

25 *Nova krila* 27-28, novembar 1995, special edition: 'Dosije: NATO letovi u zločin,' pp.7-8.

26 Holbruk, *Put u Dejton*, p.96.

27 Owen, 'The Balkans Air Campaign Study, Part 1', pp.4-25; Owen, 'The Balkans Air Campaign Study, Part 2', pp.6-27; Bucknam, *Responsiblity of Command*, pp.276-277; *Deliberate Force, A Case Study in Effective Air Campaigning*, p.483.

28 *Deliberate Force, A Case Study in Effective Air Campaigning*, p.137; Ripley, *Air War Bosnia: UN and NATO Airpower*, p.111.

29 GŠ VRS, Sektor za OBP, strogo pov. Br12/45-1143, "Obavestajna informacija", 29. avgust 1995.

30 *Deliberate Force, A Case Study in Effective Air Campaigning*, pp.483-484.

31 Interview with Lt. Colonel Ratković.

32 *Deliberate Force, A Case Study in Effective Air Campaigning*, pp.136, 162.

33 'Dosije: NATO letovi u zločin,' p.4.

34 Međović Jovo, *Jahorina 1992-1996 Dnevnik* (Svet knjige, 2001), pp.146–147.

35 'Dosije: NATO letovi u zločin,' pp.4-5, 8.

36 Interview with General Torbica; Dimitrijević, *Vazdušni Rat*,pp.286-287.

37 'Dosije: NATO letovi u zločin,' pp.4-5; Š. Hodžić, *Vitezovi i Huni* (Sarajevo, OKO, 1996), pp.218–219.

38 'Dosije: NATO letovi u zločin,' p.8; *NATO protiv Srba, Ritam zločina* (Sarajevo – Ilidža, Oslobodjenje, October 1995).

39 *Deliberate Force, A Case Study in Effective Air Campaigning*, pp.137.

40 GŠ VRS, Sektor za OBP, strogo pov. Br12/45-1143, 30. 08.1995, 'Obavestajna informacija'.

41 Interview with General Novak, Interview with General Torbica.

42 Interview with General Novak; Interview with Colonel Popovic.

43 Bošković, *Nebo na dlanu*, pp.499-502.

44 Bošković, *Nebo na dlanu*, pp.499-502.

45 Interview with Colonel Rasevic.

46 Bošković, *Nebo na dlanu*, pp.499-502.

47 Komanda 250. raketne brigade PVO VJ, pisana izjava (written statement): 'Studen Aleksandar, vodnik, komanda 250.rbr PVO, 13. septembar 1996.'

48 Komanda 250. raketne brigade PVO VJ, pisana izjava (written statement): 'Studen Aleksandar, vodnik, komanda 250.rbr PVO, 13. septembar 1996.'

49 Written statement: Studen Aleksandar.

50 Ripley, *Air War Bosnia: UN and NATO Airpower*, p.92; Chiffot, *Portes disparus, 104 jours aux mains des Serbs*, (Paris, Seuil, 1997), pp.31–36, 133; Petar Ćosović: Kako sam spasio francuske pilote (1995) <https://www.youtube.com/watch?v=rmyyiL75iuQ&t=59s>; 10. diverzantski odred VRS i francuski piloti<https://www.youtube.com/watch? v=eLxlN4_GAwE>

51 *Deliberate Force, A Case Study in Effective Air Campaigning*, pp.137-138.

52 *Deliberate Force, A Case Study in Effective Air Campaigning*, pp.148-149.

53 ICTY, General Ratko Mladić notebook No. 32, pp.156-159; Chiffot, *Portes disparus, 104 jours aux mains des Serbs*, pp.321–328; RatkoMladić – razmijena pilota, <https://www.youtube.com/watch?v=wKJGLAJiQWY>

54 'Dosije: NATOletoviuzločin,' pp.9-10.

55 Written statement: Studen Aleksandar.

56 Međović, *Jahorina 1992-1996 Dnevnik*, p.147; 'Dosije: NATO letovi u zločin,' p.11.

57 *Deliberate Force, A Case Study in Effective Air Campaigning*, pp.144-145.

58 General (ret) Hal Hornburg Talks About Operation Deliberate Force at USAFA <https://www.youtubc.com/watch?v=F2NR5mLwoJU&feature=youtu.be>

59 ICTY, General Ratko Mladić Notebook 32, pp.7–11.

60 *Balkan Battlegrounds*, p.378.

61 *Deliberate Force, A Case Study in Effective Air Campaigning*, pp.147

62 'Dosije: NATO letovi u zločin,' p.12; KemalDuraković, *Na Istoč*nom *bedemu Bosne IV, Dnevnički zapis za 1995. godinu iz donjeg Podrinja* (Dobra knjiga, Sarajevo, 2009). p.206.

63 *Deliberate Force, A Case Study in Effective Air Campaigning*, pp.150-151.

64 'Dosije: NATO letovi u zločin', pp.13-14; Međović, *Jahorina 1992-1996 Dnevnik*, p.149.

65 ICTY, General Ratko Mladić notebook 32, pp.20-21; Međović, *Jahorina 1992-1996 Dnevnik*, p.149.

66 *Deliberate Force, A Case Study in Effective Air Campaigning*, pp.156-157.

67 'Dosije: NATO letovi u zločin', pp.14-15.

68 *Deliberate Force, A Case Study in Effective Air Campaigning*, pp.152.

69 'Dosije: NATO letovi u zločin', pp.14-15.

70 Interview with Lt Colonel Ratković; Dimitrijević, Vazdušni Rat, pp.291-292.

71 Dimitrijević, Vazdušni Rat, p.292.

72 Holmes, 'Blooded over Bosnia', *Bombcat: the US Navy's Ultimate Precision Bomber*.

73 Ripley, *Air War Bosnia: UN and NATO Airpower,* pp.130–136.

74 Bilt, *Zadatak mir,* p.165.

75 *Deliberate Force, A Case Study in Effective Air Campaigning,* pp.151-152; Bucknam, *Responsibility of Command,* pp.297 and 310.

76 *Deliberate Force, A Case Study in Effective Air Campaigning,* p.152; Ripley, *Air War Bosnia: UN and NATO Airpower,* p.92.

77 *Deliberate Force, A Case Study in Effective Air Campaigning,* pp.155-156.

78 'Dosije: NATO letovi u zločin,' p.16; Duraković, *Na Istočnom bedemu Bosne IV,* p.211.

79 Interview with General Torbica.

80 Bošković, *Nebo na dlanu,* p.502. Editorial note: the "metric waves" referred to are UHF frequencies of 1-10m wavelength. Some sources claim these to be less vulnerable to detection and attack by anti-radiation missiles than other wavelengths.

81 Bilt, *Zadatak mir,* pp.165-166.

82 *Deliberate Force, A Case Study in Effective Air Campaigning,* p.154; 'Dosije: NATO letovi uz ločin,' p.18.

83 'Dosije: NATO letovi u zločin,' p.19; Međović, *Jahorina 1992-1996 Dnevnik,* p.150.

84 *Deliberate Force, A Case Study in Effective Air Campaigning,* p.157.

85 *Deliberate Force, A Case Study in Effective Air Campaigning,* pp.124, 154; Ripley, *Air War Bosnia: UN and NATO Airpower,* p.92.

86 Holbruk, *Put u Dejton,* pp.155-156; ICTY, General Ratko Mladić notebook 32, pp.31-34.

87 *Deliberate Force, A Case Study in Effective Air Campaigning,* pp.155, 157; *NATO protiv Srba, Ritam zločina,* pp.163–164.

88 Ripley, *Air War Bosnia: UN and NATO Airpower,* p.92; *Deliberate Force, A Case Study in Effective Air Campaigning,* pp.115, 158.

89 Ripley, *Air War Bosnia: UN and NATO Airpower,* p.93; AFSOUTH Fact Sheet <https://en.wikipedia.org/wiki/Operation_Deny_Flight>

90 *Konferencija za štampu Komandanta Glavnog štaba VRS,* 26. septembar 1996; Nova krila 27-28, novembar 1995, dosije: 'Nato letovi u zlocin', p.22.

91 O'Shea, *Crisis at Bihać: Bosnia's Bloody Battlefield,* pp.235-236; *Prva gardijska brigada Hrvatske vojske Tigrovi* (Zagreb, Ministarstvo obrane Republike Hrvatske, Glavni stožer Oružanih snaga RH, 2012); *Prvi hrvatski gardijski zdrug Hrvatske vojske* (Zagreb, Ministarstvo obrane Republike Hrvatske, Glavni stožer Oružanih snaga RH, 2012); Felić, *Peti korpus 1992.-1995,* pp.528-573.

92 Aralica et al, *Sto Godina,* pp.373-374.

93 DOKUMENTARNI FILM OPERACIJA SANA 95: NEDOVRSENA POBJEDA, <https://www.youtube.com/watch?v=RohHZQC62u4>

94 *Druga gardijska brigada Hrvatske vojske Gromovi* (Zagreb, Ministarstvo obrane Republike Hrvatske, Glavni stožer Oružanih snaga RH, 2012), p.356-360.

95 *Druga gardijska brigada Hrvatske vojske Gromovi,* p.356-360; Interview with General Novak.

96 Interview with Brigdair Dragan Nakić, Beograd/Banja Luka, 2016.

97 Interview with pilot 'M'; VHS footage of this mission, courtesy by Dean Čanić, Zagreb.

98 Dimitrijević, *Vazdušni Rat,* pp.332-333; Felić, *Peti korpus 1992.-1995,* pp.572-584.

99 Felić, *Peti korpus 1992-1995,* pp.572-584.

100 Interview with Brigadier Zoran Dunović, Banja Luka 9 April 2016; Felić, *Peti korpus 1992.-1995,* pp.581-582; Borojević et al, *Orlovi sa Vrbasa,* pp.176-180.

101 Dimitrijević, *Vazdušni Rat,* p.332.

102 Izetbegović, *Sjećanja, autobiografski zapis* (Sarajevo, OKO, 2001). p.254.

103 Dimitrijević, *Vazdušni Rat,* pp.332-333; Felić, *Peti korpus 1992.-1995,* pp.587-627.

104 Interview with Colonel Kecman.

105 Interview with Colonel Kecman.

106 Felić, *Peti korpus 1992-1995.* p.584

107 Interview with General Novak.

Chapter 5

1 Koljević, *Stvaranje Republike Srpske,* vol. 2, pp.353, 372–389, 401–404; Izetbegović, *Sjećanja, autobiografski zapis,* pp.259–295; Holbruk, *Put u Dejton,* pp.239–324.

2 'The Force in Aviano', *Air Forces Monthly* December 1996, pp.27-33.

3 Saunders, 'The Stars Look Down', *United States Air Force, Yearbook* (1999), pp.44-46.

4 Ripley, *Air War Bosnia: UN and NATO Airpower,* p.105.

5 Ripley, *Air War Bosnia: UN and NATO Airpower,* p.105; As an illustration of missions conducted, the 31st FW at Aviano logged 2,316 sorties in 1994-1995, plus 2065 sorties conducted while the two squadrons were part of the 86th FW in Ramstein from September 1993 to May 1994.

6 Kitfield, 'Tuzla is tough duty' (*Air Forces Monthly* December 1996), pp.60-63; Ripley, 'Tuzla Air Base', *United States Air Force, Yearbook* (1999), pp.39-40.

7 *Deliberate Force, A Case Study in Effective Air Campaigning,* pp.283-284.

8 *Deliberate Force, A Case Study in Effective Air Campaigning,* p.336.

9 *Deliberate Force, A Case Study in Effective Air Campaigning,* pp.207-239, 247.

10 *Deliberate Force, A Case Study in Effective Air Campaigning,* p.247.

11 *Deliberate Force, A Case Study in Effective Air Campaigning,* pp.258-265.

12 Ripley, *Air War Bosnia: UN and NATO Airpower,* p.111.

13 'Blooded over Bosnia', F-14 Bombcat, *Air Forces Monthly* publication, pp.14-18

14 Strickland, 'The Early Evolution of the Predator Drone', *Studies in Intelligence* Vol. 57, No. 1 (Extracts, March 2013)

15 U.S. Predator Operations – Update, Defense Technical Information Center Compilation Part Notice <https://apps.dtic.mil/dtic/tr/fulltext/u2/p010337.pdf>; Operation Nomad Vigil <https://www.globalsecurity.org/military/ops/nomad_vigil.htm>

16 Komanda 250. raketne brigade PVO VJ, pisana izjava (written statement):'Aleksic, kapetan prve klase, komanda 250.rbr PVO, Septembar 1996.'

17 Interview with Lt. Colonel Ratković.

18 'Diskusija nacelnika Uprave V i PVO puk. Radoslava Pandzica na analizi b/g za 1996. godinu' courtesy by General Torbica.

19 Borojević et al, *Orlovi sa Vrbasa,* p.181.

20 'Diskusija nacelnika Uprave V i PVO puk. Radoslava Pandzica na analizi b/g za 1996. godinu' courtesy by General Torbica.

21 Komanda V i PVO, str.pov br 03/4-95/1, 27.09 1995.

22 *Deliberate Force, A Case Study in Effective Air Campaigning,* p.199.

23 *Balkan Battlegrounds,* pp.393–395.

24 Interview with General Novak.

25 Interview with Colonel Popović.

26 Bilt, *Zadatak mir* (Beograd, Samizdat B92, 1999), p.166.

27 *Deliberate Force, A Case Study in Effective Air Campaigning,* p.507.

28 Author's interview with Richard Holbrooke, 3 October 2003, Belgrade.

29 *Deliberate Force, A Case Study in Effective Air Campaigning,* pp.164-165.

30 Bucknam, *Responsibility of Command,* p.302.

ABOUT THE AUTHOR

Bojan Dimitrijevic is the Deputy Director of the Institute for Contemporary History in Belgrade, Serbia. Educated at the Universities of Belgrade and Novi Sad, CEU Budapest and University of Bradford, he was custodian of the Yugoslav Aviation Museum before, serving as advisor to the Minister to the Serbian MoD, Minister of Foreign Affairs, the President of Serbia, and as Assistant to the Minister of Defence. His has researched the military history of Yugoslavia, and the Balkans in the Second World War, Cold War, and conflicts since, he has published over 50 books and 100 scientific articles in Serbia and abroad. This is his fifth book for Helion's @War series